Responsive Leadership
in Social Services

SAGE was founded in 1965 by Sara Miller McCune to support the dissemination of usable knowledge by publishing innovative and high-quality research and teaching content. Today, we publish more than 750 journals, including those of more than 300 learned societies, more than 800 new books per year, and a growing range of library products including archives, data, case studies, reports, conference highlights, and video. SAGE remains majority-owned by our founder, and after Sara's lifetime will become owned by a charitable trust that secures our continued independence.

Los Angeles | London | New Delhi | Singapore | Washington DC | Boston

Responsive Leadership in Social Services

A Practical Approach for Optimizing Engagement and Performance

Stephen de Groot

*Myriad Consultation and Counseling
and University of Manitoba*

Los Angeles | London | New Delhi
Singapore | Washington DC | Boston

Los Angeles | London | New Delhi
Singapore | Washington DC | Boston

FOR INFORMATION:

SAGE Publications, Inc.
2455 Teller Road
Thousand Oaks, California 91320
E-mail: order@sagepub.com

SAGE Publications Ltd.
1 Oliver's Yard
55 City Road
London EC1Y 1SP
United Kingdom

SAGE Publications India Pvt. Ltd.
B 1/I 1 Mohan Cooperative Industrial Area
Mathura Road, New Delhi 110 044
India

SAGE Publications Asia-Pacific Pte. Ltd.
3 Church Street
#10-04 Samsung Hub
Singapore 049483

A catalog record of this book is available from the Library of Congress.

ISBN 978-1-4522-9154-3 (pbk.)

Publisher: Kassie Graves
eLearning Editor: Lucy Berbeo
Editorial Assistant: Carrie Montoya
Production Editor: David C. Felts
Copy Editor: Jared Leighton
Typesetter: C&M Digitals (P) Ltd.
Proofreader: Jeff Bryant
Indexer: Kathy Paparchontis
Cover Designer: Anupama Krishnan
Marketing Manager: Shari Countryman

15 16 17 18 19 10 9 8 7 6 5 4 3 2 1

Brief Contents

Contents

Acknowledgments

I would like to thank my parents, Adrian and Sandra, for their constant patience, understanding, and support for all that I am and all that I do. I thank them for teaching me the importance of working hard and caring about the work that I do with even greater determination. Thank you.

To all of the clients, frontline workers, supervisors, and managers who have trusted me enough to share their stories, to teach me how to be a better leader—I thank you. The positive differences that have and continue to happen from what I know and how I do things would not have been possible without your feedback, support, and guidance. Thank you.

Words cannot describe the depth of heartfelt gratitude I hold for my two boys, Brayden Riley and Ethan Zane. Kind, caring, and understanding, they continue to support me so that I may support others. Thank you for your patience and the compromises you continue to make so that we can make the world better for others. Thank you.

I would like to thank my family, team members, and friends who continue to be there and help out whenever I need them. Most importantly, I want to thank them all for their patience and tolerance of my sometimes unique and unorthodox ways to make things better. Thank you.

A special thank you to the great people who took the time to review the original manuscript, provide feedback and input, and pose great questions for me to consider going forward. Thank you Tania Alameda-Lawson (Binghampton University), Gregg Allinson (Beaufort County Community College), Kathy Elpers (University of Southern Indiana), Bruce D. Hartsell (California State University Bakersfield), Judith E. Hefren (Florida State University), Leslie W. O'Ryan (Western Illinois University - Quad Cities), Raymond Sanchez Mayers (Rutgers University), and Denise K. Sommers (University of Illinois Springfield).

Your efforts were and continue to be appreciated. This work is better because of your meaningful contributions.

I would like to thank SAGE Publications for gifting me with the opportunity to make a contribution and work with other leaders to make the lives of other people better. I would like to thank my editor, Kassie Graves. Thank you for your dependability and support, your gentle and persistent reminders, but above all, I appreciate that you provided a space for me to be me. Thank you.

Preface

If your actions inspire others to dream more, learn more, do more and become more, you are a leader.

— John Quincy Adams

❖ AN IMPORTANT NOTE TO SOCIAL SERVICE LEADERS

Thank you for taking on one of the most important, challenging, and complex roles in social services. Unless one has operated in the role(s) of team leader, supervisor, coordinator, or manager in any of the varied sectors of social services, one cannot truly understand the inherent, multifarious challenges that arise from the complex roles and responsibilities of a social services leader. Thank you for committing yourself to support, supervise, and/or manage exceptionally valuable human-caring work through other people. Thank you for wanting the best and doing your best for the incredible people that work with you and for the important people that they serve and support. You cannot be thanked enough for your commitment, dedication, and hard work. Thank you, thank you, thank you.

❖ BACKGROUND

Leadership within the social services industry is gratifying and also very challenging. However, it does not have to be as difficult as it is. The work presented in this book was constructed as an effort to make your role as a leader less complex, less stressful, and much more rewarding. It has been motivated, over 20 years, by my experiences as a frontline helper, university instructor, supervisor, manager of supervisors, trainer of supervisors, and consultant to and with supervisors.

It has been inspired by my own field experience and thousands of collaborations and conversations with managers, supervisors, and frontline workers who have conveyed a need and/or desire for something BETTER—better leadership for themselves, for their work, and above all for the important people they serve.

Whether you are brand new to the role of leadership or you have been doing it for years, this book is intended to enhance the meaning, value, and quality of your leadership efforts so that you may enhance the capacities of your workers in a manner that translates into higher quality service for the people they are responsible to care for and support. It was developed to provide you and all leaders in social services with valuable insights and practical strategies for inspiring, motivating, and engaging employees and staff teams to feel BETTER, be BETTER, and do BETTER as they carry out their important work with children, youth, families, and communities.

❖ STRUCTURE OF THE BOOK

This work has been designed to build a strong case as to why a Responsive Leadership Approach is essential for approximating and achieving preferred outcomes for both employee and clients. While the discussions presented are intended to be relevant and insightful for all leaders in the various social service sectors, the real potency of this work stems from the highly practical and immediately operational leadership tools and strategies offered throughout. It is my hope that the applications offered will affirm and validate what you are already doing well as a leader and provide additional hints, tips, and strategies for developing and advancing your leadership capacities further.

The book is divided into two main parts. Part I comprises Chapters 1 and 2 and is geared toward setting the stage and building a solid case for a Responsive Leadership Approach in social services.

Chapter 1 presents an honest look at the challenging realities of the current social services system, highlighting serious impediments to preferred practice and employee outcomes. The first chapter notes the multifarious and negative implications of such impediments on the overall well-being of workers and links worker stress, intent to leave, and burnout to less-than-positive outcomes for clients. Quality supervision is presented as a major factor for mitigating many of the effects of identified organizational and work challenges; however, supervisors and quality supervision are not immune from the challenges and impacts of very tough work environments. Chapter 1 concludes by suggesting that *leadership* is the answer we might be looking for.

Chapter 2 builds on Chapter 1 and continues to compose a strong case for the leadership tools and strategies offered in Part II. The second chapter begins with a definition of leadership and suggests an important shift from supervision to leadership as inspiration. The discussion reviews a wealth of practice wisdom, scholarship, and research to demonstrate the role effective and quality leadership plays in enhanced and sustained worker engagement, motivation, and overall performance, including the positive impact these have on preferred outcomes for clients. Chapter 2 concludes by tying together what we know about quality and effective leadership with an introduction, overview, and guiding priorities of a Responsive Leadership Approach.

Part II of the book comprises Chapter 3 through Chapter 8. These sections offer a springboard from the conceptual to the highly practical by bridging the discussion established in Part I to the tools and strategies that accommodate the guiding priorities of a Responsive Leadership Approach offered throughout Part II.

Chapter 3 presents the important idea that quality and effective leadership are determined by the perception and experiences of individual members. The discussion emphasizes the benefits for leaders in learning about and engaging the unique needs, values, goals, and strengths embedded within employees' experiences. The Key Performance Motivators Scale (KPMS) and the Preferred Leadership Profile (PLP) are presented and discussed as valuable tools for enhancing and sustaining worker, engagement, motivation, and overall performance.

Chapter 4 represents a very detailed account of the importance of discovery and meaning-making within the Responsive Leadership framework. This section of the book offers leaders a comprehensive rationale and detailed process outline of the most effective communication strategy for creating a pathway to the employee and the employee's story. Several case situations are presented to illustrate the structure and process for meaning-making and discovery.

Chapter 5 is devoted solely to a strengths-based approach in leadership. The discussion opens by establishing the rationale and need for a strengths-based approach as an important method to counter the negative implications of problem-oriented approaches to supervisory training and performance development common in social services. A thorough overview, including the key components of a strengths-based approach, is presented in the context of a Responsive Leadership

Approach. The chapter offers a variety of strengths-based tools and strategies, coupled with illustrative examples of the strengths-focused methods in operation. Finally, the discussion offers a substantial list of positive and profound implications for worker and client outcomes that are a direct result of a strengths-based approach to leadership practice.

Chapter 6 offers a concentrated focus on doing inspiration and represents the most practical portion of the book. Built around the Key Performance Motivators Scale presented in Chapter 3, this segment introduces seven domains (relationship, vision and values, mission and goals, appreciative, personal/professional, feedback, and strengths) that can be accessed by leaders to enhance the motivation of most workers. Each domain offers leaders a plethora of tried-and-tested strategies to positively influence the attitudes and behaviors of workers to perform optimally.

Chapter 7 covers one of the most popular topics of interest for social service leaders: understanding and effectively dealing with employee opposition and resistance. The discussion opens up by defining and identifying various types of employee resistance and oppositional behavior. The chapter sets out competing perspectives on employee resistance and demonstrates the differential impacts these perspectives have on a leader's ability to effectively handle concerning and/or challenging behaviors. A variety of proactive approaches for decreasing and even eliminating resistance and opposition are offered throughout this segment as important considerations for all leaders. The discussion emphasizes the four core Responsive Leadership guiding principles that are foundational for dealing with employee opposition in the most efficient and effective manner. Finally, as an attempt to provide the most illustrative guide to the step-by-step Responsive Leadership Process for eliminating challenging employee attitudes and behaviors, a case situation is presented in detail. This section may represent one of the most important segments of the work as it brings to bear almost all Responsive Leadership tools and strategies offered throughout the entire book.

Chapter 8 represents a brief epilogue as the conclusion to the work offered herein. This final segment revisits the intentions and anticipated outcomes that were established at the beginning of the book. In an effort to maintain the practical disposition of the work offered, the epilogue provides the reader with some final insights and important considerations to further enhance their own leadership quality.

A Preferred Leadership Profile (PLP) and Key Performance Motivators Scale (KPMS) are available to those using this book. To access these tools, visit study.sagepub.com/degroot.

In addition to providing information and practical strategies for enhancing worker engagement, motivation, and overall performance, Chapters 1 through 7 offer the reader summaries of important points and valuable leader reflections and important considerations based on the content. These final sections of each chapter were constructed so that you may connect with your experience of the material in a manner that may fortify your capacity and efficacy as a leader, on your own personal and professional journey to enhanced leadership development.

About the Author

Stephen de Groot is a clinical and organizational consultant and author of the Relationship Based Strengths Approach (RBSA) (2003, 2013) for helping, the Empowering Social Workers Project (2006, 2010), and the Responsive Leadership Approach (2013) for Supervisors and Managers.

As an associate professor and sessional instructor, de Groot has taught in both BSW and MSW programs for seven years with the faculty of social work at the University of Manitoba. Stephen has worked with more than 200 organizations within the human services and corporate sectors and has provided support, education, and learning development to professionals working in child welfare, mental health, child and youth care, youth homelessness, addictions, justice, education, and health.

As an international trainer of more than 20,000 participants, de Groot has made it his mission not only to inspire people but to empower and equip them with knowledge and tools so that they may also inspire and transform themselves and those for whom they are responsible.

Stephen has occupied and continues to operate in a myriad of roles such as consultant, supervisor/manager, executive coach, trainer, author, and international speaker. Outside of his professional endeavors, Stephen continues to help others by devoting a great deal of his resources to giving and charity work. He is founder of the Getting to Better™ Initiative and chair of the advisory board of a global kindness movement known as Life Vest Inside™. De Groot also promotes and supports the great work of two important nonprofit organizations: See Beautiful™ and VOICES, Manitoba's Youth in Care Network.

To my brother, David John de Groot, and my friend Christopher David Surbey.
You inspired me, and you continue to do so everyday.

PART I

A Case for Responsive Leadership

1

Embracing
Social Service Realities

*Impediments to Preferred
Practice and Quality Supervision*

He has a right to criticize, who has a heart to help.

— Abraham Lincoln

❖ SOCIAL SERVICE WORKERS:
A MOTIVATED AND COMMITTED RESOURCE

To say that a social service worker is unmotivated would be similar to saying that a molecule doesn't move. Beyond being an inaccurate statement, it is actually impossible. Social service workers are among the most motivated and committed group of people that I have ever met. Helping professionals are wired to help. Their gravitation to the field of social services is no accident; they have a need to help, they value helping, and they want to help. For many workers, the decision to enter the social service field is an important and purposeful life commitment, a commitment to a profession that is very much in line with their own personal orientation, values, needs, and goals. Most workers have been helping people for many years prior to becoming profes-sional helpers. When I am asked how long I have been a social worker, I often respond by saying, "Since I was 6 years old." Like many of my social service comrades, I was very concerned with making the lives of other people better from a very early age. Like them, I held and main-tain a strong desire to help others.

This motivation and commitment to help is most evident in the beginning of a professional helper's career, amidst introductory, diploma, and degree programs for child and youth care, psychology, counseling, social work, mental health, health, corrections and educa-tion, and in a variety of courses that are geared toward enhancing the biopsychosocial well-being of children, youth, adults, families, and communities. I used to love teaching in the bachelor of social work program because this was the "starting gate," filled with excited, fresh-faced, and eager social work students, ready to take on and save the whole world! Eager to learn knowledge and skills and gain experi-ence to enhance their capacities to help, the young student-helpers were ready to go, excited and focused on how they could help and where they could help—they very much wanted to be pointed in the right direction. They were overflowing with enthusiasm, motivation, and focus. They were committed and dedicated to making the lives of other people better.

It is important to note that while all social service workers have needs, values, goals, and strengths to help, there exists a continuum of individual and unique differences among and between helpers as to what specific things motivate, excite, and contribute to higher levels of engagement with clients and with the work overall. This idea of indi-vidual worker variance regarding specific work motivation factors will be discussed further in greater detail in Chapter 3.

So what happens to that overabundance of enthusiasm and focus, the motivation and commitment to be so engaged to help? How come, as an industry, social services consistently and overwhelm-ingly maintains the highest turnover and poorest retention rates? How can it be that when touring a variety of helping sectors, one can meet so many workers who seem to be or at least appear unmotivated and/or disengaged from their work? Why do so many helpers seem exhausted, jaded, cynical, apathetic, or burnt out? What the heck hap-pened? What went wrong? As stated earlier, there is nothing inher-ently wrong with social service workers; they still want to help; they are desperate to help. Unfortunately, many workers at some point or other in their career, for many reasons, can become disconnected, dislocated, or disengaged from their most important purpose: that of helping. Before we even consider implicating them as individuals as a cause or source of this particular dilemma, it is essential that we start with the system in which they work.

While the social service industry is a well-intentioned social institution that is full of well-intentioned and well-meaning organizations geared to enhancing the physical, emotional, social, and psychological functioning of individuals, families, and communities in need of help, organizational and workplace conditions can make helping really difficult for those many wonderful, motivated, and committed workers doing the helping.

❖ SOCIAL SERVICES: A TOUGH WORK ENVIRONMENT

Most social service workers need and want to feel good about themselves and their work, to experience that they are doing the kind of work they want to do in a manner that is consistent with what they value, what they want for themselves, and what they want for the people whom they serve. When considering the apparent loss of enthusiasm, motivation, focus, and engagement of many workers in social services, it is absolutely necessary to acknowledge the realities of the challenging environments that workers operate within. Many social service sectors are characterized by challenging system, organizational, and workplace conditions that can have the potential to negatively impact a worker's perceptions and experiences of the environment, themselves, and the work overall.

It is well known that while social services work can be rewarding, it is not without its challenges. It is the toughest industry to work within, and it is no surprise that out of all occupational fields, burnout, which can result in emotional exhaustion, depersonalization, and a reduced sense of accomplishment at work (Maslach & Leiter, 2008), is more likely to occur in the social services profession (Cordes & Dougherty, 1993; Garner, Knight, & Simpson, 2007). While burnout is indeed a complex and multifaceted phenomenon (Lambert, Hogan, Barton-Bellessa, & Jiang, 2012), it is more often caused by workplace factors, and according to Maslach (2003), it is the "chronic strain that results from an incongruence, or misfit between the worker and the job" (p. 198). This concept of misfit between the worker and the job is absolutely essential to understanding what appears to be a major disconnect between how social service workers want to work and how they experience their work overall. As stated earlier and most simply put, workers have a strong desire and are wired to help; they want to make a positive difference in the lives of the people they work with so that they may feel better, do better, and live better. However, organizational and workplace conditions can make working in a preferred manner exceptionally difficult.

Generally speaking, while variable from sector to sector and work environment to work environment, similar organizational and workplace challenges have been confirmed by thousands of frontline workers and supervisors, who have collaborated with me on projects or attended many of my workshops. The various challenges posed by organizational and work conditions are also confirmed by a wealth of scholarship linking such environmental challenges to the subsequent negative impacts these challenges have on overall worker well-being, job satisfaction, and organizational commitment (Barter, 2005; Bell, Kulkarni, & Dalton 2003; Carson, King, & Papatraianou, 2011; Glisson, 2009; Graham & Shier, 2010; Herbert, 2007; Hodgkin, 2002; Kim, Ji, & Kao, 2010; Lambert, Hogan, Barton-Bellessa, and Jiang, 2012; Maslach & Leiter, 2008; Mor Barak, Levin, Nissly, & Lane, 2006; Mor Barak, Nissly, & Levin, 2001; Vinokur-Kaplan, 2009).

Organizational and Bureaucratic Challenges

> *The current era of social services has been characterised as an industry of "Deprofessionalization, contractualization, industrialization and marketization."*

— Vinukor-Kaplan, 2009, p. 233

Many frontline workers understand and experience their organizations as overly hierarchical and highly bureaucratized, concerned with and governed by rigid rules, protocols, policy, and procedures. Workers report feeling that organizational structures and rules are created in a top-down manner by legislators, boards, administrators, or managers that are out of touch with the realities of frontline service workers (Herbert, 2007). Further, in an effort to improve accountability, many agencies have increased their administrative requirements in such areas as service standards, recording, financial reporting, and information-sharing protocols (Barter, 2005). In addition to this, more than ever the call for increased efficiency, outcomes, and accountability has resulted in and added to an overwhelming demand for paperwork. Many organizations are overbureaucratized, laden with mandates, legislative requirements, and standards of practice, and can seem like paperwork is a priori, taking precedence over "peoplework." It is these organizational realities that create a major source of conflict for social workers— that organizational priorities place system needs before the needs of social workers and their clients.

Political and bureaucratic priorities and politically reactive mandate changes leave many workers feeling like they have little control over their work. This combined with highly demanding and complex caseloads makes it difficult for workers to operate in a manner that is consistent with their values, needs, and goals for helping. However, there are many other specific workplace dimensions that can negatively impact a worker's experience of the work, thereby exacerbating the stress and strain, resulting in lower degrees of motivation, commitment, and engagement with the work.

Doing More With Less

Fiscal restraints and limited resources have added to the stress experienced by a workforce that is consistently asked to do more with less. Social services are well-known as an industry with low wages and a shortage of funds for early intervention and preventative programming. High numbers of complex cases in social services intensify the workload for those carrying out the work, especially when poor retention and high turnover of staff intensify the stress and strain levels of already taxed employees. A national survey of child welfare workers in Canada overwhelmingly identified workload as the greatest impediment to good practice (de Groot, 2006, 2010; Herbert, 2007). Bureaucratic protocol, policy, and paperwork combined with high workloads and complex cases with few supportive resources can take a great deal of worker time and energy. This results in less availability for workers to carry out direct and preferred relations-oriented people-work. When you consider such environments, it is no wonder that many social service workers report that the work feels reactive and crisis-driven versus proactive or responsive (de Groot, 2006; Herbert, 2007). This can leave numerous workers feeling conflicted between workload demands and intended or preferred ways of helping.

Value Incongruence

Because many workers operate in organizational environments that are crisis-oriented, reactive, fiscally restrained, and time-crunched and where policy and paperwork take precedence over people, the time necessary for effective and quality intervention with clients is undoubtedly compromised. The little time left and supportive service available for clients are carried out in the context of predominant service models of helping. An important note here is that most intervention approaches are still highly based on and/or influenced by a biomedical model of treatment. The *Diagnostic and Statistical Manual* (DSM), with the strong backing of the psychiatric and pharmaceutical industries, continues to dominate all fields and sectors of social services. Even in an era of "strengths" as philosophically, theoretically, and politically correct, assessments that focus on risks, deficits, diagnoses, problems, disabilities, pathologies, and dysfunctions continue to govern assessment protocol and form the basis for intervention approaches. My experience, as I continue to collaborate with many frontline programs in a variety of service sectors, is that the strengths, if represented in a client's file, are hard to find, and even when there are mandatory strengths sections in files or forms, they are often sparse with information or altogether left blank. Most social services workers value a strengths-based approach and do what they can to operate in such a manner; however, the problem and pathology dominated intervention approaches provide yet another incongruence wherein workers operate out of step with their own value set and in an environment that runs counter to their need and goal to be strengths-based.

Two additional organization and workplace challenges that are prevalent and negatively impact worker motivation, commitment, and level of engagement are inadequate and/or poor quality supervision (Bell et al., 2003; Gibbs, 2001; Lizano & Mor Barak, 2012, Mor Barak et al., 2001; Mor Barak et al., 2006). Inadequate and poor quality supervision will be discussed further in the next section as a serious impediment to preferred practice and outcomes. Supervision, however, is viewed and will also be presented as the best possibility for enhancing the motivation, commitment, and engagement of frontline workers.

❖ THE LOSS OF GREAT HELPERS: IMPLICATIONS FOR EMPLOYEE AND CLIENT OUTCOMES

When considering a discussion of work environment and its impact on workers' motivation and commitment, it is important to note a simple, straightforward, and well-established fact: "Workers who perceive their organizational climate in positive terms report higher job satisfaction and greater organizational commitment to their organization" (Glisson, 2009, p. 126). Brown and Leigh (1996) indicate that a positive climate is represented by a positive work environment that does not pose a threat to the worker's identity or what is important and meaningful to the worker. It is also a workplace that is perceived by the worker to support a positive return on their investment of personal and professional work effort. Considering this perspective on the link between positive work environment and job satisfaction and commitment, is it any surprise that current social service industry work environments are actually antithetical to promoting positive worker perceptions and experiences of the workplace in which they operate?

From Burning Desire to Burning Out

The impacts of organizational and workplace conditions on frontline workers are absolutely alarming. The level and degree of job stress and strain experienced by workers across all fields of social services must be considered a serious occupational hazard and signal an industry-wide alarm. Pervasive and persistent systemic, organizational, workplace, and service challenges can have seriously negative consequences for how helpers feel about themselves and their work. It is common for workers to report low levels of morale, feeling devalued, unacknowledged, unsupported, misunderstood, and overworked. It is also common for many helpers to experience alienation, a sense of powerlessness, frustration, and hopelessness. Given the challenging and demanding working conditions workers are expected to operate in, it is not a surprise that many will experience moderate to high levels of emotional, psychological, and physical stress and eventually high levels of burnout (Kim et al., 2010).

Burnout was originally identified by Maslach (1978) as "a syndrome of emotional exhaustion and cynicism that occurs frequently among individuals who do 'people work' of some kind" (p. 99). It is important to note that Maslach (2003) implicates work factors as the main source of strain on workers that ultimately leads to burnout. The early work of Maslach and Jackson (1981) proposed three dimensions of burnout, which have been developed further and conceptualized as emotional exhaustion, depersonalization, and feelings of being ineffective at work (Maslach, Jackson, & Leiter, 1996). "In many studies burnout has been associated with various forms of negative responses to the job, including job dissatisfaction, low organizational commitment, intention to leave the job and turnover" (Maslach & Leiter, 2008, p. 499).

This is a sad and disheartening plight as no one enters the social service field with the intent of quitting, giving up, or becoming lost, disconnected from their values, purpose, themselves, work, team members, or their clients. When I consider this and my past social work students, I mourn the loss of that overabundance of motivation, excitement, and commitment many of the fresh-faced social work helpers held as they eagerly exited the training grounds to enter the tough field of social services. The unique experiences and the degree to which helpers experience poor job satisfaction and disengagement from their organizations, work, or clients are just as diverse and unique as the individual workers and the environmental/work contexts. Unfortunately, the longer workers feel overwhelmed, unappreciated, devalued, unsupported, misunderstood, and/or overworked, the greater the chances are that we are going to eventually lose them.

It is well documented that there is a direct connection between high levels of burnout among social service workers and the high rates of turnover within the organizations they work for (Carson et al., 2011; Gibbs, 2001; Kim et al., 2010; Maslach & Leiter, 2008; Mor Barak et al., 2001). High turnover can result in the inability of organizations to provide consistent, efficient, and quality supportive service for clients. Losing workers in the most common and obvious sense can be witnessed with the well-established high rate of turnover manifested in exit strategies such as early retirement, job accommodation, job transfer to other positions, or exits right out of the field of social services altogether.

However, just because people leave does not mean that they did not want to stay. I meet many workers who say, "I want to stay, but not like this," or, "I want to stay, but I can't do this anymore." Considering the three dimensions of burnout offered by Maslach and Jackson (1981), many workers reflect feelings and experiences of being exhausted, inefficient, or both. They had to leave. For many it was a matter of psychological, physical, or even spiritual survival; they just could not do the work in a manner that they were hoping for. They had to get out before it destroyed them. A common sentiment echoed by many of my child welfare colleagues who left the field altogether was articulated well in a recent conversation I had with a former coworker. He said, "I loved the people I worked with. I loved my work. I just couldn't do it in that place (work environment) anymore. I stayed as long as I could, but I had to get out or it would have killed me."

Working Wounded

Evidence suggests that prior to doing so, a worker's decision to leave the job is a deliberate and conscious choice (Mor Barak et al., 2001).

Given that the choice to leave is intentional, it has been suggested that workers may experience intent to leave for quite some time before taking any specific action (Lee, Mitchell, Holtom, McDaniel, & Hill, 1999). It is important to note, however, that while many workers may have a desire to leave the job, many do not act on their intent (Mor Barak et al., 2006). While high rates of worker turnover present a serious dilemma for the social service industry overall, what I find even more alarming is the reality that there are large numbers of workers who have been wounded, stressed, exhausted, and disengaged; those workers we have "lossed" but continue to remain with us in the field! While burnout, poor job satisfaction, and intention to leave are the strongest predictors of worker turnover (Mor Barak et al., 2006), intention to leave does not necessarily mean that workers are going to leave, and staying with an organization is an active process that is very different from not leaving (Carson et al., 2011).

For many workers that want to leave, there exist a variety of different reasons to remain in a challenging work environment. One of the most important factors mediating the decision to stay despite low satisfaction and organizational commitment, according to Mor Barak, Nissly, and Levin (2001), is a sense of responsibility and strong commitment workers have to their clients. "The conflict between organizational conditions (e.g., high caseloads) and workers' own professional expectations may lead employees to keep up with their very demanding work commitments at the expense of their own emotional health, with high levels of burnout as a result" (Mor Barak et al., 2001, p. 653).

This means that we can lose workers even though they are still among us. Some of our counterparts have become cynical, jaded, burnt out, or they have simply given up or given in. Some are doing what they can to just get through the day, to get home, or just get through to retirement. Consider my colleague's sentiment above, "I stayed as long as I could." It scares me when I consider what these stark realities mean for the quality of service for vulnerable children, families, and communities.

Impacts: Worker and Client Outcomes

It is difficult for me to think about what this might mean for overall client outcomes. There is an inextricable link between positive working conditions and preferred staff outcomes, such as job satisfaction and organizational commitment, because as discussed earlier, workers' perceptions of their work environment affect their experiences, attitudes, behaviors, and, most importantly, how they perform in that environment (Brown & Leigh, 1996; Liao & Chang, 2007). Furthermore, there is an inextricable link that exists between positive staff outcomes, practice decisions, and subsequent client outcomes. The converse is also true; there is a link between job stress and counter-productivity (Travis & Mor Barak, 2010). Simply put, when workers do well, their clients do well, and when workers' practice decisions suffer, so does the well-being of clients.

So what does this mean when a large portion of the social service workforce is not doing well? They continue to stay and work, trying their best to help despite the difficult organizational and workplace conditions that pose real impediments to preferred ways of helping. They want to do better! They want to feel better about themselves and their work. We are losing a lot of great helpers and workers. Those who remain will make up a large part of a potentially disempowered and demoralized workforce. I refer to them as the walking wounded—disengaged employees charged with the responsibility of empowering the disempowered. Indeed, this is an inadequate arrangement for essential social services to say the least.

I agree with Carson et al. (2011) when they assert that "social work currently exists in a volatile environment of changing service delivery, organizational configuration and employment arrangements and that such changes may be threatening to the health and well being of individual workers and thus diminish the sector's ability to respond to the needs of its clients" (p. 274). If organizational and workplace conditions continue to negatively impact workers' experiences of the work environment, themselves, and the work, we as a system may unintentionally be doing harm, not only to the professional helpers but also to the people that we are here to help. What a dilemma!

Where to Look for Change?

We know, due to the growing evidence, that when workers can operate in a positive work environment that is supportive and meaningful, outcomes will be better for both workers and their clients (Glisson, 2009; Vinokur-Kaplan, 2009). The central question for today's organizations and social services as a whole is "how to create organizational conditions that will lead to positive worker perceptions, attitudes and behaviours and ultimately the delivery of high quality and the most effective services" (Patti, 2009, p. 117). This query, while probably the most pressing question of all, is not at all new. This is so, just as the reality of persistent organizational and workplace conditions as hazardous to workers is not at all a new issue for the social services industry either. In fact, my professional association, the Canadian Association of Social Workers (CASW), was developed in 1926 with the purpose to improve working conditions for frontline social workers. More than 89 years later, the number one agenda item for the CASW is to improve working conditions for social workers! This has not been nor is it going to be an easy task. Furthermore, the objective of enhancing worker motivation, commitment, and engagement by improving working conditions will be extra difficult as we remain in an industry that continues to be overbureaucratic, fiscally restrained, crisis-oriented, and reactive, where caseloads, paperwork, and staff turnover are likely to remain excessive.

While large-system change may seem overwhelming and exceptionally daunting, it must remain the long-term objective. However, in the meantime, there is an urgent need for an approach, or at least a set of strategies, that can provide some immediate relief to those workers who want to feel better and do better in the context of their helping efforts.

I believe that a possible answer to this dilemma lies in a mechanism we call supervision—a mechanism that serves as an environment within the larger system, a mechanism that may be modified to cultivate, enhance, and even resuscitate workers' motivation and overall engagement.

❖ SUPERVISION: A POSSIBLE SOLUTION IN A CRISIS

When considering where to begin to effect the greatest positive change for frontline workers, the long list of workplace and organizational conditions that lead to low job satisfaction and organizational commitment and high intent to leave, turnover, and burnout can be overwhelming. I have been struggling with this for a long time as a worker, supervisor, professor, trainer, and consultant to team leaders, supervisors, managers, and directors. I believe that the quickest and most efficient solution lies in the area of quality supervision.

Supervision is the cornerstone of social services and plays the most important role in an organization's ability to carry out effective and quality service for clients. Supervision provides the environment and the mechanism for workers to learn about the work, themselves, and their clients and to integrate theory and practice, ask questions, give and receive feedback, set goals, and collaborate on their important work. Effective supervision offers workers administrative, educational, and social support (Kadushin & Harkness, 2002) and provides an environment in which workers can develop their capacities for helping further. In addition and most importantly, research indicates that effective supervision can buffer the negative effects of working in the social services industry (Kadushin & Harkness, 2002; Mor Barak et al., 2001).

Out of the identified organizational and workplace impediments to preferred practice, enhancing the quality of the worker's supervisory experience is what I believe to be the most important, realistic, and achievable option, as it is one of the workplace impediments that seems to be within our immediate control. The basis for this consideration emerges from two important realities: The first is that quality supervision is a mechanism that is critical to cultivating, enhancing, and maintaining worker motivation, commitment, and engagement, and the second is that to a large degree, workers across social services are dissatisfied with the quality of their supervision experience. These two realities pose yet another serious systemic dilemma because while supervision as a mechanism can be beneficial to staff and client outcomes, it can also be detrimental to staff and client outcomes (Mor Barak, Travis, Pyun, & Xie, 2009).

Quality Supervision and Worker Outcomes

We know more about the impact quality supervision has on staff and client outcomes than we have at any other time in our history. There is a wealth of research indicating that effective and quality supervision, among many things, is a critical factor that impacts job satisfaction, organizational culture and climate, worker commitment, staff retention, and turnover (Barter, 2005; Carson et al., 2011; de Groot, 2006; Gibbs, 2001; Mor Barak et al., 2001; Mor Barak et al., 2009; SWPI, 2011). A great meta-analysis reviewing the research on the impact of supervision on worker outcomes between 1990 and 2007 was conducted by Mor Barak, Travis, Pyun, and Xie (2009). The findings draw a direct connection between a worker's perception of the quality of supervision and their experience of competence, personal accomplishment, organizational commitment, and job satisfaction. What's key here is that whether or not supervision is determined as "quality" or effective is dependent upon the workers' perception of that experience. The importance of employees' perceptions will be covered further in Chapter 3. So what do we know about a quality supervision experience?

According to the literature on quality supervision, Mor Barak et al. (2009) conclude, "Results indicate that supervisory dimensions of task assistance, social and emotional support and supervisory interpersonal interaction are positively and statistically significantly related to beneficial outcomes for workers" (p. 3). More important is that the last two dimensions—social and emotional support and interpersonal interaction—are found to be negatively related to detrimental outcomes for workers, which I will speak to further (Mor Barak et al., 2009). Supervisory task assistance studies referred to a worker's perception that their supervisor was helpful in the learning process by assessing needs for learning (Curry, McCarragher, & Dellmann-Jenkins, 2005), providing opportunities for workers to develop their skills (Hopkins, 2002), and assisting with problem solving (Gimbel et al., 2002). Task assistance is related to beneficial outcomes such as worker retention, empowerment, and organizational citizenship behaviors (Mor Barak et al., 2009).

Social and emotional supervisory support studies demonstrate that this specific dimension is associated with job satisfaction and is linked to limiting detrimental outcomes for workers. According to Mor Barak and associates (2009), studies demonstrate that this particular supervisory dimension is consistent across a variety of social service sectors and that lack of supervisory support is significantly linked to worker turnover. Supervisory interpersonal interaction is associated with a worker's sense of personal accomplishment (Webster & Hackett, 1999), and this dimension is also linked with worker empowerment and job satisfaction when a worker experiences the supervisor relationship to be positive and beneficial to the worker in some way (Wallach & Mueller, 2006).

The research on quality supervision and positive worker outcomes is both compelling and exciting. However, my experience from speaking with thousands of frontline workers and supervisors in the field is that generally workers are less than satisfied with their supervisors and/or their experiences of supervision. As a matter of fact, for the last three years I have polled more than 3,000 frontline supervisors and managers across a range of helping services made up mostly from child welfare, child and youth care, youth justice, and mental health. In an exercise at my workshops on supervision experience, I ask participants to reflect on their "best" supervision experience ever in their careers. On average, 40% of participants have stated that they have not had a single positive one! In some places, it was close to 50%!

More and more research is demonstrating unequivocally that frontline workers are less than satisfied with the quality and effectiveness of their supervision experiences. I agree fully with Gibbs (2001) that "it is disturbing to find such a preponderance of evidence which suggests many workers are receiving insufficient supervision and that they are dissatisfied with the quality of what they get" (p. 325). Several widespread surveys from across North America confirm this reality as large numbers of frontline social workers report that they are unsatisfied with supervision (Herbert, 2007; SWPI, 2011; Whitaker et al., 2006). For many workers, inadequate or poor supervision was not only recognized as an impediment to good practice, but it was also claimed as a major factor in burnout, intent to leave, and the decision to do so (Gibbs, 2001; Kim et al., 2010; Mor Barak et al., 2006, 2009).

We know that quality supervision as perceived by workers is positively related to a sense of empowerment, accomplishment, job satisfaction, organizational commitment, and organizational citizenship behaviors, and it is negatively associated with intention to leave, turnover, and burnout. I believe that this is the biggest of all dilemmas currently existing in our social services system! The gravest of concerns is to know that quality and effective supervision directly impact outcomes for workers and clients, and as it stands right now, the current state of supervision may be the workplace factor that is having the greatest negative impact on workers and subsequently the clients they serve.

There are a multitude of complex and layered factors resulting in the poor or, more accurately, the crisis state of supervision in the social services industry. However, I would like to provide some thoughts, based on my field experience, on what I believe has led to so many workers' poor to negative experiences with supervision. Before I begin, it is critical to note that most supervisors I have met over the years want the best for their workers and also for the clients that they serve. Yes, another dilemma indeed is 100% of supervisors wanting their best for workers, yet less than 40% of frontline workers express a less-than-satisfactory experience with supervision. The three factors worth noting that I believe impede a supervisor's ability to provide a quality supervision experience for workers are related to the lack of supervisory experience, formal supervisory training, and organizational and workplace conditions. It is the combination of these factors that impact a supervisor's ability to meet workers' unique and diverse needs and goals for quality and effective supervision.

Supervisors, Less Than Ready

Many supervisors in social services have little to no experience supervising and lack formal training. It is interesting that many supervisors are brought up through the ranks in their organization due to a variety of circumstances. Many workers are promoted because they demonstrate above average skill or a set of skills as an individual contributor. Sometimes supervisors are chosen due to attrition with the result of seniority prioritizing the next person in line for the team lead. As a matter of fact, in the current state of high turnover, especially in the higher ranking positions, there are positions that require backfilling or temporary assignment. Many workers find themselves being offered a supervisory position due to an organizational need, even before they have considered taking on the role. For instance, when I was in child welfare, I became a supervisor to fill a recently vacated position until someone else was hired. I had no previous experience or any formal training. I stayed in that position for six months. One time I was offered a coordinator position of a large child and youth care program. Not to downplay my skills, but I believe it was because there were no other options. These kinds of arrangements are not uncommon in the social services industry and while more common in some sectors than others, still quite common nevertheless. This means that many supervisors lack experience or do not have adequate training. I held three formal supervisory positions for over five years prior to engaging in formal supervisory training. I use the word "engage" because I was not a participant; I was the trainer. Yes! I became a formal provincial trainer of child welfare supervisors before I had any formal training myself. However, while formal supervisory training can be very helpful in equipping supervisors with an increased capacity to provide a positive supervision experience for workers, it is worth examining how formal supervisory training can actually pose a serious barrier to quality supervision.

Formal Supervisory Training as a Barrier to Quality Supervision

Formal supervisory training occurs outside of the realities of the work environment. Often workers are required to leave the field to go to a vacuum-like, controlled, stable, and sterile room to discuss concepts, theories, and practice models of supervision. Not only are trainees away from the challenging realities in which they are expected to contend with, often the supervisory curricula is based on national or professional practice standards that can be incongruent with the realities in the field. For instance, the curriculum I was expected to deliver was developed based on the Child Welfare League of America (CWLA) standards around caseload. At the time of curricula development, approximately 20 years ago, the standard caseload for a child welfare worker was between 15 and 20 cases. The reality is that the average number of cases on the caseloads of my supervisor training participants was approximately 40 to 60! Some were higher than this. Furthermore, there rarely were transfer-of-learning mechanisms in place before and after the training to assist and support supervisors with learning, integration, and sustainability of knowledge and new skills. I have always had issues with programs and curricula that do not prepare supervisors for the realities of the work environments we send them back into.

Another way in which supervisory training can be a barrier to preferred practice and a positive supervisory experience is due to the plethora of knowledge related to the large number of theories, models, and competencies available and utilized within supervisor training. The knowledge and requisite skill sets related to all of the theories of leadership and performance management can be overwhelming. While many formal training curricula are relevant and helpful, without the transfer-of-learning supports following the training, it often results in a serious loss of the formal training knowledge. Many frontline social service workers find it difficult to keep up with their own workloads, let alone try out newfound information and skills from training. Furthermore, without adequate supports for supervisors returning from training eager to try out new approaches, a potential helpful and exciting experience can turn into increased stress and strain, adding to and exacerbating already overwhelming work conditions.

One of the most important roles of social service managers is to develop the capacities of staff so that they can perform the most effectively and efficiently when carrying out the organization's mission and goals of service delivery (Vinokur-Kaplan, 2009). Therefore, a great deal of formal supervisor training focuses on motivating, developing, and managing worker performance. It is my belief, however, that while the many theoretical and technical orientations to motivating worker performance can provide insights and assistance to supervisor trainees, they may actually detract from a positive experience of quality supervision (back in the field) for both worker and the supervisor. How could this be? Unfortunately, we have been misled to a large degree by a behaviorist approach to performance development and especially performance management. Yukl (2010), when speaking to the complexities of leadership and performance, posits that "there are serious weaknesses in much of the behavioural research conducted during the past two decades" and adds that there has been "a tendency to look for simple answers to complex questions" (p. 75).

The theoretical approaches to motivating work performance were developed to provide supervisors with insight for analyzing performance, assessing problems, and planning intervention to extinguish poor behavior and enhance desired or preferred performance. The inherent problem with most of these theories is that they are grounded in human behavior theory and purport to explain and predict worker motivation and performance. The problem with formal supervisor training is that trainees are taught to interpret behavior and manage it. In addition to this, many curricula that deal with addressing poor performance or employee opposition and resistant behavior are geared toward starting with and addressing undesirable behavior, negatives, deficits, or performance weaknesses. Two things are often left out of the training: (1) how to allow for and incorporate the subjective experience and perceptions of the worker involved in the problem and (2) a strengths-based approach for dealing with problems, even as simple as a focus on worker strengths—what a worker does or is doing well.

Up to this point, I have mentioned that many supervisors in social services have little to no experience prior to becoming a supervisor. Also, I have pointed out that formal supervisor training can be incongruent or inadequate for meeting the demanding realities of the workplace environment. In addition to this, I have raised the concern that supervisor trainees are taught to interpret and manage worker performance outside supervisor knowledge of worker experience, perceptions, and strengths. So how can these things negatively impact a quality supervision experience for both worker and supervisor? It is likely to happen when the consequences of such arrangements occur in the context of the already taxing and stressful social service work environment.

Supervisors Are Not Superhuman

Supervisors are not immune to the organizational and workplace conditions that lead to stress, exhaustion, burnout, intention to leave, and turnover. As a matter of fact, they are contending with the exact same conditions and organizational environments as workers, but also have the added responsibility of supervising their team members simultaneously. The role of a supervisor in social services is exceptionally complex and demanding under "normal" circumstances. The vast value-based knowledge, skills, and competencies expected of supervisors in social services can seem overwhelming, even when categorized into the three supervisory functions of administration, education, and support, originally outlined by Kadushin (1976). According to the many conclusions formed regarding the complex roles of supervisors at a recent National Association of Social Workers (NASW) Social Work Policy Institute (SWPI) symposium on supervision was that "real world practice would indicate that it is difficult to actualize all of these roles simultaneously and it may not be feasible to expect to find all of these attributes in one individual" (SWPI, 2011, p. 1). According to the findings from the symposium, supervisors are having difficulty keeping up with fulfilling their administrative, educational, and supportive functions as supervisors (SWPI, 2011).

This is not at all surprising to people who work in the industry, especially supervisors who feel the crunch of their various roles and demands every day. In light of this discussion, poor supervision quality as expressed by workers in the field and specified in the literature should also be of little surprise. However, the question I have been struggling with is, out of the entire set of complex, interconnected, and mutually impacting work conditions, which have the greatest negative implications for a worker's experience of the quality of supervision? Generally speaking, it is the current state of supervision itself that is the biggest problem.

In the complex and multifaceted world of social service supervision, I have always appreciated the three-part supervisory functions of administration, education, and support developed by Kadushin (1976) and further expanded upon by Kadushin and Harkness (2002) and Shulman (1993, 2010). They are helpful in many ways in conceptualizing and compartmentalizing the various roles and modalities of supervisors in social service settings. However, I have always struggled with the order of importance, mostly of which the functions are categorized and subsequently prioritized; this has become a more important struggle recently due to the greater knowledge of the importance of the supervisor–worker relationship and positive outcomes for workers and clients, The supportive function receives third billing—the lowest priority—in relation to administrative and educative functions respectively, according to Kadushin and Harkness (2002). Since the beginning of empirical validation, the definition and categorization of the three supervisory functions demonstrated that supervisors involved in various studies were placing a large portion of their time and energy within the responsibilities related to the administrative function of supervision (Kadushin & Harkness, 2002). In some studies, administrative and educational tasks took the greatest priority while the supportive function took the lowest priority

(Poernter & Rapp, 1983; Shulman, 1982). And according to Kadushin and Harkness (2002), "tasks related to supportive supervision," in some studies, "were rarely if ever identified" (p. 24).

A Need for Change

What does all of this mean for a worker's experience of quality supervision? Based on what we know from the literature and from what workers are reporting, we should take a moment to speculate on some of the realities of the current state of supervision. This will be helpful in determining where to go from here. We know that there are many supervisors in the field that have little to no experience with supervision and probably also come up from the ranks of the large numbers of workers who were largely dissatisfied with their own supervision. What type of quality and effective supervision can we expect of new supervisors who are thrown into a crisis-oriented, time- and energy-constrained working environment that places administrative over supportive functions as priorities?

We also know that supervisors who are formally trained are taught to rely on deterministic and reductionist models of supervision, performance development, and performance management, which predominantly take a behaviorist approach to working to develop and manage staff. In a time- and energy-constrained environment, there is a tendency for supervisors to interpret and manage their workers' behavior rather than getting to know the employees' experiences. Individual performance plans are often the first mechanism to fall to the wayside in supervision as a majority of time is taken to put out fires, manage difficult cases, or deal with performance problems. Performance management in most social services, like the word *discipline*, does not have a positive connotation. It is often associated with a focus on performance deficits or weaknesses. In addition to this, all supervisors, regardless of being new, seasoned, untrained, or trained, operate in an environment that encourages problem-focused supervision and a progressive-discipline approach to performance management, with little if any emphasis on subjective experiences or worker strengths.

It is in this light that we can begin to understand the many reasons why there is such a prevalence of poor quality and overall dissatisfaction with workers' experiences of supervision. For many of the thousands of workers I have spoken with who are dissatisfied with supervision, they report experiences that reflect some or all of the following about their experience of supervision:

- It doesn't feel good.

- It goes against the values and expectations of how to work with clients.

- It's not what is needed.

- It's not what is wanted.

- It's not meaningful.

- Overall, it is just not helpful.

I am learning more and more that supervisors are subjected to working conditions not conducive to getting to know their workers' subjective experiences of the work and how they experience themselves within the work. They are unintentionally dislocated from the most important aspects of their most important resource: what a worker values, what they need, what they want, and what their strengths are. I also believe that due to this disconnect, supervisors are unable to respond to the unique and diverse values, needs, goals, and strengths of their workers in the process of facilitating and working toward the organizational mission, objectives, and service delivery. It is my point that this reality and the subsequent implications are major contributors to an overall poor or ineffective supervision experience for many workers.

The poor state of supervision experiences for a majority of social service workers and the deleterious consequences for both worker and client outcomes signifies a dire need for change. We need to take a serious look at supervision as the greatest mechanism for supporting and developing the capacities of workers to carry out their important roles as helpers. Currently, supervision is in crisis. Workers need more than supervision as we know it. They require a process for support and capacity development that places the greatest emphasis on the supportive aspect of supervision. Workers require a supervision process that places their individual values, needs, goals, and strengths as priorities and as avenues to enhance motivation, commitment, and engagement that enhances overall job satisfaction and organizational commitment. This can be a process that results in the approximation and achievement of preferred outcomes for both worker and clients simultaneously.

Frontline social service workers require more than supervision as we know it; they require leadership!

❖ SUMMARY OF IMPORTANT POINTS

- Social service workers are an extremely committed and highly motivated group of people.

- While social service work is rewarding, there exist a multitude of workplace and organizational impediments to preferred practice and supervision, impacting worker job satisfaction, motivation, and overall performance.

- Impediments to preferred practice and supervisory support can have negative impacts on both worker and client outcomes.

- The challenge for supervisors is not how to get workers motivated and engaged but how to keep them motivated and engaged.

- Many workers experience burnout, and many others experience intent to leave. Many remain in the field, working wounded.

- Supervision is a mechanism that can mitigate the negative effects of a tough work environment, thereby enhancing both employee and client outcomes.

- Unfortunately, the current state of supervision is in crisis as many workers report poor quality and/or inadequate supervision.

- A possible solution is to enhance quality supervision by focusing on quality leadership.

❖ PERSONAL LEADER REFLECTIONS AND CONSIDERATIONS

- Consider a time when you were most engaged and motivated. What contributed to that time?

- Consider your own work environment. Which of the above impediments to preferred practice and supervision can you identify? Which are within your control and/or may be influenced by you?

- Consider asking team members about their experience of supervision. What are they saying about their experiences of supervision?

- What has your own experience been like with respect to quality supervision?

- From what you know and/or what you are hearing from others about their experiences with supervision, what changes may be considered to enhance supervision quality?

❖ REFERENCES

Barter, K. (2005). *Working conditions for social workers and linkages to client outcomes: A literature review*. Ottawa, Canada: Canadian Association of Social Workers.

Bell, H., Kulkarni, S., & Dalton, L. (2003). Organisational prevention of vicarious trauma. *Families in Society: The Journal of Contemporary Social Work, 84*, 463–470.

Brown, S. P., & Leigh, T. (1996). A new look at psychological climate and its relationship to job involvement, effort and performance. *Journal of Applied Psychology, 81*(4), 358–368.

Carson, E., King, S., & Papatraianou, L. H. (2011). Resilience among social workers: The role of informal learning in the workplace. *Practice: Social Work in Action, 23*, 267–278.

Cordes, C. L., & Dougherty, T. W. (1993). A review and an integration of research on job burnout. *Academy of Management Review, 18*, 621–656.

Curry, D. H., McCanagher, T., & Dellmann-Jenkins, M. (2005). Training, transfer, and turnover: Exploring the relationship among transfer of learning factors and staff retention in child welfare. *Children and Youth Services Review, 27*, 931–948.

de Groot, S. (2006). *Empowering social workers in the workplace: A strengths based strategy for child welfare*. Ottawa, Canada: Canadian Association of Social Workers.

de Groot, S. (2010). *Empowering social workers in the workplace: A strengths based strategy for child welfare: Facilitator manual*. Winnipeg, Canada: General Child and Family Services Authority and the Canadian Association of Social Workers.

Garner, B., Knight, K., & Simpson, D. (2007). Burnout among corrections-based drug treatment staff. *International Journal of Offender Therapy and Comparative Criminology, 51*, 510–522.

Gibbs, J. A. (2001). Maintaining front-line workers in child protection: A case for refocusing supervision. *Child Abuse Review, 10*, 323–335.

Gimbel, R. W., Lehrman, S., Strosberg, M. A., Ziac, V., Freedman, J., Savicki, K., & Tackley, L. (2002). Organizational and environmental predictors of job satisfaction in community-based HIV/AIDS services organizations. *Social Work Research, 26*(1), 43–55.

Glisson, C. (2009). Organizational climate and culture and performance in the human services. In R. J. Patti, *The handbook of human services management* (2nd ed.) (pp. 119–142). Thousand Oaks, CA: Sage.

Graham, J. R., & Shier, M. L. (2010). The social work profession and subjective well-being: The impact of a social work profession on overall subjective well-being. *British Journal of Social Work, 40*, 1553–1572.

Herbert, M. (2007). Creating conditions for good practice: A child welfare project sponsored by the Canadian Association of Social Workers. In I. Brown, F. Chaze, D. Fuchs, J. Lafrance, S. McKay, & S. Thomas-Prokop (Eds.), *Putting a face on child welfare: Voices from the prairies* (pp. 223–250). Regina, Canada: Prairie Child Welfare Consortium and Centre for Excellence in Child Welfare.

Hodgkin, S. (2002). Competing demands, competing solutions, differing con-
structions of the problem of recruitment and retention of frontline rural
child protection staff. *Australian Social Work, 55*(3), 193–203.

Hopkins, K. M. (2002). Organizational citizenship in social service agencies.
Administration in Social Work, 26(2), 1–15.

Kadushin, A. (1976). *Supervision in social work.* New York, NY: Columbia
University Press.

Kadushin, A., & Harkness, D. (2002). *Supervision in social work.* New York, NY:
Columbia University Press.

Kim, H., Ji, J., & Kao, D. (2010). Burnout and physical health among social
workers: A three-year longitudinal study. *Social Work, 56*(3), 258–268.

Lambert, E. G., Hogan, N. L., Barton-Bellessa, S. M., & Jiang, S. (2012).
Examining the relationship between supervisor and management trust
and job burnout among correctional staff. *Criminal Justice and Behavior, 39*,
938–957.

Lee, T. W., Mitchell, T. R., Holtom, B. C., McDaniel, L. S., & Hill, J. W. (1999).
The unfolding model of voluntary turnover: A replication and extension.
Academy of Management Journal, 42, 450–462.

Liao, H., & Chang, A. (2007). Transforming service employees and climate: A
multilevel, multisource examination of transformational leadership to
building long-term service relationships. *Journal of Applied Psychology, 92*,
1006–1019.

Lizano, E. L., & Mor Barak, M. E. (2012). Workplace demands and resources as
antecedents of job burnout among public child welfare workers: A longitudinal study. *Children and Youth Services Review. 34*, 1769–1776.

Maslach, C. (1978). Job burnout: How people cope. *Public Welfare, 36*, 56–58.

Maslach, C. (2003). Job burnout: New directions in research and intervention.
Current Directions in Psychological Science, 12, 189–192.

Maslach, C., & Jackson, S. E. (1981). The measurement of experienced burnout.
Journal of Occupational Behaviour, 2, 99–113.

Maslach, C., Jackson, S. E., & Leiter, M. P. (1996). *Maslach Burnout Inventory
manual* (3rd ed.). Palo Alto, CA: Consulting Psychologists.

Maslach, C., & Leiter, M. P. (2008). Early predictors of job burnout and engagement.
Journal of Applied Psychology, 93, 498–512.

Mor Barak, M. E., Levin, A., Nissly, J. A., & Lane, C. J. (2006). Why do they
leave? Modeling child welfare workers' turnover intentions. *Children and
Youth Services Review, 28*, 548–577.

Mor Barak, M. E., Nissly, J. A., & Levin, A. (2001). Antecedents to retention and
turnover among child welfare, social work, and other human service
employees: What can we learn from past research? A review and meta-
nalysis. *Social Service Review, 75*, 625–661.

Mor Barak, M. E., Travis, D. J., Pyun, H., & Xie, B. (2009). The impact of supervision on worker outcomes: A meta-analysis. *Social Service Review, 83*, 3–32.

Patti, J. R. (2009). *The handbook of human services* (2nd ed.). Thousand Oaks,
CA: Sage.

Poertner, J., & Rapp, C. A. (1983). What is social work supervision? *Clinical Supervisor, 1*(2), 53–65.

Salamon, L. M. (1993). The marketization of welfare: Changing nonprofit and for-profit roles in the American welfare state. *Social Service Review, 67,* 17–39.

Shulman, L. (1982). *Skills of supervision and staff management.* Itasca, IL: Peacock Publishers.

Shulman, L. (1993). *Interactional supervision.* Washington, DC: National Association of Social Workers.

Shulman, L. (2010). *Interactional supervision* (3rd ed.). Washington, DC: National Association of Social Workers.

Social Work Policy Institute. (2011). *Supervision: The safety net for front-line child welfare practice.* Washington, DC: National Association of Social Workers.

Travis, D. J., & Mor Barak, M. E. (2010). Fight or flight? Factors influencing child welfare workers' propensity to seek positive change or disengage from their jobs. *Journal of Social Service Research, 36,* 188–205.

Vinokur-Kaplan, D. (2009). Motivating work performance in human services organizations. In R. J. Patti, *The handbook of human services management* (2nd ed.) (pp. 209–238). Thousand Oaks, CA: Sage.

Wallach, V. A., & Mueller, C. W. (2006). Job characteristics and organizational predictors of psychological empowerment among paraprofessionals within human service organizations: An exploratory study. *Administration in Social Work, 30*(1), 95–115.

Webster, L., & Hackett, R. K. (1999). Burnout and leadership in community mental health systems. *Administration and Policy in Mental Health, 26,* 387–399.

Whitaker, T., Weismiller, T., & Clark, E. (2006). *Assuring the sufficiency of a front-line workforce: A national study of licensed social workers: Executive summary.* Washington, DC: National Association of Social Workers.

Yukl, G. (2010). *Leadership in organizations* (7th ed.). Upper Saddle River, NJ: Prentice Hall.

2

Responsive Leadership

From Supervision to Inspiration

Circumstances are beyond human control, but our conduct is in our power.

— Benjamin Disraeli

❖ LEADERSHIP DEFINED

According to Northouse (2004), who conducted a survey on leadership in social services, "There are almost just as many definitions of leadership as there are people who have tried to define it" (p. 2). He goes on to define what I prefer as one of the most simplistic and straightforward definitions of leadership, describing it as "a process by which an individual influences a group of individuals to achieve common goals" (p. 4). However, while I prefer simplicity, one may say that Northouse's definition of leadership can also fit as a simplified definition of supervision. Supervision is not necessarily leadership, and not all supervisors are leaders. So in the spirit of the sentiment above and as a way of clearly differentiating leadership from supervision without complicating things further, I would like to throw my definition of leadership into the pool of definitions. The following definition of leadership has evolved from my experience of great leaders, what I have learned from conversations on leadership with thousands of workers and supervisors, and research on leadership. More recently, however, my view of leadership has been influenced tremendously by the following quote:

> *If your actions inspire others to dream more, learn more, do more and become more, you are a leader.*

— John Quincy Adams

I will therefore define leadership as *a process by which an individual or individuals inspire the attitudes and behaviors of others to engage in value-based and purpose-critical efforts in order to accomplish a set of shared objectives*. A leader inspires. For the purpose of this discussion *inspire* means to stimulate to action, motivate, be the cause or source of, or bring forth. Leadership is about inspiration! It is much more than an elaborate definition, a set of qualities or prescribed roles. Leadership is about a meaningful, significant, and valuable experience for both the leader and, more importantly, the person who is being led. Given the general state of poor-quality supervision across social services, workers need an approach to leadership that will connect with, inspire, and enhance worker motivation and commitment to feel better, be better, and do better as they carry out their role of helping.

Leadership and Accountability

It is important to note here that it was purposeful to make "value-based" and "purpose-critical" concepts an explicit aspect of the leadership definition. This is so because often values (vision and guiding principles) and purpose-critical processes and tasks (directly tied to mission and organizational objectives) are often implicit and left out of the scope of the definition and overall conception of leadership. When these two items are not named, they cannot be claimed. Great leadership is about holding oneself and others accountable. Organizational priorities and objectives are geared to driving the purpose of the work. Purpose-critical objectives help workers answer the questions, "Why do I have to do this?" and/or, "What's the point?" Values and guiding principles help workers answer the question, "Why do I have to do the work in this way?" while they carry out the work of helping. When workers can clearly answer, "What is the point?" and, "Why are we expected to do it in this way?" they are able to hold themselves and each other accountable to quality and effective helping. I believe, as I will elaborate further in Chapter 3, that guiding values and purpose-critical responsibilities are foundational to both accountability and motivation, and if left implicit or unclaimed, holding individuals responsible can be an elusive and frustrating process, more so within a highly bureaucratic, politically reactive, and crisis-oriented environment.

Leadership goes beyond what may seem to be, as I describe it, quality supervision. This is so mostly because social service supervision as we know it in the simplest way is composed of administrative, educational, and supportive functions (Kadushin & Harkness, 2002). Effective leadership as it will be discussed for the remainder of the book will focus primarily, as an absolute priority, on relationship quality between the leader and the person or persons being inspired as a key factor in the leadership process. I will refer to the person being inspired as member, employee, or worker rather than the common terms follower or subordinate. The latter two terms are less than flattering and connote a hierarchy of sorts.

A leader by the definition I put forth can be anyone who is responsible for directing, guiding, and supporting the work of others and has been identified as a leader by a particular individual or group. Such a definition of leadership opens up the possibilities for leadership by people in various roles such as colleague, mentor, supervisor, manager, director, and more, allowing for varying types of leadership arrangements such as coleadership or shared leadership among a group of individuals. The term supervision will remain in use as the mechanism, the interpersonal interaction and/or dyadic interface wherein leader and member come together in the structure and process of the leadership arrangement. Furthermore, it is not my intention to change the language we have come to know as most everybody understands what I am referring to and maintains their own experience of the mechanism of supervision.

A Practical Approach to Quality and Effective Leadership

Just as it is not my intention to change all of the terms and definitions that we have come to understand within a traditional supervision arrangement, it was definitely not my plan to put forth another model of leadership. It is my purpose, however, to offer insights and practical strategies for leadership that will inspire workers to feel better, be better, and do better in their work—to experience quality leadership, a strong sense of job satisfaction, and organizational commitment. In order to fulfill this objective, it will be necessary to articulate what

I believe are the two most important aspects of quality and effective leadership. The first and most important determining element of quality and effective leadership is the employee's perception of the leader–member relationship as positive, meaningful, and supportive. The second key variable that determines quality and effective leadership is a leader's capacity to learn about, understand, and respond to the unique needs, values, goals, and strengths of individual team members. By illustrating the important cornerstones of quality and effective leadership, I will offer relevant research, practice wisdom, and evidence-based practice examples to support and strengthen the rationale for the insights and practical strategies offered to leaders throughout the book.

Quality Leadership as an Experience

For the last decade, I have been working with thousands of supervisors in a variety of social service sectors to assist with the motivation, commitment, and engagement of workers. In particular, I wanted to help with those workers who seemed "less motivated," resistant, oppositional, or, as I referred to earlier, those employees that appeared disconnected, disengaged, and/or burnt out. For the most part, I have relied on the practical experience gained from what thousands of frontline workers and leaders have said contributed to quality leadership and, subsequently, preferred staff and client outcomes. In addition to relying heavily on what my social service comrades referred to as "doing what works," I supplemented my understanding of positive and not-so-positive experiences of supervision with knowledge from a variety of human behavior theories, models of leadership, and performance management approaches.

I began to understand that there was a strong connection between a worker's experience of quality supervision and two very important factors. The first was that workers who described a quality or positive experience with their supervisor often referred to the supervisor–worker relationship as a major factor. The relationship that contributed to a positive supervision experience was often characterized by key ingredients such as trust, respect, understanding, and integrity. The second prominent consistency was the strong correlation that existed between a worker's positive supervision experience and the expression by the worker that the experience was meaningful and or valuable, often because, in the workers' view, to some degree individual values, needs, and/or goals were being supported and/or accommodated by the supervisor.

Conversely, an opposite story was beginning to form with those workers that reported poor-quality or a negative supervision experience; that is, they reported an unsatisfactory supervisor–worker relationship and, unsurprisingly, low levels of trust, respect, understanding, or perceived integrity. In some instances, all of these ingredients were reported as hampered to some degree or missing all together. In addition to this, workers with a poor or conflicted relationship with their supervisors often expressed feeling misunderstood or unsupported by their supervisors. That was it! Workers with a positive supervision experience were feeling satisfied, motivated, and engaged; they were inspired. This was leadership. Those that reported a poor or negative supervision experience were less satisfied, motivated and engaged than their counterparts.

Changing the Environment Through Quality Leadership

One of the most profound realizations that hit me hard was that both satisfied and unsatisfied workers were working in similar working environments. This led me to question whether or not we could affect positive changes in worker motivation, commitment, and engagement if we could not change the larger systemic challenges and realities that negatively impact most social service work environments. The answer is a resounding yes! I began to look to the research on effective leadership and the connection to worker motivation, satisfaction, and organizational commitment. A great deal of literature and formal research on effective leadership and the positive impacts for workers and clients confirmed what I was experiencing in my interactions with frontline workers on the ground as key elements that differentiated quality and poor supervisor–worker experiences.

The evidence is overwhelming. We may not be able to alter the larger systemic challenges, but we can indeed enhance the overall quality of the supervisor–employee experiences by focusing on the capacity development of supervisors and managers to *lead*—to inspire workers and enhance performance.

It is in light of this strong revelation that I believe leadership, as an organizational dimension, is the primary source mediator of employee satisfaction, motivation, commitment, and engagement. Therefore, it reasons that the leader–member relationship is the greatest mechanism for fostering and facilitating overall employee performance toward the achievement of organizational and service outcomes. However, it is not necessarily the relationship per se but the perception of the quality of the leader–member relationship by the member that creates the greatest positive impact on employee satisfaction and performance.

While it is true that all employees, to some degree or another, have a relationship with their leaders, interpersonal and relational variance lies within the individual members' experience of the quality of that particular relationship. It is the employee's perceived quality of the leader–member relationship that characterizes and influences the member's level of satisfaction, motivation, and engagement with their job. In essence, high-quality leader–member relationships result in high-quality performance!

❖ QUALITY AND EFFECTIVE LEADERSHIP: KEY INGREDIENTS

Practice Wisdom and What We Know

Approximately 15 years ago, I began to develop frontline-practice training curricula from an appreciative and strengths-based perspective. I would often ask participants to reflect on and share a time in their career when they felt their best and were doing their best. What surfaced immediately as a consistent theme was the positive connection that existed between their best times at work and their best experience with a team leader, supervisor, manager, or director. Most people recounted their best times as being the time when they had the greatest quality leader–member relationship experience! This phenomenon was consistent and led to me to inquire specifically about their greatest leadership experience ever.

I would ask individuals and group participants to answer the following questions regarding their career history and experiences of past supervisors and/or managers:

- When was it the best?
- What made it the best?
- Who made it the best?
- What was it about your leader's behavior—their actions and/or interactions—that made your experience so great?

It is these questions and subsequent reflections that I have posed for years, in one-on-one interviews or small groups, to thousands of frontline workers and managers. I like to start many of my leadership trainings off with this type of appreciative inquiry in order to substantiate the important place relationship plays in the context of an employee's greatest leadership experience ever. What I find so fascinating is that, embedded within and throughout the thousands of diverse and unique stories, four key ingredients have surfaced to the top of the list every time. These four elements that have contributed to so many employees' greatest leadership experiences ever are *trust, respect, empathy*, and *integrity*. While the individual manner and meaning in which these ingredients are defined and discussed can vary, they are clearly evident in many employee statements regarding their best leadership experiences.

The term *safety* is one that surfaces quite often in the discussion of great leaders and great leadership experiences. Sometimes, it is referred to generally at first and, when described in more detail, combines and reflects one or more of the four key ingredients above. While many employee responses have pointed to a variety of informational, educational, supportive, administrative, and organizational factors that were in operation and clearly contributed to the best leadership experiences ever, the most essential were those qualities that are and were interpersonal and relation-oriented in nature. The *relationship* is absolutely essential for a great leader–member experience. Quality relationships and quality leadership are inextricably linked.

The following statements were captured from participant responses with in a "greatest leadership experience ever" exercise from one of the many leadership training seminars I have conducted. There are clear and evident reflections of *trust, respect, empathy*, and *integrity*, and contributing factors of a *safe* experience are also present in the reflections.

- "My supervisor was a great listener and remembered what was important to me."
- "I was safe to take risks in my new job without being criticised, judged or blamed."
- "My manager was approachable; I could see her for almost anything. I needed that."
- "I was asked my opinion and it was taken seriously."
- "My supervisor just gets it; he's been there and understands how hard it can be."
- "I had the autonomy I wanted, but if I needed something he was there."
- "She was dependable and reliable; I could trust her that she would follow through."

- "I had a manager that always started with what I was doing well; that made it easier to tackle the harder stuff, because I didn't feel like a total 'screw up.'"

The above statements are valuable because they reflect and speak to the importance of *trust, respect, empathy, integrity,* and an overall sense of *safety.* In addition to this and just as important is that each statement also reflects a realization and/or accommodation of what is important for individual members—their needs, values, goals, and strengths! What is consistent is that most workers and supervisors report that their leader really knew them and had an understanding of their perceptions and experiences, what they needed, what was important to them, and what they wanted for themselves and their clients. Their leaders were able to be responsive in the process of leadership.

In this light, it is not at all surprising that these employees were feeling their best and doing their best at work at a time in their career when they had the greatest quality leadership experience ever!

Research and What We Know

The last chapter pointed out that many frontline workers are dissatisfied with supervision and that a poor-quality supervision experience was implicated in worker burnout, intent to leave, and exiting behavior. We now know that quality supervision, which I refer to as a mechanism of effective leadership, has a significantly positive impact on both staff outcomes and outcomes for clients.

There is considerable research from a variety of nonprofit, for-profit, and corporate sectors demonstrating unequivocally the importance and positive implications of quality leader–member relationships as an important antecedent to overall leadership effectiveness. Furthermore, available research also points to variables, such as trust, respect, empathy, integrity, and overall safety, within the leader–member relationship that contribute and are connected to favorable employee experiences of work and themselves within the work. Favorable, positive work environments and attitudes increase motivation and job satisfaction and enhance organizational commitment and organizational citizenship behavior.

Research on leader–member exchange (LMX) theory illuminates and reinforces the importance of a quality supervision experience through an effective leader–member relationship. LMX theory posits that leaders develop an exchange relationship over time with each member (Dienesch & Liden, 1986; Graen & Uhl-Bien, 1995). According to Mahsud, Yukl, and Prussia (2010), "In a high exchange relationship there is a high level of trust, liking and respect" (p. 561). Also, in a high-exchange relationship, the leader is able to provide desired outcomes of the subordinate, and "in exchange the subordinate is expected to be committed to the work and loyal to the leader" (Mahsud et al., 2010, p. 561–562). Leaders who are able to develop high-quality exchange relationships with members are likely to be more effective than leaders who are less able to develop a high-quality leader–member exchange (Graen & Uhl-Bien, 1995). According to Mahsud et al. (2010), there is a great deal of empirical evidence demonstrating a strong positive correlation between LMX quality and leader effectiveness (e.g., Graen & Uhl-Bien, 1995; Harris, Wheeler, & Kacmar, 2009; Schriesheim, Castro, & Cogliser, 1999; Schriesheim, Neider, & Scandura, 1998). In a meta-analytic study of member–leadership exchange correlates, Gerstner and Day (1997) found that high exchanges were related to higher member satisfaction, greater organization commitment, better job performance, and lower turnover.

According to Mahsud et al. (2010), leader–member relationships that contribute to leader effectiveness are of high quality and characterized by a high level of trust and respect. This is an important point because this also confirms what many frontline workers and supervisors are saying contributes to a quality supervision experience. *Trust, respect, empathy*, and *integrity* are key ingredients in a quality supervision experience and effective leadership. This is not surprising, especially in light of the research and empirical evidence confirming the important place the qualities of trust, respect, empathy, and integrity hold for frontline workers, their supervisors, and the overall success of the organization. While these four variables are intertwined and mutually reinforcing of one another, it is important to have a look at them separately in order to understand the impact of each but also to shed light on the combined, subsequent implications of their simultaneous operation within the context of a leader–member relationship.

Trust and Integrity

Trust is the number one ingredient listed by workers—the most important aspect of a quality supervision experience—and is identified as the most important leadership variable that contributes to their best leadership experience ever. Robinson (1996) observed trust as "expectations, assumptions or beliefs about the likelihood that another's future actions will be beneficial, favorable, or at least not detrimental to one's interests" (p. 576). According to Caldwell and Dixon (2010), trust belongs among the most important factors influencing interactions in organizations as well as organizational success.

Trust and *integrity*, while sometimes noted by workers as separate leadership variables, are indeed intricately connected. Lambert, Hogan, Barton-Bellessa, and Jiang (2012) describe trust as the belief that there will be a congruency between what is said and what is done. The connection between trust and integrity has been confirmed in research on worker perceptions of trust. Perceptions of honesty and reliability (Kramer, 1999; McAllister, 1995) as well as perceptions of fairness and consistency (Mayer, Davis, & Schoorman, 1995) are key factors that contribute to trust in a leader–member relationship. The alignment between a person's words and deeds as perceived by another person is referred to by Kannan-Narasimhan and Lawrence (2012) as behavioral integrity. Behavioral integrity by a leader forms a strong source for leader–member trust. According to Kouzes and Posner (2002), leader integrity builds when leaders "practice what they preach" or "walk the walk"; that is, they do what they say they will do and follow through. This has been referred to as the acronym, DWYSYWD, which stands for "do what you say you will do" (Kouzes & Posner, 2002).

There is ample evidence on the positive effects and impact of trust and behavioral integrity for frontline workers and organizations overall. Organizations with workers who trust those in charge are more successful in the long run than organizations with workers who do not trust those in charge (Robinson, 1995). Workers who trust their supervisors and mangers are more satisfied in their jobs (Yang & Mossholder, 2010). Trust in a supervisor will often lead to reciprocal behaviors and positively affect work behavior outcomes and is linked with greater productivity of employees (Mayer et al., 1995; Mayer & Gavin, 2005). There is also evidence pointing to a link between worker trust and workers' willingness to be more open to feedback (Lambert et al., 2012). Trust is also linked to feedback in that workers who trust their leaders are more willing to provide feedback on important matters related to the work or the workers' experiences of the work (Wong & Cummings, 2009). Just as trust can have a positive impact on overall worker satisfaction, performance, and organizational commitment, the absence or breach of trust can have the opposite effect. Lack of trust can be a serious stressor for workers, and because it is a known buffer to burnout, the shortage or absence of trust has been linked to a whole host of negative employee outcomes (Lambert et al., 2012).

Respect

Respect, like trust, has been positively associated with workers' job satisfaction and organizational commitment (Laschinger & Finegan, 2005). Clarke (2011) points out that trust and respect are highly correlated and interrelated in a leadership situation and that the ability of the leader to convey caring, attentiveness, and support increases the likelihood of respect. Respect is a central element of the leader–worker relationship and directly tied to overall leader effectiveness (Clarke, 2011). From a behavioral perspective, respect, according to Clarke (2011), is less of a quality and more a result arising from specific behaviors of the leader. Yukl (1999, 2010) also speaks to the importance of relation-oriented behavior in leadership and emphasizes its importance in generating and maintaining respect. Early research on the importance of relation-oriented behaviors and leadership consistently confirmed the importance of behaviors related to consideration and supportive leadership and found that there was a correlation between this type of behavior and member satisfaction with the leader (Mahsud et al., 2010). One of the most important relation-oriented leadership behaviors that is key to a caring and supportive experience is empathy.

Empathy

Empathy is gaining a great deal of attention in research across a variety of disciplines regarding effective leadership and preferred worker and organizational outcomes. Like trust and respect, empathy has been identified as an important quality that is correlated with effective leadership and positive worker outcomes, including job satisfaction, organizational commitment, and enhanced performance. In addition to being identified as critical to effective leadership, empathy is identified as being correlated and interrelated with trust and respect and is defined as the ability to recognize and understand the emotions, feelings, and needs of others (Holt & Marques, 2011; Mahsud et al., 2010). When workers feel listened to and understood, there is likely to be an increase in trust and respect within the leader–member relationship. In addition to this, there is a great deal of research on the importance of leader empathy and the importance of emotionally attuned and expressive leaders.

Successful and effective leaders are not only sensitive to the needs and emotions of their members, but they can also regulate their emotions as well (Rajah, Song, & Arvey, 2011). A leader's ability to identify and display appropriate emotions to accommodate the needs of members assists those members with their own social and emotional regulation (Mayer & Salovey, 1997; Rajah et al., 2011). According to Rajah and associates (2011), in times of negative affect and high stress, which are commonplace in social service environments, leaders who are able to understand the group's emotions and regulate them prove to be among the most effective. Further, "when managers are able to empathize with followers' emotional reactions to stressful situations, and are capable of regulating these emotions, these often lead to desirable outcomes such as lower stress levels, increased job satisfaction, and better work performance" (Rajah et al., 2011, p. 1113).

Safety

I stated that many frontline workers and supervisors alike have mentioned safety as a quality of a great supervision or supervisor–worker experience. Often the word safety is used in this respect to describe a general feeling and, when elaborated on further, the description of the experience of safety produces concepts and/or images that relate directly to trust, respect, empathy, or integrity. Sometimes it is a combination of these factors that are used together to describe a worker's sense of safety within the supervisor–worker relationship. Safety, then, is a key element of the leader–member relationship and contributes to effective leadership. This is not surprising given the research on quality relationships and the importance of relations-oriented behaviors on worker and client outcomes.

There is evidence that the perception of the leader's character influences the followers' sense of trust and vulnerability to the other party's actions (Dirks & Ferrin, 2002). When supervisors listen, show consideration and caring, and are fair, consistent, reliable, and supportive, among many other types of relations-oriented behaviors, workers are more likely to feel safe—safe to ask questions, safe to be open to feedback and instruction, safe to give feedback to the leader, and safe to say, "I'm scared," "I don't understand," "I need help," or, "I don't know what I'm doing." Safety in the leader–member relationship is critical because the important people being served and supported by frontline helpers require that the workers are providing the most effective and highest quality service possible. Safety in the leader–member relationship creates an environment wherein workers can learn and develop optimally, which will assist them in performing to their greatest potential.

Quality Leadership and Relationship as a Pathway to Worker Experience

In light of the combined practice wisdom and research, it is clear that *trust, respect, empathy*, and *integrity* are undeniably key factors that contribute to effective leadership and quality supervision experiences. The leader–member relationship based on these factors is critical for enhancing job satisfaction, commitment, and overall engagement. The relationship is also essential for accessing a worker's story—his perceptions and lived experiences of work and himself within that work. I mentioned in the first chapter that while formal training can be helpful for leaders, current stress-laden and crisis-oriented work conditions coupled with less time for worker–leader interactions can lead unintentionally to the interpretation and management of employee behavior. When we get to know our workers outside of our own biases, generalizations, assumptions, past experiences, human behavior theories, and models of performance management approaches, we can gain greater access to the things about work and about them and their experiences of work that motivate and engage them to perform at their best. I also stated earlier that the number one piece of advice I give leaders is "Get to know your staff." A relationship built on the four key factors creates an avenue or pathway to learn the most about what, why, and how certain things are important to workers. What motivates them, why does it motivate them, and how can we as leaders keep them motivated, enhance their motivation, or resuscitate their resources and sources for motivation within the current challenging work conditions.

❖ THE ROAD TO A RESPONSIVE LEADERSHIP APPROACH

One of the last things I wanted to do when I became a social worker was to put forth yet another approach to leadership. However, the reality for me was that the area of supervision within social services, what I believe to be the most salient mechanism available for helping workers feel better and perform better in their work, was actually a detriment to preferred practice, workers themselves, and their clients. It is my intention to take an honest look at what we know to be certain about the challenging realities of social services supervision as well as the subsequent negative implications for employees in order to develop the simplest and most practical, efficient, and impactful approach to leadership. I want to create an approach that will accommodate and mediate the effects of those challenges on workers in a manner that enhances preferred outcomes for them and the important clients they serve and support.

We know that social service workers are a motivated group of individuals with varying needs, values, goals, and strengths for helping. We know for certain that workers' perceptions of their work environment directly affect their experiences, attitudes, behaviors, and, most importantly, how they perform in that particular environment. We also know that when social service employees operate in an environment that is perceived to be positive, meaningful, and valuable, outcomes will be better for both workers and their clients. We know that when workers find their work and work environment to be congruent with their values, accommodating of their needs and goals to help, and affirming and reinforcing of their strengths and capacities, they do better and their clients do better also.

However, we also know that the social services are not without serious systemic, organizational, and workplace realities that pose serious impediments to preferred ways of working and preferred outcomes. In addition, we know that myriad environmental challenges negatively impact many workers' experiences of the work and of themselves, leading to high levels of physical, emotional, and mental exhaustion, burnout, intent to leave, and turnover. For many workers who remain working in environments that may be challenging, they are not immune to the negative impacts on their own experiences of job satisfaction, motivation, engagement, commitment, and overall performance. Among the many challenging realities listed in Chapter 1 are some that may seem difficult if not impossible to change, like bureaucratic structure and hierarchy, political reactivity, fiscal restraint, mandated and legislated paper priorities, and more. However, there is a need to look to places within the system where immediate and impactful change can indeed be made. I pointed out in Chapter 1 that our greatest possibility for change may exist in what we commonly know as the mechanism of supervision.

Supervision: An Environment Within an Environment

Supervision as a mechanism can operate as an environment within an environment, as a pod-like shelter to protect workers from the detrimental effects of harsh working environments. Supervision can provide a type of necessary protection so that workers may be held up and built up, supported and developed in a manner that enhances their resiliencies to cope and work simultaneously to achieve meaningful and valuable results as they carry out their role of helping. We know that effective supervision can buffer the negative implications and effects of working in the social service industry. We know that supervisory social and emotional support and quality interpersonal supervision interactions result in a host of beneficial employee outcomes such as overall job satisfaction, organizational commitment, and organizational citizenship behaviors. We know that when employees are motivated, engaged, and committed to their work and their organization, when they feel better and perform better, preferred outcomes for clients are also more likely.

Unfortunately, generally speaking, supervision in social services is in a serious state of crisis. To a large extent, many workers are dissatisfied with supervision and report that their experiences of supervision are often inadequate, of poor quality and/or lacking in meaning or value. We know that inadequate or poor-quality supervision is a major factor in burnout, intention to leave, and high worker turnover. We also know that quality supervisor interactions and supervisory social and emotional support are negatively related to detrimental outcomes for workers. Given what we know about the inextricable link between workers' well-being and client outcomes, the current state of supervision and its consequences are absolutely alarming!

Enhance Support in the Support Component of Supervision

A major part of the problem leading to this dilemma is that the supportive aspect of supervision is given little priority in training or supervisory capacity development overall. In addition to this, supervisors are not given the skills to enhance the interpersonal, relations-oriented, and supportive capacities for quality supervision. Supervisor training curricula often prioritizes theories, models, and performance management strategies necessary for interpreting and managing the behavior of employees, inadvertently leaving little room for micro-practice skills necessary for connecting with and engaging the subjective experiences and strengths of workers. Furthermore, the supportive aspect of supervision is not only largely missing from training and development, but also as a practice priority, it tends to play third fiddle to the administrative and educational supervisory functions on the ground and can be almost nonexistent in the supervision experience of many frontline workers. When these realities are combined with the fact that many inexperienced supervisors operate in a stressful, complex, and crisis-oriented system that demands more and more from them, it becomes exceptionally clear how a quality and supportive supervision experience that is both meaningful and valuable can be lacking for many workers in the field of social services.

The current state of supervision does little to inspire workers to feel better, be better, and perform better in the role of helping. I believe that attempting to dismantle and reconstruct what we know as supervision may be a daunting and arduous task. How can we effect change? Where can we start to do this? I propose a simple proposition based on an important and well-known reality: When workers can operate in a positive work environment that is meaningful and supportive, outcomes will be better for employees and their clients. So therefore, I agree with Patti (2009) and believe that our priority for effecting the greatest change is to create organizational conditions that will lead to positive perceptions, attitudes, and behaviors that will lead to the highest quality and the most effective services possible. We may not be able to change the environment altogether, but we may indeed have the capacity to change the perceptions and experiences workers have of the environment that they operate within.

Accept What We Can't Change and Change What We Can

I think that quality supervision and a quality supervision experience can be enhanced if we adopt an approach to leadership that embraces the challenging impediments to preferred practice and prioritizes what we know to be the mechanism within our control to effect the greatest change—that is, the environment within the larger system environment, the mechanism of supervision. It is this idea of an environment within an environment that makes change more manageable and possible. Instead of focusing on the whole system and its challenges, how about placing the focus on an approach to leadership that prioritizes the individual experience of one worker at a time? By enhancing the overall job satisfaction, motivation, engagement, and performance of each worker within the context of supervision, we can impact the larger team and organizational environments in which they operate.

It is this thinking combined with the idea that social service employees require more than supervision that led me down the path of constructing an approach that will result in the most effective and highest quality leadership experience possible. Social services require an approach to leadership that will acknowledge, enhance, preserve, and even resuscitate frontline employees' motivation, engagement, and commitment. Workers require an approach to leadership that is simple, practical, and impactful and supports their needs, values, goals, and strengths in a manner that positively enhances their work and the experiences of themselves within the work. In addition to these things, the model of leadership must embrace and accommodate the challenging realities of the current social service environment in order to prioritize the preservation of the most valuable resources of time, energy, and funding.

❖ THE BUILDING BLOCKS OF A RESPONSIVE LEADERSHIP APPROACH

Earlier in the chapter, I defined leadership as a process by which an individual or individuals inspire the attitudes and behaviors of others to engage in value-based and purpose-critical efforts in order to accomplish a set of shared objectives. A leader inspires. How do leaders inspire? We know already that a quality leader–member relationship and a quality supervision experience are inspiring and have contributed to the stimulation of many workers to feel better, do better, and perform better in their work. Earlier in the chapter, I indicated that practice experience, research from leader–member exchange theory, and research on effective leadership point to the importance of trust, respect, integrity, and empathy behaviors as critical to developing a positive and quality leadership experience for the employee. Keep in mind, it has been well established that it is the employee's perception of the leadership that dictates the quality for that particular worker's experience to be both meaningful and valuable. This will be discussed further in Chapter 3.

Worker as Expert

While a quality leadership experience is indeed inspiring for most people, purposeful inspiration can be difficult for a leader to accomplish and maintain unless the leader knows what it is that inspires individual employees to feel, be, and perform better. Therefore, tuning into the employees' experiences of the work and their experiences of themselves within the work is the only way a leader can learn about and know for certain the unique needs, values, goals, and strengths of employees. Knowing and understanding a worker's experience is only one aspect of the Responsive Leadership Approach. Responding to what a leader understands with the right response at the right time is what makes the approach the most effective and impactful with and for employees. An accurate response by a leader to accommodate the perceived subjective experience of the member is what sets Responsive Leadership apart from other approaches to supervision. So what is it that leaders are responding to in their role as supervisor or manager? The employee experience of the work and their experiences of themselves within the work.

The Importance of Needs, Values, Goals, and Strengths

You may have noticed by now that when I discuss getting to know employees and their subjective experiences, I often refer to four main areas: needs, values, goals, and strengths. This is so for two important reasons. First, for the last decade I have been supporting supervisors and managers to tune into these particular areas, as I have come to understand them, as key sources of information for learning about and understanding what motivates workers to perform optimally. And rather than encourage an interpretation and management approach to professional development and/or performance management, I would encourage supervisors to work to understand the subjective experiences of a worker's needs, values, goals, and strengths—to respond to those key areas the most accurately, in a facilitative and engaging manner,

Because I had been out of the academic arena for many years, focusing my attention *in* the work versus *on* my work, I wasn't really aware until recently of the scholarship that had accumulated and evolved in the field of work motivation theory (WMT). WMT scholarship is what brings me to the second reason for my emphasis on a diligent focus on employees' needs, values, goals, and strengths. A great compilation of WMT and research by Latham and Pinder (2005) has increased my understanding of the powerful role individual needs, values, and goals play when it comes to motivation at work. I was surprised that a focus on strengths is missing altogether within the discourse regarding WMT; however, I have seen firsthand the powerful influence a strengths focus has on worker motivation and overall performance enhancement. I will discuss the positive implications of a strengths focus in leadership further in Chapter 5.

Work motivation is a set of energetic forces that originate both within as well as beyond the individual's being to initiate work-related behavior and to determine its form, direction, intensity, and duration (Pinder, 1998, p. 11). This definition speaks to the important implication of both the individual and the environment as impacting motivation and, more importantly, the interaction between the worker and the worker's environment. I have always known that needs, values, and goals were separate concepts yet were also intricately related. The work offered by Latham and Pinder (2005) presents a clear conceptualization of the interconnectedness of these three motivation factors. They write, "Values are rooted in needs and provide the principal basis for goals. . . . Goals are the mechanism by which values lead to action" (Latham & Pinder, 2005, p. 491). In this light, needs are at the root of most behavior and, according to Kanfer (1991), are internal tensions that influence and mediate cognitive processes which result in behavior variability. Behavior variability refers to the differences that exist between and among individuals. This point emphasizes the need and importance for leaders to get to know the unique needs, values, goals, and strengths of their members so that they can respond to and accommodate those preferences, to the extent possible in the context of the work and work environment.

A great deal of scholarship and research clearly point out that effective leaders are those supervisors and managers who get to know and understand the unique needs, values, and goals of their workers (Latham & Pinder, 2005; Mahsud et al., 2010; Maslach & Leiter, 2008; Mor Barak, Travis, Pyun, & Xie, 2009; Rajah et al., 2011; Vinokur-Kaplan, 2009; Yukl, 1999, 2010). Getting to know workers is only part of the equation. More important is what happens as a result of that knowledge, especially when we consider that work motivation emerges not only from within the individual but also from the interaction between the individual and the environment. It is critical that leaders, to be the most effective, understand what needs, values, and goals are important to workers in order to look for opportunities and resources available within the work environment to fulfill those needs, align with values, and accommodate goals, to the extent possible. Furthermore, effective leaders that know and understand their members well can choose appropriate relations-oriented, supportive, helpful, and developmental responses to increase the meaning and value of the work and their experiences of self in the work for members. I refer to this as a leader's capacity to choose the right response at the right time to accommodate and/or approximate the unique needs, values, goals, and strengths of workers in a way that inspires them to perform at their absolute best as they carry out the role of helping.

❖ THE GUIDING PRIORITIES OF RESPONSIVE LEADERSHIP

The Responsive Leadership Approach was developed out of my understanding of stories regarding best leadership experiences gathered from thousands of frontline staff, supervisors, and managers. Responsive leadership builds on leader–member exchange (LMX) theory, work motivation theory (WMT), and has been influenced by both my clinical and organizational knowledge and experience. Responsive Leadership represents an approach to leadership that prioritizes quality leader–member relationships as critical to enhancing employee job satisfaction, organizational commitment, and organizational citizenship behavior. Responsive Leadership encourages leaders, through a relations and strengths orientation, to learn about and engage with employee needs, values, goals, and strengths in order to optimize motivation, employee satisfaction, and overall performance. Furthermore, Responsive Leadership, through the enhancement of employee outcomes, aims at the simultaneous approximation of enhanced climate and culture as well as preferred outcomes for children, families, and communities.

The following represent the guiding priorities of a Responsive Leadership Approach to supervision and management. In order to achieve optimal leadership quality and effectiveness, to positively impact employee motivation, engagement, commitment, and overall performance, a responsive approach to leadership must

- focus on the mechanism of supervision (dyadic interface) as the primary level for leadership development,

- make quality leader–employee relationships an essential focus,

- promote the operationalization of trust, respect, integrity, and empathy to enhance the meaning and value of a quality leadership experience,

- emphasize interpersonal and communication skill development,

- utilize relations-oriented and strengths-based tools/strategies for accessing the employee and the employee's story,

- encourage the accurate identification and engagement of employee needs, values, goals, and strengths through a variety of responsive tools and strategies,

- strive for greatest "fit" between employee experience and environment in order to optimize worker motivation, engagement, and overall performance, and

- work to improve and attain preferred outcomes for both staff and clients.

In addition to the guiding priorities, one of the most important objectives of the Responsive Leadership Approach is that it was constructed to be simple, practical, and impactful. It was developed as a way of uncomplicating leadership. The concepts and processes involved are simple and quite basic, the tools and strategies highly concrete and tangible, and the impact immediate and transformative. The Responsive Leadership Approach truly epitomizes the saying, "The whole is greater than the sum of its parts."

The individual parts of the approach are helpful, but it is the way that the pieces of the perspective work together to mutually and reciprocally influence the other aspects of the approach that gives it profundity. This is the part where some people wonder if my excitement and my statements are embellished. However, to date I have utilized this approach to leadership with more than 2,500 supervisors, managers, and executives across a variety of social service sectors. One hundred percent have reported a positive change in their leadership development and overall experience. More importantly, 100% of the managers trained and supported in this approach have also reported that the Responsive Leadership strategies, tools, and processes have resulted in an increase in individual worker and team morale, motivation, engagement, and performance. Furthermore, most have reported the by-product of major savings in time, energy, and money. In an environment where time and money constraints are endemic, these particular by-products of the Responsive Leadership Approach were unexpected yet welcomed gifts.

Overall, Responsive Leadership posits that leaders are responsible for inspiring workers to feel better, be better, and perform better in their role of helping. The remainder of the book will offer simple, practical, and transformational concepts, tools, and strategies for putting into practice the guiding priorities of a Responsive Leadership Approach.

❖ SUMMARY OF IMPORTANT POINTS

- Leadership is about inspiration—to stimulate, motivate, and bring forth greater worker motivation, engagement, and overall performance.

- Quality and effective leadership is defined by the perceptions and experiences of the worker.

- Greatest leadership experiences are built on the key qualities of trust, respect, integrity, and empathy.

- Quality supervision through effective leadership can positively alter a worker's perception of the work environment, leading to better outcomes for both employees and clients.

- A responsive approach to leadership sets leader–member relationships as the highest priority.

- A responsive approach to leadership encourages supervisors to engage and understand worker needs, values, goals, and strengths.

- A responsive approach to leadership can enhance worker motivation, engagement, and overall performance.

❖ PERSONAL LEADER REFLECTIONS AND CONSIDERATIONS

- Consider a time in your career when you had the greatest leadership experience. When was it the greatest? What made it so great? Who made it so great? What was it about your leader's behavior—their actions and/or interactions—that made your experience so significant?

- Consider how your perceptions and experiences of great leadership were related to operationalized qualities such as trust, respect, integrity, and empathy.

- Consider what you do in your role as a leader to promote, endorse, and/or foster the qualities of trust, respect, integrity, and empathy.

❖ REFERENCES

Caldwell, C., & Dixon, R. D. (2010). Love, forgiveness, and trust: Critical values of the modern leader. *Journal of Business Ethics, 93,* 91–101.

Clarke, N. (2011). An integrated conceptual model of respect in leadership. *Leadership Quarterly, 22,* 316–327.

Dienesch, R. M., & Liden, R. C. (1986). Leader–member exchange model of leadership: A critique and further development. *Academy of Management Review, 11,* 618–634.

Dirks, K. T., & Ferrin, D. L. (2002). Trust in leadership: Meta-analytic findings and implications for research and practice. *Journal of Applied Psychology, 87,* 611–628.

Gerstner, C. R., & Day, D. V. (1997). Meta-analytic review of leader-member exchange theory: Correlates and construct issues. *Journal of Organizational Behavior, 22,* 789–808.

Graen, G. P., & Uhl-Bien, M. (1995). Relationship-based approach to leadership, development of leader–member exchange (LMX) theory of leadership over 25 years: Applying a multilevel multi-domain perspective. *Leadership Quarterly, 25*, 219–247.

Harris, K. J., Wheeler, A. R., & Kacmar, K. M. (2009). Leader–member exchange and empowerment: Direct and interactive effects on job satisfaction, turnover intentions, and performance. *Leadership Quarterly, 20*, 371–382.

Holt, S., & Marques, J. (2011). Empathy in leadership: Appropriate of misplaced? An empirical study on a topic that is asking for attention. *Journal of Business Ethics, 105*, 95–105.

Kadushin, A., & Harkness, D. (2002). *Supervision in social work.* New York, NY: Columbia University Press.

Kanfer, R. (1991). Motivation theory and industrial and organizational psychology. In M. D. Dunnette & L. M. Hough (Eds.), *Handbook of industrial and organizational psychology* (pp. 75–170). Palo Alto, CA: Consulting Psychologists Press.

Kannan-Narasimhan, R., & Lawrence, B. S. (2012). Behavioral integrity: How leader referents and trust matter to workplace outcomes. *Journal of Business Ethics, 111*, 165–178.

Kouzes, J. M., & Posner, B. Z. (2002). *The leadership challenge* (3rd ed.). San Francisco, CA: Jossey-Bass.

Kramer, R. (1999). Trust and distrust in organizations: Emerging perspectives, enduring questions. *Annual Review of Psychology, 50*, 569–599.

Lambert, E. G., Hogan, N. L., Barton-Bellessa, S. M., & Jiang, S. (2012). Examining the relationship between supervisor and management trust and job burnout among correctional staff. *Criminal Justice and Behavior, 39*, 938–957.

Laschinger, H., & Finegan, J. (2005). Using empowerment to build trust and respect in the workplace: A strategy for addressing the nursing shortage. *Nursing Economics, 23*(1), 6–13.

Latham, G. P., & Pinder, C. C. (2005). Work motivation theory and research at the dawn of the twenty-first century. *Annual Review of Psychology, 56*, 485–516.

Mahsud, R., Yukl, G., & Prussia, G. (2010). Leader empathy, ethical leadership, and relations-oriented behaviors as antecedents of leader-member exchange theory. *Journal of Managerial Psychology, 25*, 561–577.

Maslach, C., & Leiter, M. P. (2008). Early predictors of job burnout and engagement. *Journal of Applied Psychology, 93*, 498–512.

Mayer, R. C., Davis, J. H., & Schoorman, D. F. (1995). An integrative model of organizational trust. *Academy of Management Review, 20*, 709–734.

Mayer, R. C., & Gavin, M. B. (2005). Trust in management and performance: Who minds the shop while the employees watch the boss? *Academy of Management Journal, 48*, 874–888.

Mayer, J. D., & Salovey, P. (1997). What is emotional intelligence? In P. Salovey & D. J. Sluyter (Eds.), *Emotional development and emotional intelligence* (pp. 3–31). New York, NY: Basic Books.

McAllister, D. (1995). Affect- and cognition-based trust as foundations for interpersonal cooperation in organizations. *Academy of Management Journal, 38,* 24–60.

Mor Barak, M. E., Travis, D. J., Pyun, H., & Xie, B. (2009). The impact of supervision on worker outcomes: A meta-analysis. *Social Service Review, 83,* 3–32.

Northouse, P. (2004). *Leadership: Theory and practice* (3rd ed.). Thousand Oaks, CA: Sage.

Patti, R. J. (2009). *The handbook of human services management* (2nd ed.). Thousand Oaks, CA: Sage.

Pinder, C. C. (1998). *Work motivation in organizational behavior.* Upper Saddle River, NJ: Prentice Hall.

Rajah, R., Song, Z., & Arvey, R. D. (2011). Emotionality and leadership: Taking stock of the past decade of research. *Leadership Quarterly, 22,* 1107–1119.

Robinson, S. L. (1996). Trust and the breach of the psychological contract. *Administrative Science Quarterly, 41,* 574–599.

Schriesheim, C. A., Castro, S. L., & Cogliser, C. C. (1999). Leader–member exchange (LMX): A comprehensive review of theory, measurement, and data-analytic practices. *Leadership Quarterly, 10,* 63–113.

Schriesheim, C. A., Neider, L. L., & Scandura, T.A. (1998). Delegation and leader–member exchange: Main effects, moderators, and measurement issues. *Academy of Management Journal, 41,* 298–318.

Vinokur-Kaplan, D. (2009). Motivating work performance in human services organizations. In R. J. Patti, *The handbook of human services management* (2nd ed.) (pp. 209–238). Thousand Oaks, CA: Sage.

Wong, C., & Cummings, G. (2009). The influence of authentic leadership behaviors on trust and work outcomes of healthcare staff. *Journal of Leadership Studies, 3,* 6–23.

Yang, J., & Mossholder, K. W. (2010). Examining the effects of trust in leaders: A bases-and-foci approach. *Leadership Quarterly, 21,* 50–63.

Yukl, G. (1999). An evaluation of conceptual weaknesses in transformational and charismatic leadership theory. *Leadership Quarterly, 10,* 285–305.

Yukl, G. (2010). *Leadership in organizations* (7th ed.). Upper Saddle River, NJ: Prentice Hall.

PART II

From Concepts to Practice

Responsive Leadership Strategies and Tools

3

Perception Is Everything

We do not see the world as the world is, we see the world as we are.

— Stephen Covey

❖ PERCEPTIONS OF EFFECTIVE SUPERVISION AND QUALITY LEADERSHIP

The last chapter provided research and many accounts on the importance of and significant role individual perceptions play in shaping our experiences with leaders and work environments. We know for certain that it is the workers' perceptions of leaders' behavior and character that will determine whether a worker will trust, respect, and subsequently "follow" or be inspired by that particular leader. There is a direct connection between workers' perceptions of the quality of leadership and their experience of competence, personal accomplishment, organizational commitment, and job satisfaction. Therefore, whether or not leadership is determined to be of quality and/or effective is dependent upon the workers' perception of that experience.

Individual perceptions and the impact on a workers' experience of work and of themselves within the work extends beyond the immediate leader–member relationship. We also know that workers who perceive their immediate work environment as positive experience greater job satisfaction and organizational commitment. When workers perceive their work climate to be positive, meaningful, and supportive, outcomes will be better for both the worker and the clients they serve. Worker perceptions of the leader, leadership, and the work environment therefore directly impact their experience, their attitudes, their behaviors, and, most importantly, how they perform at work.

I have witnessed firsthand the significant role worker perceptions play in shaping and determining the worker experience of leadership and of the work overall. Among many of my important learning experiences as a supervisor and trainer of supervisors and managers over the years, there are three situations in particular that stand out as "lightning-bolt moments." It was these specific instances that contributed to and solidified my understanding of the importance of employee perceptions, a quality leadership experience, and subsequent impacts on employee engagement, motivation, and performance. I will share a brief overview of each situation, including insights, themes, and important lessons learned that have influenced and continue to influence the primary importance I place on employee perceptions and the employee's story—their lived experience.

Situation 1: We may not know what we think we know.

Like most supervisors in the social services, I began supervising clinical therapists and residential group care workers long before I had any formal training as a supervisor, other than a field-placement training course, which I taught! I had a great deal of supervision experience but lacked formal training or any type of feedback on the quality and effectiveness of my supervisory efforts. At one point in my career, I was responsible for supervising the staff in a large residential youth care program: seven clinical therapists, 22 program managers, and approximately 125 frontline child and youth care workers. Without a direct supervisor or manager myself, it was not long before I realized that providing quality and effective supervision for everyone might be absolutely impossible! It was desperation and necessity that led me to enlist my clinical therapists to help with supervision of staff. Also, because the program did not have time or money to provide formal supervision training, I planned to train my team to supervise as an aspect of their professional development through their individual supervision sessions with me.

Now I think it is important to note that up until this particular time, I would state confidently that I was a great supervisor. It was my perception that I was doing everything well; for years, my teams seemed happy and productive, and I had never heard otherwise. So confidently I began to prepare my clinical team members to be supervisors and encouraged them to consider their preferred supervision approach. It wasn't until I asked them to do this that I realized I had never considered mine. In addition to this, it was not until this point that I had ever stopped to think, "How do I prefer to be supervised?" and, "How do I prefer to supervise?" These were not easy explorations. It took me some time to connect with what, why, and how I preferred to supervise. I had never ever stopped to consider this before. Wow!

Through exploration and various reflections, I discovered that I supervised the individuals on my team the way that I preferred to be supervised, which was directly linked to my own needs, values, and goals. In addition to this, I supervised everyone on my various teams the same way—same structure, same process, same format, same questions, and so on. I learned that I just pieced together what I had learned from my own past supervisors over the years and combined it with what I "liked" from the supervision courses I was teaching at the university. Like most supervisors, I was doing what I liked and what made the most sense for me.

This represented a very important yet challenging and meaningful eye-opening journey. It seemed as though I had to start from the beginning again, which was a little embarrassing because I had been supervising some of my team members for years. I asked each of them these questions:

- Tell me when supervision was the best or most helpful for you at any time in your career?

- What made it so meaningful or valuable?

- How would you prefer supervision?

- What would be the most helpful for you?

Interestingly, just as I struggled to figure out what, why, and how I liked to be supervised, it was difficult for my team members also. It was as though we were all on autopilot. In sharing perspectives, we were able to figure out specific individual preferences for what we each defined as a quality supervision experience.

Thankfully, I found out that I was doing a lot of things right, such as being trustworthy, respectful, a good listener, and a role model; however, there were things I could have been doing differently that would have made a significant differences for each of my team members. For instance, Lindsay preferred more supervision, not less, and preferred it early in the day, when she was alert and energized. She preferred a more structured, organized, supervisor-led supervision session with a clear agenda and concrete objectives and activities focused primarily around cases and clinical intervention. Small talk and getting off topic was not a favorable occurrence for Lindsay as she wanted to use the time most efficiently. However, personal check-ins were very important as was Lindsay's preference for having her strengths identified and feelings affirmed and validated. These were just some of the many insights I gained around Lindsay's preferences for the most meaningful and valuable supervision. Raegan on the other hand wasn't as concerned with formality, structure, or format and preferred a collaborative back-and-forth dialogue that was led mostly by her. She valued supervisor input that was relevant and concrete. Rather than following a set agenda, Raegan preferred a quick review of cases so that there was more time to discuss pressing matters as they related to clients, the team, the organization, or her own professional development. Raegan believed that less supervision was better for her at that particular juncture in her career and within the present work environment.

I began to learn that despite my team members' common purpose for being in this field, they maintained unique needs, values, and goals for supervision and the work overall that if and when accommodated made a significant difference for them and their work. This knowledge enhanced my work in a number of ways. I found individual supervision sessions became more focused, effective, and meaningful. Furthermore, because effectiveness and quality were enhanced, individual supervision sessions were shorter in length and were required less frequently. From a practical standpoint, we were saving valuable time and energy, which are what I refer to as nonrenewable resources in the social service industry.

This particular situation surfaced important themes that were positively impactful then, and the insights gained continue to influence my understanding of the importance of perception on effective supervision and overall leadership quality. Some of these themes are

- many supervisors don't know what they think they know,

- supervisor perspectives often differ from their workers,

- often supervisors don't know what they are doing that works well with staff and/or what needs to be changed,

- worker perceptions and experiences hold the key to worker preferences for effective supervision and quality leadership,

- supervisors and workers may not know their own preferences for supervision,

- worker perceptions on effective supervision may be different than their supervisors' perceptions, and

- perceptions of trust, respect, and empathy are important to most workers.

Situation 2: All is not as it seems.

Early on in my career as a provincial trainer of supervisors and managers in child welfare, I began to learn of a gap in perceptions that existed between those of the supervisors and of their individual members. The advantage of training in a small province as a trainer of frontline workers and managers is that there are times when one week I would have frontline workers as attendees, and later that month, I would have their direct supervisors in training on supervision. This proved to be an interesting situation because often frontline staff would talk about experiences with their supervisors. Also, managers would be encouraged, as part of their training curriculum, to talk about specific staff concerns, especially in the three-day program designed to assist supervisors on how to effectively manage "difficult" employees.

One day, a supervisor who I will refer to as Barb showed up early for the "how to manage difficult employees" training. She informed me that she had been waiting for this training for months because she really wanted to learn how to "fire a problem staff member." I reminded her that the curriculum was designed to assist with understanding and managing challenging behaviors. She boldly stated, "Nothing will help this guy I inherited. He has got to go!" Despite my efforts to encourage her to use the curriculum strategies to gain an understanding of the presenting issues, she was adamant that nothing was going to change her mind. On more than several occasions over the three days, I had to interrupt the group work at her table because she capitalized on the working time to enlist five other participants to sympathize with her plight. She continually focused on the negative aspects of her situation and built her case with colleagues at the table to fire this particular staff member.

Barb consistently listed all of the behaviors that bothered her. She stated that her staff person was lazy and avoidant. According to her, he was spending less time at work, and when he was at work, he would leave unit meetings and group supervisions early. He was withdrawn and passive in individual supervision sessions. According to her, she didn't know if he was even listening as he consistently "did not take direction well." She stated that she had reprimanded him on several occasions and indicated that he must attend all unit meetings and individual and group supervision sessions. In describing her staff member and his behavior, Barb used words like lazy, uncommitted, uncooperative, insubordinate, passive-aggressive, and poor team player. Throughout the training sessions, I did my best to assist Barb on working to understand the employee's behavior. She was adamant that she had done all that she could. Her staff action plan stated, "Fire Brandon!" in bold letters across the entire staff development document.

Flash forward one month. I am training 70 frontline workers in a relationship-based strengths approach to child welfare intervention. In the back of the room is a participant that catches my attention. He is active and engaged, asking great questions, and responding to the material in an operationally consistent manner that was well in line with the curriculum values and preferred practice. Not only did he know this approach, it was obvious that he was a skilled practitioner also. He stood out so much that I became curious to know where he had trained, and I was also interested as to whether he had or would consider training workers in this approach. I had lunch with him.

What I learned blew my mind! As I listened to his story, I heard that training was one of the few contexts in the field where he still felt good and confident in his abilities anymore. He went on to say that he loved his job as a community support worker but was feeling very unsatisfied at work over the past year. He claimed that he did not have a good relationship with his supervisor, stating that he had little respect for her as a leader. He mentioned that he entered the field to work with people, not to spend his time in meetings and group supervisions. He stated that he appreciated team functions but not too many; nor did he like meetings that went on too long or were irrelevant to his work or his professional development. He noted that although he didn't feel good about it, he had been avoiding team functions in order to make more time for the clients on his caseload. He indicated that this had caused a great deal of tension between him and his supervisor. In his words he stated, "I don't trust her. I think she is lining me up to be fired." His name was Brandon! Oh my goodness, it hit me: This was Barb's problem staff member! I was in a bind because I could not breach confidentiality; however, I offered to help. He declined as he was feeling hopeless and felt as though he had tried everything. He considered putting in for a transfer to another department. I heard from my professional contacts that Brandon was terminated six weeks later.

This was another lightning-bolt moment. How could the person described by Barb as the worst social worker ever be experienced by me and/or other supervisors as the social worker we would love to have on our team? We need workers like Brandon in the field. He was a great worker—motivated, engaged, and wired to make a positive difference. Regardless of the details, there was a serious problem with perceptions. What is astounding is that the more I listened to Barbs and Brandon's stories, the more I learned that they actually wanted the same thing: to work in a manner that was best for clients and the team. They both wanted to get the job done and to do their best by the clients they served.

This experience hit me hard and deeply as a person committed to developing the best capacities of both frontline workers and their leaders. I also share the desire to do the best for the children, families, and communities we serve. Quality client service and support is dependent upon workers and their leaders. Remember, there exists a set of inextricable links between quality leadership and positive worker experience of self and the work, between positive employee experiences and quality practice decisions, and between good practice decisions and preferred outcomes for clients. We need workers like Brandon to feel better and to perform better. We need supervisors like Barb to be less frustrated, angry, and exhausted. While I will discuss similar leader–member dilemmas in Chapters 4 and 7 in the context of understanding and approaching resistance and oppositional behavior, it is important to note that the gap in different perceptions/experiences between supervisors and employees is very common, and the space can range from minor and insignificant to absolutely massive. I sometimes refer to the big ones as the "Grand Canyon gaps" in perceptions, issues that can lead to increased stress and conflict and all sorts of problems for leaders, their staff, and eventually for their clients.

This particular situation, like many other similar situations that followed in my career, surfaced important themes that were positively impactful then, and the insights gained continue to influence my understanding of the importance of perception on effective supervision and overall leadership quality. Some of these themes are as follows:

- Often supervisors and workers, despite differences, want the same things: better working relationships and preferred client outcomes.

- Supervisors and workers can have very different perceptions of the same situation.

- Large differences in supervisor and worker perceptions can cause stress and conflict.

- Conflict caused by differences in supervisor and worker perceptions can negatively impact trust, respect, the leader–member relationship, and overall performance.

Situation 3: One small difference can make BIG differences.

I have had the privilege of working on some amazing projects that were geared toward enhancing social work team capacity. One project in particular, the Empowering Social Workers (ESW) Project (de Groot, 2006), was directed at empowering child welfare workers through a strengths-based approach to embrace and alter challenging workplace realities in a manner that would result in increased optimism, morale, empowerment, and team cohesion. A significant point to mention is that the ESW Project was initiated at the same time as what people refer to as the "worst time in child welfare in our province's history." The project was launched days prior to the discovery of an atrocious child death and the subsequent negative and tumultuous child death review that followed. This is important not because many project participants stated that it was the worst time to be working in child welfare in their entire careers but because the project demonstrated that we can effect positive change even at a time when workers in a system are feeling the most devalued, unsupported, and demoralized.

There were a number of purposeful and unintentional insights gleaned from the project. The hypothesis that we could effect positive changes in worker experience and overall workplace climate was confirmed in our work. This was exciting as it affirmed and validated the idea that we could positively affect workplace climate even if political, bureaucratic, fiscal, organizational, and workplace challenges continued to persist. However, despite the intentional deductions gathered, there were two significant surprises that occurred, one during the project and the other during project follow-up. The first surprise that occurred within the project was the importance the supervisor played in the experiences of workers and of the workplace climate overall. Many project participants reported being dissatisfied with supervisory support and/or supervision due to a variety of factors. Some of these factors included a new supervisor being placed with the team, the team not knowing the supervisor, the supervisor not knowing all of the team members, diverse and differential staff support and supervision needs, trust and safety requiring more effort and work, little acknowledgment or validation by the supervisor, and workplace challenges making it hard on the supervisor (de Groot, 2006, p. 121).

It is important to note that when the project supervisor learned of this information following the project report, he was surprised and his feelings were hurt. However, like many great leaders, he agreed to team building in order facilitate a better understanding and accommodation of individual team members' needs and preferences for supervisory support and supervision. He wanted to do the best for his members and staff. I was asked to facilitate the initiative. I referred to the exercise as "Preferred Supervision: Identifying Needs to Succeed." This process was very successful and initiated steps the supervisor could take to enhance overall leadership quality for individual team members. At the time, I did not know that it was this process that stimulated the early development of the Preferred Leadership Profile (PLP), which I will discuss further in this chapter.

The second and most surprising revelation occurred during project follow-up and debriefing. Because the ESW Project was measuring changes in key areas such as worker feelings of optimism, empowerment, morale, and team cohesion, the evaluation design required two groups: the project group and the control group. The two groups were as identical as possible in size, location, number of team members, types of clients, number of cases, years of experience, and so on. What I found to be fascinating were the differences in overall worker satisfaction and workplace climate between the two teams. The control group reported a significantly higher level of morale, optimism, and team cohesion. What did most of them attribute it to? It was in large part due to the perceived supportiveness and supervision quality of the supervisor! This was exciting: an insight that confirmed the importance employee perceptions have on worker experiences and workplace climate. More importantly, the greatest insight was that these two teams operated in similar environments with similar and persisting organizational and workplace challenges, yet due to positive worker perceptions of leadership quality, things were much better overall for the control team and its members.

This particular situation surfaced important themes that were positively impactful then, and the insights gained continue to influence my understanding of the importance of perception on effective supervision and overall leadership quality. Some of these themes are as follows:

- Worker perceptions and experiences of supervision have a significant impact on optimism, morale, job satisfaction, and workplace climate.

- Supervisors, by tuning into worker needs and preferences, can enhance the quality of supervision and support for workers.

- Effective supervision and quality supervisory support can buffer workers against the stress and challenges of a trying and difficult work environment.

Each of the three scenarios, in unique ways, demonstrates the role worker perceptions play in their experience of supervision and perceived supervisory support. While all of the lessons learned, including themes that emerged from the situations presented above, are valuable, it is the final bullet of the third scenario (*Effective supervision and quality supervisory support can buffer workers against the stress and challenges of a particular work environment*) that I find the most fascinating and profound. Situation 3 continues to confirm for me the power that quality leadership can have on workers' perceptions and experiences of the work and the work climate. I have been referring to supervision as a mechanism of leadership and have made reference to the context of supervision as representing an environment within an environment. Situation 3 clearly speaks to these ideas. Supervision as a mechanism can operate as a safe-haven for workers, especially during extremely difficult and challenging times. It reinforces the idea that while we may not be able to change or alter many of the bureaucratic, political, fiscal, and/or organizational impediments to good practice, as mentioned in Chapter 1, quality supervision and supervisory support can positively enhance workers' experience of themselves, the work, and the organization overall.

It is in the context of these scenarios that we may have a partial yet profound solution to the question posed by Patti (2009). That is, how do we create organizational conditions that will lead to positive worker perceptions, attitudes, and behavior in order to bring about the highest quality and the most effective service? It is through a quality leadership experience wherein the leader places primacy on the importance of the workers' perceptions of themselves and the work but above all their perceptions of the quality of supervision and supervisory support.

❖ THE EMPLOYEE AND THE EMPLOYEE'S STORY

Up to this point in the discussion, I have referred to the terms *perception* and *worker experience* to indicate how social service employees come to interpret and understand leader behaviors and their work environments overall. Perceptions are the key to experience. When making reference to the perceptions and experiences of workers, I often refer to the terms employee story or worker story.

I like to use the narrative concept of story to refer to the lived experience of individuals and/or groups. In the simplest manner, a person's story is his or her subjective experience of everything—of self, people, and situations. Our stories are made up of how we think and feel about ourselves and everything in the world around us. Our stories are shaped by our needs, beliefs, values, attitudes, and goals, and they are informed by our past, present, and future. How we make sense of our stories and the meaning that the stories maintain in large part determines the attitudes we hold and the behaviors we choose in our interactions with different people and/or in a variety of situations.

I mentioned in Chapter 1 that if asked for advice on how to be a better leader, my standard response is, "Get to know your employee!" I also highlighted an important and consistent theme which has surfaced from both practice wisdom and research: When employees and managers refer to their experiences of effective and quality leadership, it is not uncommon for them to attribute those experiences to the fact that their leader really knew them and had an understanding of their perceptions and experiences. Effective leaders are those leaders who are in tune with what workers need, what is important to them, and what they want for themselves, their team members, and the clients they serve. Getting to know the employee and the employee experience is absolutely essential if leaders are going to provide effective leadership and a quality leadership experience for the members that they lead.

In order to stress the absolute necessity of getting to know the employee and the employee's story for enhancing a quality leadership experience and motivating workers to perform optimally, it is important to place this discussion in the context of the definition of leadership offered in Chapter 2. Leadership was defined earlier as a process by which an individual or individuals inspire the attitudes and behaviors of others to engage in value-based and purpose-critical efforts in order to accomplish a set of shared objectives. An emphasis is placed on the leader's ability to inspire, motivate, stimulate, or bring to action certain attitudes and behaviors that result in the optimization of worker performance and enhanced quality service. That's great, but the question becomes how do you inspire workers to be motivated and engaged as they carry out their work, especially when they are operating in challenging work environments that present serious barriers to preferred practice?

The answer to this question is at the heart of a Responsive Leadership Approach. Leaders can inspire their employees when they cultivate and connect with the experiences and perceptions of workers—perceptions of their work, their work environment, and their experiences of themselves within that particular context. The Responsive Leadership Approach places primary emphasis on establishing a respectful, trusting, and safe relationship that is, in and of itself, engaging, satisfying, and motivating. More importantly, however, such a relationship is critical as it creates what I refer to as a pathway to the employee's story—their lived experience. Why is the employee story so important? Because it is within the employee's perceptions and lived experiences that important needs, values, goals, and strengths lay. These are the key sources of individual motivation, engagement, commitment, and overall performance. This concept is built on the idea that the only way a leader can inspire is if he knows what it is that inspires each individual employee.

Consider the three scenarios above. While very different stories, there is a common consistency that holds them together: To varying degrees there existed barriers to the access of the employee's experience. We the supervisors were all missing important information. I was missing important information regarding the needs, values, and goals of my team members. Barb was missing large chunks of important information and meaning around her "challenging" employee. The project supervisor was also missing information as it pertained to the perceptions of his team members regarding work, supervision, and the relationship with him as the supervisor. As I stated earlier, it is this missing information and meaning that can lead to a variety of experiences and situations that can range from relatively minor to annoying, all the way to serious stress and conflict between the supervisor and employees. An important note worth restating is that in each situation, other than Barb's because it was probably too late, it was accessing employees' perceptions and experiences that led to a better experience of quality supervision, a better leadership experience, and enhanced work overall.

What Motivates Social Service Workers?

What if supervisors could access that information—the employee story and the meaning embedded in it—earlier? What if managers can discover important information before gaps in perception cause any difficulties in the leader–member relationship? What if supervisors could learn about employee needs, values, goals, and strengths right from the beginning of the leader–member working relationship? If so, wouldn't we be able to minimize the potential for stress and/or conflict with employees and the subsequent challenges that may arise in work and service as a result? Wouldn't access to this important information and meaning enhance the quality of the employee experience with their leader and the work overall? Wouldn't the cultivation and engagement with important aspects of the employees' story enhance their experiences of the work thereby lead to better practice decisions and preferred client outcomes? These are the questions that I pursued over the last 15 years in my work with supervisors, managers, and leaders. The answer to all of these questions is a resounding YES! Absolutely!

It was this inquiry that provided impetus for seeking out, through research and interviews with thousands of employees and supervisors, what information from the employee's story is the most essential to access. What information is necessary to enhance a leader's capacity to inspire greater motivation, engagement, commitment, and overall performance from all employees? My findings helped shape my understanding of specific domains that are key sources of motivation for social service employees. In addition to this, the plethora of information from workers was used to develop a tool: the Preferred Leadership Profile. It was constructed to assist workers and their leaders in the discovery and documentation of important employee needs, values, goals, and strengths as they relate to preferences for leadership and the work overall.

Different People, Different Motivators

As stated in Chapter 1, social service workers are an exceptionally motivated group of people who value and desire making the lives of those less fortunate better. However, the plethora of organizational and workplace realities presented earlier challenge many workers' connection to and engagement with the things that motivate them the most. It is critical for leaders to understand and connect with the various elements and dynamics that contribute to fostering and sustaining employee motivation and engagement. Over the years, I have come to learn that social service employees are motivated by a variety of different things as they relate to the work and the employees' experiences of themselves within the work. These "things" are very much tied to employees' needs, values, goals, and strengths. The following items, which will be revisited in Chapter 6, represent worker preferences that are key sources of motivation and quality engagement for most employees. They are

- quality relationships characterized by trust, respect, integrity, and empathy;
- to work in step with their personal and/or professional values;
- to have and hold a shared vision and mission with others;
- to engage in tasks and objectives that are important to them, or that they at least see the value in,
- to have some aspect of themselves or their work acknowledged, appreciated, and/or admired;
- an environment that supports personal and professional growth;
- to see results;
- to have positive and constructive feedback;
- to have a sense of personal power or control over some aspect of the work; and
- to have strengths identified and built on in the pursuit of important objectives.

This list, which will be the main focus of Chapter 6, represents an array of motivation sources for many employees; however, the degree to which each item is motivating and engaging has to deal with the unique preferences and experiences of each individual employee. For some employees, like myself for instance, working in step with my values is very important for me. I also like to see results. My colleagues may not hold the same preferences. My office-mate years ago was not concerned as much with values but focused most of his energy on opportunities that supported his personal and professional growth.

It is very important to note that if at anytime workers lose connection to important and preferred factors that keep them motivated and/or engaged, there is a likelihood that they will begin to lose motivation, focus, and engagement with the work. The longer a disconnection from such preferences persists, the more apt employees are to experience a disconcerting feeling; the longer a disconnect persists, the more likely that disconcerting feeling may shift to disillusionment and possibly demoralization. The more a leader knows about employee preferences and sources of motivation, the better able he will be to respond and accommodate, to the extent possible, the various needs, values, goals, and strengths embedded within the unique employee perceptions and experiences of those preferences. In addition to this, the longer and more fully a leader assists employees with a connection to their needs, values, goals, and strengths, the longer employees will stay motivated and engaged with the work.

The Key Performance Motivators Scale

Understanding key sources of motivation preferences for employees has been very helpful for myself and other managers for learning, understanding, and responding to the various needs, values, and goals embedded within the meaning of those preferences. Prior to developing the Preferred Leadership Profile, I created a simple tool I refer to as the Key Performance Motivators Scale (KPMS), which can be found as Appendix A. It was developed to help workers and supervisors alike to identify and connect with their own and others' preferences for the things that motivate and engage them as they carry out their work. The KPMS is short, straightforward, and simple to use. It can be completed and discussed between supervisor and employee, and it can also be used in groups as a team-building exercise for surfacing and discussing important individual and team discoveries. While the KPMS offers supervisors an avenue for getting to know their employees better, I often suggest that the supervisors I work with use the Preferred Leadership Profile to gain a more comprehensive understanding of the employee and their story—their needs, values, goals, strengths, and preferences for support.

❖ THE PREFERRED LEADERSHIP PROFILE: PURPOSE

While the next chapter will detail a variety of barriers and challenges that exist to accessing and engaging the employee experience and offer tools and strategies for mitigating such impediments, I feel it is important to introduce the Preferred Leadership Profile tool at this juncture of the discussion. It is my intention that the PLP overview provided here will enhance your understanding of and reference to the tool, including such things as employee preferences as they relate to leadership and various aspects of the work. The PLP tool can be found in Appendix B.

In the most practical sense, the PLP enhances the leader's ability to get to know, understand, and respond to the unique needs, values, goals, and strengths of employees in a manner that leads to the greatest development of employees and essentially the greatest delivery of preferred staff and client outcomes. The main role of any leader is to deliver on service and client outcomes by inspiring the attitudes and behaviors of others to carry out effective and quality work. In order to *deliver*, a leader must *develop* the capacities of the employee and the team overall. And because delivery of outcomes is dependent upon development, the most effective employee development is dependent upon thorough and accurate *discovery*. I refer to discovery, development, and delivery as the three Ds of responsive leadership. When a leader discovers the unique needs, values, goals, strengths, and overall preferences of employees, optimal development, motivation, and engagement is possible and delivery of preferred staff and client outcomes much more likely.

The PLP tool was developed to provide both leader and members with opportunities to discover and connect with preferences and key motivation sources so that work may be a more meaningful and valuable experience for everyone involved. In addition to this, the PLP structure and process offer both leader and member opportunities to strengthen the leader–member relationship, to assist in a quality leadership experience and enhanced satisfaction with overall supervision and supervisory support. We know from previous chapters that enhanced supervision and quality leader–member relationships as perceived by the employee are foundational for enhancing the meaning and value of the employee work experience. In addition, the more a leader knows and understands what employees need, what is important to them, what they want, and what their strengths are, the better able the leader is to create the best fit between workers' preferences and capacities and the work overall. We know that such experiences enhance not only the worker's perception of leadership and supervision but also the perception of work and a work environment as positive, meaningful, and valuable. Therefore, the PLP tool can be instrumental in enhancing worker motivation, engagement, job satisfaction, organizational commitment, and organizational citizenship behavior.

❖ THE PREFERRED LEADERSHIP PROFILE: STRUCTURE AND PROCESS

What the PLP Contains

The PLP is a 10-page document housing four main categories with a variety of informative sections pertaining to key work preferences and motivators common to many social service employees. The four main categories of the PLP are *Values and Purpose, Preferred Outcomes, Strengths,* and *Preferred Performance Supports.*

Values and Purpose is the first category of the PLP. This section encourages workers to connect with and identify aspects of the organization or program's vision, mission, and values that are important to them and their work. This PLP area also guides employees to make connections between organizational objectives and their own personal purposes. An important aspect for understanding worker motivation is to know an employee's individual reasons behind taking and remaining in a particular job. In addition to this, the *Values and Purpose* section solicits from the worker information pertaining to their own WIIFM, an acronym which means "What's in It for Me?" The WIIFM can provide the supervisor with insight into one or more particular payoffs related to a worker's purpose in carrying out his or her role of helping.

Desired Outcomes is the second major category in the PLP. This realm of the PLP brings purpose and objectives together as it encourages employees to consider specific goals—what they want for their clients, for themselves, and for the team overall. For most workers, these areas are key sources of motivation, focus, and engagement.

The third major category is the *Strengths* category. This section encourages employees to consider their own strengths as they pertain to both professional and personal domains. The strengths section is great for workers and supervisors alike. For employees, claiming strengths can be a positive, affirming, and hope-instilling process. In addition to this, it can assist employees in their own development as strengths are key to uncovering resources from past and present successes and are great for focusing on future successes also. For the supervisor, knowing employee strengths can help with professional development and motivation as strengths can be built on and leveraged in the pursuit of important goals and professional development. A strengths focus will be elaborated on further in Chapter 5.

The fourth and final category of the PLP is *Preferred Performance Supports*. It is the largest of the four profile categories as it contains a host of employee preferences geared toward enhancing professional development, learning, quality supervision, and communication. Employees are to consider and identify preferred goals for their own professional development. Additionally, employees are offered an opportunity to consider whether they have strengths that they would like to develop further. Employees are asked to reflect on their specific preferences for learning and to consider what qualities and/or ingredients would lead to quality supervision and support. This section of the PLP also offers employees the opportunity to outline preferences for structure and process within the context of supervision. Finally, the *Preferred Performance Supports* category of the PLP offers workers a place to outline and specify their own preferences for the most effective communication and feedback.

Introducing the PLP and Ensuring Buy-In

One of the greatest impediments to preferred practice echoed by social service workers is that there is too much paperwork. This is one of the most common challenges and sources of resistance that surface when trying to introduce the PLP tool to individual employees and teams. Prior to introducing the PLP, it is critical that employees see the value in the tool. How do you get staff to see the value in the PLP tool? You consider their needs, values, and goals as a means to connecting the PLP to what they want for themselves, for their work, and, above all, for the clients they serve. Helping employees answer the questions, "What's the point?" and, "Why should I take the time to fill this out?" is critical for buy-in and engagement with the tool. If the answers to these questions illuminate that the PLP tool can indeed accommodate one or more of the employee's needs, values, and/or goals, he or she will be more likely to complete the PLP tool.

Another suggestion I make for supervisors and managers is to inform employees that the PLP tool will assist in greater quality supervision and better leadership overall. I suggest that leaders convey to their team members the following message: "I really want to be a better supervisor/manager. This PLP tool can help me with this." I have yet to hear employees argue with wanting to have better supervision or an enhanced leadership experience at work. This is another great way to introduce the PLP and increase the likelihood of buy-in by team members.

The PLP can be introduced to individual members in the context of a meeting or supervision session, or it can be introduced to the whole team at a unit meeting. Either way, time should be provided for a discussion of the PLP, the value of it, and the intended positive implications of its use.

The following chapter on communication and accessing the employee story will provide insights, tools, and strategies that will assist with introducing and discussing the PLP tool with members.

Completing the PLP

On average, the PLP takes approximately two hours to fill out in its entirety. However, when and how a PLP is completed can be decided upon by both the supervisor and the employee. Because it is not mandated or legislated, the PLP tool can be completed and used in a manner that accommodates the realities of a particular work environment. Most employees that have completed the tool have preferred to take it home to fill it out.

Some, however, have completed the PLP if and when time permitted at work, within work hours. While most people have preferred to fill out the tool in its entirety, others have chosen to complete the tool in parts and pieces. Some supervisors have used various sections of the PLP for team-building exercises, by utilizing specific sections for group discussions and processes. Regardless of how the PLP is completed, it is important that the employee submit a copy to their direct supervisor or manger. It is up to the supervisor or manager to follow-up—to have a discussion with the worker regarding the PLP, including that worker's experience of his or her own discovery process within the context of completing the form.

The PLP Discussion Is Critical

It has been emphasized and will continue to be that it is absolutely essential that the supervisor and/or manager have a good discussion with the team member as soon as possible, following the completion of the PLP. This discussion offers the leader an opportunity to learn more about the employee and the employee's needs, values, goals, strengths, and preferences for support. In addition to this, the leader is able to gain some insight into the members' experiences of filling out the PLP tool. Some important points for discussion are as follows:

- What was filling out the tool like for the member (their experience)?

- Were there areas of the tool that were familiar and/or comfortable to complete?

- Were there areas of the tool that were more difficult and/or challenging to complete?

- Were there areas of the tool that were most meaningful and/or valuable?

- Was anything new learned and/or confirmed in the process of filling out the tool?

The above questions are suggested as provisional guides for supervisors and managers and have been helpful in facilitating a deeper and more meaningful understanding of the employee and the employee's experience as it relates to his or her needs, values, and goals. It is also a suggested that supervisors who utilize the PLP tool and engage in a PLP follow-up discussion with their workers utilize the communication process for *meaning making* offered in the next chapter.

The PLP is a living document and can be revisited by the employee from time to time in order to add, enhance, or even modify the information as it pertains to the employee's experience and the various sections of the tool. I encourage supervisors and employees, as key information is revealed, to make changes immediately as the discovery process is ongoing and continuously unfolding.

❖ ENSURING SUCCESS: THE DOS AND DON'TS OF THE PLP

In order to approximate successful use of the PLP in a manner that is consistent with the intent and preferred outcomes of the tool, there are some important dos and don'ts that require attention.

Preferred Leadership Profile Dos

Do complete your own PLP first.

This is absolutely essential for many reasons—the biggest being integrity. Great leaders do not ask or expect their members to do something that they haven't done or are not prepared to do themselves. In addition to this, one of the first questions many employees ask their supervisors is, "Have you completed it?" If the answer is no, employee buy-in of the PLP will likely be seriously compromised, if not altogether negated. More importantly, completing your own PLP will enhance your understanding of the PLP structure and process, including your own discovery process. By completing the PLP, you will also be able to answer many questions employees may have about the structure or process involved with the PLP tool.

Do encourage your members to see the value in the PLP.

This was discussed earlier and is critical for buy-in and subsequent success with the PLP. Engagement, cooperation, and motivation to complete the PLP are tied to whether or not the employee sees the value in the tool. Does it have meaning? Does it hold value? Remember that it is critical, prior to expecting the staff to complete the PLP, that they be able to answer the questions, "Why am I filling this thing out?" and "What's the point?" If there is no point, then there is no point. It would be ridiculous to expect an employee to connect and meaningfully engage with more paperwork when there is no point. However, when employees can connect the PLP to the accommodation of their needs, values, and/or goals, they will be much more motivated and engaged to complete the tool. Ensure that employees understand the value and see meaning in the PLP prior to your expectation that they complete the tool.

Do provide members with generous and flexible opportunities to complete the PLP.

Given the fast pace and heavy workloads characteristic of most social service environments, additional paperwork is often not a priority for most workers. However, if employees see the value in it, they are more likely to do what is necessary to get it done. It is important that supervisors provide a variety of generous and flexible opportunities to complete the PLP tool. Generous and flexible mean that workers are given realistic and achievable opportunities that consider the realities of their particular work and workplace demands. Opportunities to complete the PLP can be collaboratively discussed between the supervisor and employee. As discussed earlier, opportunities can be found at work, on shift, at breaks, in between shifts, at home, or during allocated time off designated specifically to support the completion of the PLP tool.

Do negotiate a completion date for the PLP.

While it is important to offer generous and flexible opportunities, a completion date is also important. This is so because, amidst the competing work and caseload priorities, the PLP can be set aside or lost in the multifarious demands of the social service work environment. And because the PLP represents more paperwork in a sea of documentation requirements, it may be less than appealing for some workers even if they see the value in it. Therefore, be sure to set a specific check-in date and/or completion date to have the PLP tool completed and submitted. If more time is required, be sure to renegotiate this with the worker and clarify an alternate date for completion.

Do have follow-up discussions with employees regarding the PLP.

Following up on the PLP is an essential *do!* It is not uncommon for many workers to roll their eyes or sigh when having to engage in a new work-related practice, standard, or tool. For many workers in social services who live and work in environments that are constantly shifting and changing in terms of standards, protocols, procedures, and mandates, there are many times when new tools are introduced and not followed up or through on. This can add to a type of learned apathy around the perceived integrity and the organization's commitment to new tools. Many workers who take the PLP tool seriously are often looking forward to the follow-up part of the process. They can also be looking for a return on their own investment of the time, energy, and commitment that went into completing the PLP.

I have heard workers in situations where the PLP has been completed but not followed up or through on state, "I wish I would have never filled it out." Keep in mind that the PLP tool can create hopeful and optimistic expectations about enhancing work and the work environment overall. Due to the personal nature of the PLP tool, a worker's commitment to fill it out goes beyond time and includes a personal investment and a risk to trust the leader and the process—that it will be an endeavor that will be favorable to the employee.

Follow-up on a tool that has been promoted by you as meaningful and valuable is essential if for nothing at all for your integrity. Keep in mind that integrity is a key to quality leadership. Effective leaders "do what they say they will do." Not following through on the PLP tool will undoubtedly be a breach to your leadership integrity.

Do expect some resistance to the PLP tool.

I have introduced the PLP tool to approximately 1,000 supervisors and managers. Many of them have gone on to introduce and utilize the tool with more than 7,000 social service employees in a variety of sectors. To some degree, all of the leaders experienced resistance with one or more of their employees. This is common, and it is OK! While resistance and opposition will be elaborated on more thoroughly in Chapter 7, it is important to highlight some of the common reasons for resistance and or opposition to the PLP tool and the process overall.

The most common reason contributing to PLP reluctance has to do with issues regarding trust. Sometimes it can be difficult for workers to trust that the PLP tool will be used within the context of the spirit and intent with which it was developed, introduced, and explained. Unfortunately, in the past, workers have been asked to fill out tools, assessments, questionnaires, and/or surveys with the intent to enhance quality and/or efficiency of individual performance, team functioning, organizational development, or client outcomes, and their experience following completion or engagement was less than positive. In some instances, little to nothing was made of their efforts, meaning there was no follow-up or follow-through.

For some employees, their experiences may have ranged from neutral to negative after the completion of a document that held personal information, including their perspectives and opinions. I have heard many stories of workers who stated that they were reprimanded following the sharing of their opinions. Others social service employees have shared stories of confidentiality breaches and/or negative repercussions from supervisors after sharing personal opinions and perspectives regarding various aspects of the work.

Another major reason that contributes to reluctance with PLP completion and engagement in the process has to do with whether or not workers see the value in the tool. As stated above, it is critical that workers can answer the two questions, "Why am I doing this?" and, "What is the point of this PLP?"

Preferred Leadership Profile Don'ts

Don't forget to follow up or follow through on the PLP tool.

Although this is covered in the *do* section above, it is critical to mention again. Forgetting to follow up on the tool may seriously compromise your leadership integrity and the level of buy-in and commitment of employees on the team. In addition, not following up or through on the PLP may also jeopardize the leader–member relationship and be perceived by employees as "more of the same" social service rhetoric, further perpetuating and impacting a negative view of you the leader and the work environment overall. Not following up or through on the PLP actually has the opposite effect for which it was intended.

Don't use the PLP as an evaluation or performance tool.

The PLP tool contains a wealth of personal and professional employee information all in one place. It can be tempting for some supervisors to want to use the PLP as a means of performance evaluation or performance management. The PLP was not intended or developed to be used as such. The PLP is a tool for discovery of important needs, values, goals, strengths, and other key sources of motivation. Information pertaining to goals and strengths from the PLP can indeed be used and integrated into performance evaluation processes and frameworks. However, when the PLP is used as a performance evaluation tool, it does not fit, and it can be confusing and awkward for both the supervisor and the employee. In addition to this, most performance appraisal and evaluation processes are often less than inspiring for most workers, and utilizing the PLP in this manner may result in a worker's experience of the PLP and the process around it to be less than positive and engaging.

Don't use the PLP as a means to discipline employees.

The reluctance that many workers have in engaging with and completing a tool like the PLP is often tied to a not-so-good experience with a similar tool or process from the past. Unfortunately, for some workers, the professional or personal information has been held against them in some manner; sometimes information is judged, criticized, or even delegitimized in the context of a verbal and/or behavioral response from their direct supervisor. I have heard terrible stories wherein workers have been reprimanded, faced consequences, and/or experienced repercussions as a response to the information they have shared in the PLP tool. In some instances, when employees have been involved in a disciplinary situation, information from the PLP has been brought into the meeting to be used to support the disciplinary action and/or to help build a case for disciplinary action. This is not what the PLP is intended for, and if utilized in this manner, it will undoubtedly result in implications that are diametrically opposed to the spirit and intent for which the PLP tool was developed.

❖ SUMMARY OF IMPORTANT POINTS

- Leadership is determined to be effective and high quality by the individual perceptions and experiences of each worker.

- Workers who perceive their work environment as positive, meaningful, and supportive experience greater levels of job satisfaction and organizational commitment than their coworkers that don't.

- Worker perceptions and experiences hold the key to worker preferences for effective supervision and quality leadership.

- Supervisors and workers can have very different experiences of the same situation.

- Worker perceptions and experiences of supervision have significant impact on optimism, morale, job satisfaction, and workplace climate.

- Effective supervision and quality supervisory support can buffer workers against stress and challenges of a particular work environment.

- All workers have a variety of diverse and unique Key Performance Motivators.

- When supervisors and managers get to know the needs, values, goals, strengths, and preferences for support, they are better able to enhance and sustain motivation, engagement, and optimal performance.

❖ PERSONAL LEADER REFLECTIONS AND CONSIDERATIONS

- Consider your own preferences for effective supervision and quality leadership. What do you need? What do you value most? What do you hope for?

- Consider asking your team members to share their preferences for effective supervision and quality leadership. What are you doing well? What might you need to work on?

- Review the Key Performance Motivators list. What stands out as important and/or meaningful for you?

- Consider sharing and reviewing the Key Performance Motivators Scale with one or more team members.

- Review the Preferred Leadership Profile. Consider what areas stood out for you as most meaningful.

- Consider introducing (in parts or as a whole) the Preferred Leadership Profile to team members, individually or as a group.

❖ REFERENCES

de Groot, S. (2006). *Empowering social workers in the workplace: A strengths based strategy for child welfare.* Ottawa, Canada: Canadian Association of Social Workers.

Patti, R. J. (2009). *The handbook of human services management* (2nd ed.). Thousand Oaks, CA: Sage.

4

Meaning Making

*Practical Strategies for
Understanding and Accessing
the Employee Story*

*The humble listen to their brothers and sisters because they
assume they have something to learn. They are open to correction,
and they become wiser through it.*

— Thomas Dubay

❖ DISCOVERY AND THE EMPLOYEE STORY

Because the delivery of quality and efficient supportive services is
dependent upon the optimal development of workers to be motivated, engaged, committed, and competent, accurate discovery of the
employee's story is essential. As stated in the previous chapter, accurate discovery by the leader is about arriving, to the extent possible,
at an understanding of the unique needs, values, goals, and strengths
of the employee as they relate to work and their experience within the
work. Simply put, the more a leader can discover the meaning and
value within what workers need, what they want, what is important

to them, and what they are good at, the more a leader is able to inspire that worker to connect with the things that will foster, promote, and maintain the greatest motivation, engagement, and commitment in the processes of worker development and delivery of preferred outcomes.

There are a myriad of benefits to accurate discovery of the employee's story that are critical to enhancing both employee and client outcomes. In addition to promoting the connection to key motivators and developing optimal employee capacity, accurate discovery provides the leader with important insights into what leader behaviors and interactions may offer keys to create the best quality leader–member relationship. Moreover, practical insights gleaned in the ongoing process of discovery may assist the leader in identifying and accommodating, to the extent possible, the needs and goals employees have for quality supervision and overall supervisory support. We know from practice wisdom and research that effective and quality supervision will enhance the meaning and value employees place in work and will also likely improve the overall experience of the work environment as positive. Accurate discovery of the employee's story is also critical in assisting leaders to find the best fit between the worker's needs, values, goals, and strengths and the specific roles, responsibilities, and expectations required within the context of the employee's respective work environment.

We know that when employees are connected to key motivators, have opportunities to feel valued and successful at work, experience quality supervisory support and a quality leader–member experience, and perceive their work environment as being positive and having meaning, they are much more likely to be motivated and engaged and perform optimally. Research also demonstrates that these workers will subsequently be buffered from stress and less susceptible to burnout.

❖ BARRIERS TO AN ACCURATE UNDERSTANDING OF THE EMPLOYEE STORY

Despite the wonderful intentions of all supervisors and managers to want and do the best by their members, there exists a myriad of serious barriers to accessing the important information and meaning regarding the employee and his or her story. Unfortunately, when access to an accurate understanding of needs, values, goals, and strengths is blocked, the incredible efforts of leaders, including time, energy, knowledge, and skills, to develop and deliver cannot be fully realized.

Consider for a moment the three scenarios offered in the last chapter. In all three of the situations, despite the good intentions of all supervisors, there was important information and meaning from the workers' stories that if and when known by the supervisors made positive differences in how they experienced the work and themselves within the work. In addition to this, when discovered, all supervisors had access to information and meaning that could be used to enhance the worker experience of supervision, supervisory support, and work overall.

Just as it is important to claim the organizational and workplace impediments to good practice, so too is it important to identify and claim the potential barriers that exist to gaining access to an understanding the employee story. Each item listed as a barrier or barriers have the potential to challenge the discovery process and accurate understanding of the employee story. However, when they are in operation simultaneously, the blockade can be formidable. The following barriers are important to identify and embrace if we as leaders are going to be able to navigate, accommodate, and respond to the challenges that they pose. These barriers, presented below, have been identified as *Organizational and Workplace Impediments, Theories and Models, Our Story, Assumptions, Generalizations, Labels, Diagnoses, and the Personnel File.*

Organizational and Workplace Impediments

Many organizational and workplace realities and their consequences were identified in the first chapter of the book. How does the highly bureaucratic, politically reactive, fiscally constrained, crisis-driven environment wherein workers are consistently expected to do more with less impact access to the employee's story? Well, we already know that such environments can have a negative impact on the quantity and quality of supervision and overall supervisory support. Two common challenges that are often uttered by supervisors and managers in social services are "There is not enough time!" or "There is not enough money!" Many of the reasons provided in answer to the questions "How come supervision doesn't happen more often?" or "How come we don't meet more regularly as a team?" are often connected to a lack of time, energy, or money. From a practical vantage point, opportunities to access the employee's story are limited when face-to-face contact is limited due to the various organizational and workplace challenges. In addition, when the quality of leadership through effective supervision and supervisory support are diminished, it is not uncommon for the quality of relationships and communication between leader and employee to suffer also. When and if this happens, it can be a recipe for all sorts of stress and potential conflict.

Due to the fast pace and high workloads characteristic of most social service workplaces, it is not uncommon for supervisors and managers to become, to varying degrees, disconnected from important information and the meaning of an employee's story. So then, the question becomes, if and when quantity and quality of supervision and supervisory support are compromised, how do supervisors come to know and understand the meaning of the experiences and specific behaviors of the employee? There are a variety of sources from which leaders draw information in attempts to understand the perceived attitudes and behaviors of employees.

It is important to note that the following identified barriers, listed below, can indeed be helpful at times to inform leaders about the attitudes, behaviors, and/or interactions of the employees as they carry out the work. However, the caution and the term *barrier* has been arrived at because overreliance on the following items as ways of interpreting attitudes and behaviors can lead to unintentionally missing of the meaning within the employee's experience, sometimes slightly or other times completely. Below, I will define each barrier and then provide two concrete examples that illustrate the interplay and operation of the barriers as they pertain to challenging the access to and attainment of an accurate understanding of the employee's story.

Theories and Models

Theoretical constructs and the models that are derived from them are the cornerstones of formal social services education and training programs. Human behavior theories and their orientations have been and continue to be very helpful in guiding intervention, support, and overall work with clients for social service employees. As leaders, theories of performance development and performance management, including the many theoretical orientations of leadership, can be helpful for interpreting and managing the performance of employees to be motivated and engaged and to perform in a manner that results in preferred outcomes for clients. However, while leadership theories and models of performance development and management can be helpful, they can be an exceptional and formidable barrier to an accurate understanding of a worker's story, their lived experience.

The perspective I'm about to share here is just that—my perspective. It is a perspective that threatens some of my colleagues and causes slight discomfort for others. It has been derived from my experience as a facilitator of many performance management orientations and from my experience consulting on hundreds of situations with managers, executives, human resources personnel, representatives from unions, and arbitrating lawyers when dealing with employees that have presented as exceptionally "challenging" and/or "difficult."

My perspective is this: I believe that we have been unintentionally and unfortunately misled by a behaviorist approach to dealing with unique and complex human issues. I touched on this idea somewhat in Chapter 1. Formal supervisor and management training, as it pertains in particular to performance management, is most often geared toward two main avenues for shaping performance: interpretation and management. The first thing social service supervisors and managers are taught to do is to interpret the behavior of their employee—to consider the attitude or behavior in the context of a theoretical or set of theoretical constructs and models. Once interpretation has been accomplished and "understanding" reached, leaders are encouraged to manage the behavior. The approach to intervening to shape behavior is often informed by the particular orientation or models being used to interpret the behavior of the employee. This is often done outside the involvement and/or the story of the employee.

Early on in my career, I bought into interpretation and management of employee behavior; this is the way I was taught and later what I was teaching to supervisors and managers. Furthermore, when consulting on "difficult" and/or "challenging" employee behaviors, interpretation and management was the standard way to go. What was also common in both the teaching arena and the consultation on difficult employee situations was that the employee being discussed was most often not present at the meeting and/or not a part of the discussion!

I am purposeful in my omission of making reference to any specific theoretical orientations and/or models geared toward the management of employee behavior. Most of the theories and models have been and can be helpful. My point is not to argue about the psychometric integrity or validity of any particular orientation or approach but to bring attention to the potential pitfalls and negative implications that may ensue when we use the models to interpret and manage employee behavior without important information and meaning from his or her story.

Therefore, it is important to note that the problem does not lie necessarily in the theoretical orientations and the models but in the process of interpretation and attempted management of the behavior outside the perspective and/or subjective experience of the employee. The main problem with behavioral approaches to performance management is that the process gives leaders little if any access to or understanding of the employee's experience—the meaning, the behavior, and the overall context hold for that employee.

The potential pitfalls and negative implications that ensue from interpreting and managing employee behavior outside the meaning of his or her story and how to avoid such consequences will be discussed further in this chapter and elaborated on more thoroughly in Chapter 7.

Our Story

Just as employees have their own needs, values, and goals that are operating within their subjective experience of their work and of themselves within the work, so too do the managers that supervise them. Think about it: When leaders lead, the main tool being utilized is themselves. Their own stories comprise a complex culmination of their personal and professional life experiences—family, community, school, church, and work. They have and maintain their own beliefs, values, culture, ideas, opinions, and goals, and more that have been shaped and influenced throughout their lives.

Often when interpreting and managing the behavioral performance of an employee, it is not uncommon for the perspective of the leader to be influenced by his very own story. If not aware of this dynamic, her own subjective lens may unintentionally block out, undermine, or even delegitimize the subjective experience of the worker. In addition to this, if the manager is not fully aware of his own needs, values, and goals operating in a situation, another potential and unintentional consequence is that the needs, values, and goals of the worker's story may be eclipsed by those of the leader. This dynamic and the potential challenges that ensue will be discussed further in the chapter on resistance and opposition.

Assumptions

Assumptions are operating all the time. Also developed out of our personal and professional life experiences, we have assumptions about everyone and everything. Assumptions usually inform our thinking and feeling on what certain people may or may not be capable of at certain times, in interaction with other people, or in particular situations. A typical assumption among millions that people tend to make is that women are better at relationship building than men. Another common assumption is that resistant employee behavior is often the result of a fear or unwillingness to change. If leaders are not aware of the assumptions that are operating in the process of interpretation of an employee's behavior, there may be serious blocks to the accurate access and understanding the meaning of an employee's experience. When this happens, the intervention chosen within the approach to performance management may be based on inaccurate or even fictitious information!

Labels

Many of us use labels to describe certain behaviors and even people. Often labels are derived from our interpretation and/or understanding of a person's behaviors. Labels that are applied to employees by supervisors in an interpretation and/or description of the behavior can be either positive or negative. Some common positive labels for employees are go-getter, star performer, strong willed, top dog, straight shooter, compliant, and team player. Some common negative employee labels are lazy, manipulative, stubborn, noncommittal, passive-aggressive, aggressive, and insubordinate. While labels can be helpful as descriptors, they can also block access to an understanding of the person's subjective experience of her own behavior within a situation. Furthermore, the major problem with labels is that whether they are positive or negative can have the tendency to categorize and/ or pigeonhole people, thereby limiting the perceived capacity of an individual to change an attitude or behavior.

Diagnoses

Seeing this category may encourage you to stop and ask yourself, "Are we talking about employees or clients here?" Yes, we are discussing employees; however, given the prevalent use of formal *DSM* diagnosis in the social service sector, it is not uncommon for the language to overflow or seep into the interpretation and description of employee behaviors. Terms such as ADHD or obsessive–compulsive have been used to describe some workers who appear extremely energetic, focused, and meticulous about work structure and process. Terms such as antisocial, narcissistic, and oppositional have been used to describe the certain behaviors and people, usually in the context of challenging or less-than-desirable situations. While these references are far from formal diagnoses, a major problem I have with diagnoses is that once they are made, the search for alternative explanations or meaning can be limited if not altogether abandoned. In addition to this, diagnoses, like labels, have the tendency to generalize a person's behavior and limit others and one's own perceived capacity for change and growth. Diagnoses, when used, pose serious limitations to access and accurate understanding to the meaning of specific employee behaviors and interactions.

Personnel File

The employee personnel file houses all the information known by the organization about a particular employee. While personnel files are intended to support the journey of the employee within and through her respective organization, the data contained in an employee's file is often the information gathered within a busy system and made up of narratives that are shaped by the aforementioned areas—supervisors' stories, performance plan information, assumptions, labels, and so forth. When employee records are developed within such a context, it is not uncommon that there are important aspects of the employee experience as they relate to specific needs, values, and goals missing altogether. In addition to this, there is also a good chance that many employee files are missing an identification of worker-specific strengths and successes. I would say that such a personnel file represents an unintentional and unfortunate misrepresentation of the employee and his story.

The last point represents a dilemma that I often try to bring to the attention of leaders and HR professionals alike. I have them consider the question: When are supervisors and managers most often encouraged to document something in an employee's file? Take a moment yourself to consider when you or a colleague were encouraged to "make sure you document that." I can tell you that from my experience, it was usually when something was "wrong" or needed to be fixed or when I was being encouraged to "cover my butt" for accountability purposes. In addition, I was consistently encouraged to "document, document, document" in the process of discipline or working with challenging and undesirable employee behaviors. I cannot remember a time in my career when I was ever encouraged to document the strengths, successes, or potential of an employee! The sad and unfortunate aspect of this dynamic is that even if an employee messes up just two or three times in a seven-year career, those moments will stand out more as a representation in the file than the thousands of times the employee was performing well or even optimally!

It is for these reasons that the employee file can become a barrier to accessing the details of important aspects of the their respective needs, values, goals, and strengths—essential aspects of the employee's story.

❖ WELL-INTENTIONED AND UNFORTUNATE PITFALLS: TWO VERY DIFFERENT CASE SITUATIONS

I have mentioned that all leaders want the best for their employees. They want them to be motivated, engaged, and committed to their clients and the work overall. However, as stated above, there are many barriers to accessing an accurate and clear picture of the employee and her story. Unintentionally, supervisors get caught up in the process of interpreting and managing an employee's behavior in order to increase motivation and enhance performance. Often when we interpret and attempt to manage behavior, we are operating outside the meaning within the employee's story. When we are missing meaning around what workers need, what is important to them, what they want, and what they are good at, there is a good chance that we will not be able to accommodate and/or respond in a manner that is meaningful and valuable to them. When this happens, the consequences can range from minor and insignificant to outright stressful and conflictual.

The following two scenarios are offered to illustrate common approaches to influencing employees to do better as they carry out their work of helping. The two examples provided below are exceptionally different as the first is a typical and fairly positive situation common to most social service settings, and the second is a less-than-positive scenario as it relates to a more serious and challenging situation of employee opposition and resistive behavior.

Situation 1: A Challenge for Valerie

Background Information: Valerie has been a community mental health worker for 16 years in the same office. For the first five years, she was actively involved in the community as an outreach worker. Over the last 10 years, she has been working in the intake unit where she is responsible for intake, assessment, and referral. Over her career, until recently, she has been motivated, committed, and engaged in the work despite the persistent challenges of a work environment characterized by rotating managers and high staff turnover. Just recently, she mentioned to one of her codirectors that although she still loves her job, she feels as though she would like to be challenged more in her work. The director was concerned about this because Valerie is a long-time employee who is exceptionally valuable to the organization. He did not want to lose her. He was worried and did not know what to do, so he scheduled a meeting with the other codirector to try to problem-solve. The following is what I have experienced as a typical well-intentioned conversation as the directors engage in the process of interpretation and premanagement of Valerie's attitude and her behavior.

Director 1:   *I'm really worried about Valerie. She says that she needs to be challenged in her work. I don't think she is as committed as she used to be* (Assumption).

Director 2:   *Well, we all get like that after many years on the job* (Our Story, Assumption). *Plus, it's been difficult on her without consistent leadership in the unit* (Assumption).

Director 1:   *Ya, all good points, and remember after that team building we realized that Valerie needs to be in control and prefers structure* (Theories/Models). *She can be a bit of a control freak and a little anal about how things get done* (Labels). *Don't get me wrong; I like Valerie, and that's what we need in her unit. I think that's why she prefers intake* (Theories/Models, Assumption).

Director 2:   *Hmmm. What we need? You know that we have the supervisor position open again. Maybe Valerie would feel better if she was in that role* (Assumption). *She said she still likes her job and needs a challenge. This would be a great challenge* (Assumption).

Director 1:   *That's a good idea. You know it would also demonstrate to her that we value her here* (Assumption). *I remember when I was offered the supervisor role, it really gave me a confidence boost* (Our Story, Assumption). *It was definitely a challenge.*

Director 2:   *Come to think of it, isn't she taking a master's course in leadership? I'm pretty sure I read that as part of her performance-appraisal plan.*

Director 1:   *Yes, I recall that she might be. This is perfect then* (Assumption)*! Let's offer her the supervisor position!*

Director 2:   *Great. Why don't we call her in on Monday and let her know that we value her work and that we believe she would be perfect for that role!*

Director 1:   *Done!*

These two directors are well intentioned and really care about responding to Valerie in a manner so that she can feel valued and more challenged in her work. However, as you can see, they are operating without Valerie present and without access to her experience, her story. They are using information gathered from their observations, assumptions, their own stories, theories/models, labels, and the personnel file to inform their interpretation and their response to managing Valerie and her situation.

This scenario is fictitious; however, it is generated from a culmination of many of the scenarios I have witnessed, experienced, and heard about. Although following the scenario through further on this particular trajectory is beyond the scope of this particular illustration, I will inform you that the decision was made to offer Valerie the team supervisor position. She accepted. Eleven months later, Valerie submitted her resignation and took a job as an intake worker at the community addictions center just down the road. You may be just as confused as Valerie's directors were.

We will return to Valerie's situation further in the chapter when I outline the priorities, tools, and strategies of a Responsive Leadership Approach. My intention is to illuminate a more accurate understanding of Valerie's situation as we work to make meaning of her experience. Together, we will work to create a pathway to Valerie's story so that we may better understand and engage Valerie in a responsive manner that results in her feeling better and performing better at work.

Situation 2: Getting James Back on the Floor

Background Information: James is a youth service officer who works in a secure-custody setting for youth. He has worked in the field for more than 15 years. James is well known to HR and to the union as he has a history of being moved around every couple of years due to difficulties with clients, coworkers, and supervisors. James was moved to his current position two years ago. Early in his career, he was assaulted and injured in a physical altercation with a youth. James was placed on *work accommodation,* which is the term used to describe his placement on desk and paperwork duty to accommodate his injury and challenges to working directly on the floor with youth. However, James has been better physically for a considerable time, and other employees are requesting a rotation to James's current position. In addition to this, James's supervisor fears that the longer James stays on accommodation that it may appear to others as favoritism and further impact the already low morale on the team. According to HR and the supervisor, it is time for James to get back onto the floor and back to working with the youth in the unit. James states that he is not ready to get back on the floor and is refusing to do so.

The following represents what I would refer to as a common conversation between the supervisor and an HR member regarding an attempt to deal with James and his serious reluctance to get back onto the floor.

Supervisor: *I'm not sure what to do about James. He is still refusing to get off accommodation and get back to work with the youth. The guy has a serious history of insubordination* (Personnel File, Label). *I don't think I've ever had such a lazy and resistant staff member* (Labels). *He's here for himself and no one else* (Assumption).

HR Person: *C'mon, we've seen these guys before* (Our Story, Assumptions). *He's got his ass covered by the union* (Assumption). *And he is doing just what he needs to do to get by* (Assumption). *He's quite manipulative* (Label). *Most of the clients on the unit are diagnosed with antisocial personality disorder and oppositional defiant disorder. How did the psychiatrist miss James* (Diagnoses)? *Ha ha! Just kidding.*

Supervisor: *I know. He seems to take more of my energy than some of the kids on the unit, and actually, his file is probably bigger than some of our clients' files* (Personnel File).

HR Person: *Well, it doesn't help that he has been moved around for the last 12 years by the last HR director. He's resistant* (Label), *he doesn't have any work aspirations* (Assumption), *and he doesn't want to change* (Assumption). *He is just plain comfortable like all the guys we've seen that are just cruising to retirement* (Our Story).

Supervisor: *So what do I do?*

HR Person: *Well, we have to start holding him accountable. Document, document, document! Let's build a case that he is not doing what you need him to do. Let's put the pressure on; maybe start by developing a strong performance-management plan. We can't move him again because there is nowhere left in the organization to place him.*

Supervisor: *Ya, well, we've got to do something. I'm getting tired of this. It's got to stop. It's affecting me and the team, and if the stress from this continues, it will soon affect the kids.*

HR Person: *OK. Let's get started. Let's bring James in next week and inform him of the plan.*

Supervisor: *OK. But we have to be prepared for the union to attend* (Assumption) *as James will not agree to a meeting alone with management* (Assumption).

HR Person: *OK. I better give them a heads up and probably get some legal advice. This is probably going to go south* (Assumption). *We've seen this before* (Our Story).

Clearly, the supervisor and the HR person want something better for James, the team, and the clients. Unfortunately, they seem quite negative and overwhelmed with James and his behavior. Although this scenario is quite different from the preceding situation with Valerie, the similarity lies in the supervisor and HR working to interpret and manage the situation outside the presence of the employee and the employee story.

Like the first situation with Valerie, this scenario is fictitious also; however, it is generated from a culmination of many of the scenarios I have witnessed, experienced, and heard about. Although following the scenario through further on this particular trajectory is beyond the scope of this illustration, I will inform you that the decision was made to place James on a progressive discipline program. James took a six-month stress leave. Upon his return, he accused management of harassment. Following a one-year arbitration process, James was awarded compensation and moved to a job answering phones and organizing files at a youth community program within the same organization. James's superiors were left feeling frustrated and exceptionally angry.

We will return to James's situation further in Chapter 7 when I outline the priorities, tools, and strategies of a Responsive Leadership Approach to understanding and dealing most effectively with employee resistance and oppositional behavior. My intention is to illuminate a more accurate understanding of James's situation as we work to make meaning of his experience by implementing the various components of the Responsive Leadership Approach. Together we will work to create a pathway to James's story so that we may better understand and engage James in a manner that results in him feeling better and performing better at work.

Information Is Not Meaning

Something that I have learned from working with so many leaders and their employees in the context of performance optimization and service outcome enhancement is that often the information leaders use in decision-making regarding employees is exactly that—information. It is not necessarily meaning. This is something that I often encourage leaders to consider.

Consider the above situations of Valerie and James. Whether the circumstances were positive or challenging, there was a lot of information being considered. However, what was missing was the meaning of that information, which can only be found within the employee's story. A great deal of information being used to consider and manage the situations came from the sources listed above as barriers to the employee story. This often happens when conversation, planning, and goal setting occur outside the involvement of the employee and the employee's perspective. The meaning that is missing is related to the employee's perception and experience of two things: the situation and how he or she experiences the situation. In particular, the four areas that are critical to meaning making are the specific needs, values, goals, and strengths of the employee. It is essential that leaders search for meaning by considering what it is that the worker might need, what it is that is important to him, and what it is that he hopes for in this particular moment and/or situation. These areas hold important meaning and insight for the most effective leader response, to positively influencing a worker to be engaged and motivated and to perform optimally as she carries out her important role of helping.

❖ THE IMPORTANCE OF RELATIONSHIPS AND COMMUNICATION

It is my experience that problems and challenging situations as they relate to worker morale, motivation, and overall performance arise not so much from miscommunication but misunderstanding of the meaning within a particular situation. Accurate discovery is only possible by accessing the meaning within the story of the employee or employees involved in a particular situation. However, lack of or misunderstanding of the meaning a particular situation holds for workers is often at the center of issues related to poor morale, lack of motivation, undesirable performance, and so forth.

Communication is the primary means to accessing an employee's story. As a matter of fact, quality leader–member relationships combined with effective communication are the keys to creating conditions to access a pathway to the employee's story, in particular his or her needs, values, goals, and strengths.

The combination of effective communication and quality relationships is critical for all leaders to acknowledge and respect. While effective communication in and of itself is helpful for getting to know and understand the meaning of an employee's experience, it is the context of that communication that is the most essential aspect of the equation. The context that I am referring to is the leader–member relationship.

Often, the degree to which a worker is open or willing to express personal and professional needs, values, goals, and strengths is dependent upon the perceived sense of trust, respect, and overall safety to do so. Also, workers' openness and willingness to give or receive feedback is also dependent upon the level of safety in the leader–member relationship. As discussed in Chapter 1, a sense of safety within a leader–member relationship is tied directly to the qualities of trust, respect, integrity, acceptance, and understanding experienced by the employee in the context of the working relationship with their direct supervisor and/or manager.

❖ GETTING TO BETTER BY ACCESSING THE EMPLOYEE STORY

In my training, consultation, and coaching with leaders, I often use the metaphor *getting to better* to illustrate the importance accurate *discovery* has on the *development* of an employee to *deliver* optimal performance and service delivery outcomes for clients.

In the context of performance development, leaders and workers alike often understand, to some degree, what it is they would like to improve upon or get better at. It may be to get better in competence, confidence, or specific capabilities. It may be a little better or a lot better. I like the idea of the term better because it is a general reference that refers to forward motion toward an important employee goal or set of goals. Also, I like the term better because I'm not sure what the terms *best* or *perfect* are or whether they are at all attainable. Finally, I like the use of the term *getting to better* because it can encourage small steps or increments of better that are relevant, realistic, and achievable in arriving at the destination or the goal of better.

We Can't Leave a Place Unless We First Arrive

This is a statement that I often use in the context of the *getting to better* analogy. While at first it may sound strange or confusing, like some paradoxical proverb, the concept is actually quite simple and has proven very helpful for many of the leaders I work with.

Prior to performance development, workers experience or exist at a certain level of confidence, competence, and overall capability. The main objective of the leader in this process is to move them forward in their overall development—to inspire them in a way that enhances focus, motivation, engagement, and/or overall performance development toward the delivery of preferred service outcomes. Consider for a moment Valerie and James. According to my perspective, their leaders cannot assist them in their developmental journey to better unless they first arrive at the meaning of Valerie and James's stories—what is important to them, what they need, and what they desire with respect to their work and their goals for performance enhancement. Before leaders can leave a place, which is an employee's current level of job satisfaction, motivation, engagement, capacity, and ability to perform, they must first arrive at an accurate understanding of the employee's needs, values, goals, and strengths. Once they arrive, they can begin to move to *better*.

Unfortunately, despite good intentions, many leaders, in their efforts to motivate or enhance employee performance, engage in the interpretation and management of behavior based on information, not meaning. As demonstrated in the scenarios presented in Chapter 3, when decisions are made outside of the meaning of the employee's experience, the consequences can range from minimal and insignificant to outright challenging, leading to all sorts of stress and conflict and a myriad of other problems.

❖ RESPONSIVE LEADERSHIP: PRIORITIES, STRATEGIES, AND TOOLS

As discussed repeatedly, the key to a leader's ability to inspire—to influence the attitudes and behaviors of employees to be motivated and engaged and to perform optimally—is accurate discovery of meaning within the employee's story. As stated in the last chapter, knowing and understanding a worker's experience is only one aspect of Responsive Leadership. Responding to what a leader understands with the right response at the right time is what makes the approach the most effective and impactful with and for employees.

The remainder of this chapter will identify and discuss key components of a Responsive Leadership Approach: relational and communication priorities and tools and strategies for optimizing the conditions to access and make meaning of the employee experience. The priorities, tools, and strategies discourage leaders from interpreting and managing employees' behavior and instead encourage relational engagement and accurate understanding of the employee and the employee's story.

Relational Priorities: Operationalization of Trust, Respect, Empathy, and Integrity

Responsive Leadership places the leader–member relationship in highest regard, and so relations-oriented behaviors are key priorities for developing quality leadership experiences for workers. Chapter 2 illustrated the profound and impactful role *trust, respect, integrity,* and *empathy* have on an employee's experience of great supervision, supervisory support, and leadership overall. As a matter of fact, these four ingredients are essential and central to all great leadership experiences; that is, they were operating when workers experienced feeling better and doing better in their work. Research and stories from thousands of workers has evidenced the importance *trust, respect, integrity,* and *empathy* play in a quality leadership experience for both supervisor and employee.

However, the concepts of *trust, respect, integrity,* and *empathy* can be hard to define as they are amorphous, global, and often tied to an individual's situation or set of experiences. More difficult than defining these concepts is articulating what they look like in operation. How does one do trust? How do we do respect? Operationalization of the four key factors is central to the Responsive Leadership Approach and necessary for creating quality leader–member relationships. Operationalization of values can be a challenging endeavor for many supervisors and managers. The effect of this can be heard in a response to the question I once posed to a CEO, "How do you do *respect* with your team?" Below is an illustration of the response I received and the brief discussion that was stimulated by the question.

Steve: *Can you tell me how you do respect with your team?*

CEO: *I show them respect every day.*

Steve: *Yes. I hear that. Can you tell me how you show them respect?*

CEO: *By being respectful.*

Steve: *Yes. I am hearing that you are being respectful. Can you give me an example of what you mean by this?*

CEO: *I talk to my employees in a respectful tone. I behave respectfully in meetings . . .*

Now, I don't want to come across as saying this CEO is not respectful—not at all. As a matter of fact, if you followed this particular CEO around for one day, you would witness him engaging with his members and teams in dozens of very respectful ways. Most of us can look back on our behavior and pick out what may or may not have been respectful or trust building. However, the key to operationalizing values is in the proactive and purposeful choice of behavior prior to the interaction. It is not the fault of managers and executives that they struggle with the operationalization of values. There are few training programs or courses that teach us how to operationalize values. It takes practice, and it gets easier.

Operationalization of values is something that I spend time on in my training courses with workers and leaders. I often say that when we do not operationalize important guiding values from a Responsive Leadership Approach or, specifically, the guiding principles from our organizations' visions, the values just become words on dust-covered plaques on the wall—meaningless. Therefore, I try to simplify the operationalization of values, with three easy steps: (1) define the values, (2) negotiate a shared understanding, and (3) identify value-based behaviors in operation.

Step 1: Define the values.

Defining a global and/or amorphous value can be a great first step in identifying what it is we are all talking about. A clear definition helps by giving the value shape and substance and makes it more tangible. Before it can be claimed, it must be named. The following definitions of *trust, respect, integrity,* and *empathy* have proven helpful to many of the supervisors and managers that have attended the Responsive Leadership training I provide.

Trust: A sense of security and comfort that are the result of actions and/or interactions by a leader, which are favorable or at least not detrimental to the member.

Respect: The demonstrated or expressed consideration of and/or support for another person's physical, emotional, mental, social, and/or cultural well-being.

Integrity: When a person's actions are aligned with their stated values, and when that person follows through on what they say they will do.

Empathy: The ability to tune into and reflect the emotions and subjective experiences of another person in a manner that conveys acceptance and understanding.

Step 2: Negotiate a shared understanding of the value.

While a clear definition of a concept or value is a great start, it is just that. It is important to do what is possible to gain some insight into the understanding or meaning these key factors have for members and the team overall. I have met some leaders and workers in my journey who understand respect very differently from me. Some people associate respect with compliance, fear, and/or loyalty. This is reflected in such statements as "Show some respect and do what you're told!" and "If you respected me, you would do what I ask and not question my authority." It is important to clarify such big differences in the perceived meaning of important values as they have the potential to cause confusion, stress, and conflict.

The best way to begin negotiating a shared understanding is to talk to members and teams about the definition of a particular value and what it means to them. I encourage leaders to ask their members very directly, "What does *respect* mean to you? What does it look like? How do you know *respect* is happening? How do we all understand *respect* in the context of our work with our clients and in our work together with each other?" Answers to these questions are a great way to gain understanding into what *respect* means and what it looks like for workers. We can take this approach with other important values such as *trust, integrity, empathy,* and/or other guiding values that are contained in the vision and mission of the agency.

Step 3: Identify specific value-based behaviors in operation.

Once a value is defined and a shared understanding established, the next step in operationalization is to be purposeful in the consideration and choice of behaviors that would support, endorse, and/or foster that particular value. A couple of process-oriented questions I encourage leaders to consider are "How will what I am about to say or do demonstrate *respect* or build *trust*?" and "Which behaviors will be better to foster or develop *trust* further with members and/or the team overall?" The questions can be simplified even further.

"Will this demonstrate *respect*?" Or "Will this build *trust*?" If the answers to these questions are "no," the leader better consider another behavior if his intent is to uphold any or all of the identified and important relation-oriented values.

It is important to note that operating from our personal, professional, and organizational values 100% of the time is virtually impossible. This is especially true in environments plagued by fiscal and time constraints, bureaucratic and political priorities, legislated mandates and changing standards of practice, and competing organizational and program priorities that challenge even the most value-based professional to operate within a set of guiding principles. This is why, in my support for and encouragement of leaders to be value-focused, I ask them to consider these four words when operationalizing values: to the extent possible. I use this tactic because, while it may not always be possible to operate within or from a certain value set, we must do what we can to align ourselves to the extent possible. An example of this is when a leader operates from the value of collaboration. It may not always be possible to get input from the staff on everything; however, he will do what he can to have them involved in the process, to the extent possible.

Meaning-Making Questions

The operationalization of the aforementioned core values is critical for developing and establishing quality leader–member relationships and for creating conditions, a pathway to the meaning within the employee's story. I continuously differentiate between information and meaning. Information is not meaning! Information is the stuff that interpretations are made of—the pieces that we gather from the personnel file, assumptions, our story, labels, and more. I have referred to meaning as being an accurate understanding of the needs, values, goals, and strengths that are operating within the story of the employee's experience. It is impossible to access the meaning without the direct involvement of the employee we are considering or working with.

Three Important Meaning-Making Questions

I have discovered three questions that are critical if leaders are going to avoid the potential pitfalls and perils of employee-behavior interpretation and management. I call them *meaning-making questions*. The questions automatically implicate the experience of the employee as they are impossible to answer without the worker's participation in the discussion. The three questions are as follows:

1. *What do we know about* this *from this person's perspective?*

2. *What do we know about their experience within this?*

3. *What are the needs, values, goals, and strengths operating for this person?*

The *this* that is emphasized in the first question is whatever it is the leader is considering and/or concerned about. It could be a statement, a behavior, or even the context of a particular situation. Once again, it is impossible to answer the question without the involvement of the particular employee being considered and/or discussed. What I find absolutely fascinating is how difficult this question can be for many supervisors to answer. There are many reasons for this, among which are that supervisors and managers have been taught to interpret and manage behavior and are expected to do it in an environment that is often crisis-driven, where there is less time and fewer resources to see frontline workers face to face.

Let's consider James and Valerie's situations from above. If the managers were taught or encouraged to start with a *meaning-making question* prior to their own interpretation of the information, they may have been able to access important information and meaning to respond to the respective experiences in a way that led to a better outcome. Let's take the scenarios a little further to incorporate me as the person being sought for support. I will illustrate how useful the first *meaning-making question* can be for saving much needed time and energy and for initiating a more accurate process for accessing and understanding Valerie's experience.

Revisiting Valerie's Situation

Director: *I'm really worried about Valerie. She says that she needs to be challenged in her work.*

Steve: *Really? Valerie says she is not challenged in her work?*

Director: *Ya, I don't think she is as committed anymore.*

Steve: *Really? Is that what she said? What do you know about what she meant by "she is not challenged in her work" from her perspective?*

Director: *Well, she's been here for 15 years, and she is getting stagnant.*

Steve: *Did she say that things are getting stagnant?*

Director: *No, but lots of people would after 15 years in the same unit.*

Steve: *Are we talking about a lot of people or Valerie? What do we really know about this from her perspective?*

Director: *Hmmm. Nothing I guess.*

Steve: *Ya, you might want to check that out with her before we do anything else.*

This process appears so simple, yet it is much more difficult than it seems. Often when supervisors who are considering specific employee attitudes and/or behaviors that they find concerning, it is not uncommon for them to struggle with accurately answering *meaning-making questions*. It is much harder when there is stress and conflict and/or the supervisor–employee relationship is strained, as it is in the case above with James. We will revisit James's scenario in Chapter 7.

Because there are two main parts to every situation—the individual's perception of the situation and the individual's subjective experience of that situation—the second and third *meaning-making questions* ask the leader to consider the employee's experience within a particular behavior and/or situation.

*What do we know about his or her
experience within this? What are the needs,
values, goals, and strengths operating for this person?*

Like the preceding *meaning-making question*, this focus encourages those searching for meaning to consider the subjective experience as it relates specifically to the needs, values, goals, and strengths of the person and behavior being considered. Why are needs, values, goals, and strengths so important? Because, as mentioned in the previous chapter, it is my perspective that needs, values, and goals are operating in every single situation. Strengths are operating in a different manner than are needs, values, and goals and are integral in the accommodation of the other three priorities. Strengths will be discussed much further in the next chapter.

The Preferred Leadership Profile: Insights Into the Employee Story

Introduced in the last chapter, the PLP is a tool developed and used for *discovery* of a worker's subjective experience as it relates to needs, values, goals, and strengths. In addition to this, the PLP can help leaders identify and gain an understanding of key motivating sources for enhancing worker engagement and overall performance. Further, the

PLP tool, while developed for the purposes of *discovery*, simultaneously offers a process for building *trust, respect, integrity,* and *empathy,* thereby strengthening the leader–member relationship and establishing a pathway to the employee's story.

Consider Valerie's situation again but this time with the PLP tool in mind. Had Valerie's directors utilized and referred to her PLP, they would have gained some insight into what things may or may not be important to Valerie. Valerie's PLP would have been helpful to the directors as they could have developed a more responsive approach to Valerie's situation. As a matter of fact, there are several key areas from Valerie's PLP that definitely would have been helpful and provided insight for her codirectors prior to their unilateral attempt at interpreting and managing the situation. The following four items were taken from Valerie's PLP.

Valerie's PLP

PREFERRED OUTCOMES

1. What is it that brought you to your current position?

   "I've always wanted to be a MH outreach worker as long as I can remember, since wanting to be a social worker anyway. I love having involvement in my own community because that is an important value for me and my family."

2. What are the things that keep you there?

   "I love the face-to-face personal contact with the people of my community. I like to hear their stories. I like to know that I am providing a valuable service and that I am making a difference. I also like to be in charge of the referrals so that I can ensure they get connected to the right programs."

3. What's in it for me (WIIFM)? This is not a selfish question. We are all in certain roles or jobs at different times for different reasons. Sometimes it can be about

   a. making a positive difference,
   b. working to advance in one's career,
   c. earning a living,
   d. gaining experience,
   e. enjoying a challenge, or
   f. fostering personal growth.

   "It's that simple. I enjoy a challenge, and I really need to know I am making a difference. Working close to the frontline, as close as I can to the people in my community, and hearing the stories firsthand are my big WIIFMs."

PERFORMANCE SUPPORT PREFERENCES

1. What goals or aspirations do you have for yourself as they relate to professional performance and growth? These should be what you feel are important, not what others have defined as important. Please list at least two.

   "I would like to learn how to work a little better independently. Given the high turnover of team members and leadership, I would like to learn how to self-assess my own performance and work on my own development. I am not interested in a supervisor position as I don't feel it is my preference, and it will take me further from what I love: working closely with my people."

   "I would like to get more skilled using a strengths approach in intake and assessment."

The value of the PLP cannot be overstated. Sometimes even a little information can provide valuable insights into important employee motivators and work preferences. In this particular instance, the several areas from Valerie's PLP offered above may have assisted the codirectors in a more accurate assessment of her story, more so than their own interpretation. For instance, one can see from Valerie's profile that face-to-face client contact is important to her. She also states very clearly in her own words that being a supervisor is not her preference and that it also may take her further from what she loves the most: *"working closely with [her] people."* These important tidbits of information may have been enough to convince the codirectors to seek more clarification prior to interpreting and attempting to manage Valerie's situation without her input, without the meaning within her story. In addition to the use of a PLP, the codirectors may have also benefited from a *responsive approach to communication* while engaging in *relations-oriented discovery*.

❖ RESPONSIVE COMMUNICATION AND RELATIONS-ORIENTED DISCOVERY

Some years ago, I was involved in working simultaneously on a youth-engagement strategy for child welfare in one province in my country and a staff-engagement strategy in a youth justice setting from another province. When I was writing the final reports, something quite surprising stood out to me. If I were to cover up the word *worker* in the staff engagement report and the word *youth* in the youth-engagement report when reading the sections of each report on perceptions and experiences, it would seem as though I was reading the same report. What was astounding to me was how similar client experiences were to the employees that served and supported them. Similar themes, such as the importance of trust, respect, following through (integrity), and having a voice and a choice in matters affecting them, were also very important to both groups. What stood out the most for me were the themes that surfaced in both reports. According to the youth and staff involved in the explorations, the people identified as responsible for care and support *did not listen,* they *did not understand,* and they often *seemed not to care!* This was shocking and unsettling as I know from my experience that adults who work with youth and most supervisors/managers want the best for those that they support. They do care!

I have also been a part of a variety of staff-morale surveys and interviews, and many of these themes, including staff perceptions of a lack of understanding, appreciation, validation, and recognition by supervisors, are also common themes that lead many social service employees to feeling misunderstood, undervalued, and unappreciated.

Challenges and Barriers to Listening and Relations-Oriented Discovery

To this point, I have described many current social service work environments as fast-paced, crisis-driven, and fiscal and resource restrained where people are expected to do more with less. When these environments are combined with supervisors/managers who have little supervision experience or formal supervision training and who have been taught to interpret and manage behavior in the process of staff member development, it is not surprising to hear that employees are reporting in large numbers that they are not feeling heard, understood, or even cared for. In this light, it is also less surprising that social service workers are feeling dissatisfied with their supervision experience and quality leadership overall.

As stated earlier, there are many organizational and workplace impediments to preferred supervision practice that we cannot control. However, there is something that we can do, and it is 100% within our control. We can listen!

The Power of Listening

When speaking with thousands of frontline workers about their best supervisor or manager experience, it is not uncommon to hear many say, "She really listened to me," or "She really seemed to understand me," or, "He really cared." Listening is the first critical step in people feeling listened to. It is necessary that we listen if we are going to understand. It is when we understand others that they begin to feel valued and cared for. Listening is absolutely critical.

It is not uncommon to hear people make statements that minimize listening; an example is, "I didn't do much; I just listened." The power of listening cannot be underestimated, especially when there is an army of social service workers in dire need of exactly that! When a supervisor/manager listens effectively, he is operationalizing the values identified in quality leadership and the very behavior also identified in what most social service employees describe as their best leadership experience ever. Listening takes patience and focus and requires a person to be present. Listening conveys respect, caring, and compassion, among many other things. Listening builds trust, demonstrates respect and integrity, and paves the way for empathy; all of these foster great leader–member relationships and create a pathway to the employee's story, their lived experience.

However, with all that said, I still experience a range of a little to a lot of resistance when I introduce listening techniques in my leadership training workshops. I often hear expressions such as, "This is basic," "We took this stuff years ago in university," or, "These techniques are common sense." Most of the sentiments are correct; most of us have taken listening-skills training years and years ago, and the techniques are also quite basic. However, it is the last comment that I have struggled with the most because while it seems like common sense, if more supervisors and managers were practicing good-to-great listening, the numbers of workers stating that their superiors do not listen, understand, or care would be considerably lower. I think I have recently come to understand what people have been trying to say when they utter, "Paraphrasing and empathic responding are common sense." I think what they mean is that such listening techniques *make sense*. However, I would argue that the use of such skills is not that common, at least in the experiences and perceptions of many social service workers.

Personal Barriers to Listening Effectively

Our Assumptions

We have assumptions about everything. Many of our assumptions are developed out of and based on our own values, beliefs, and life experiences. Earlier in the chapter, assumptions were posited as barriers to accessing meaning within the employee's story. In addition to this, many of the other barriers identified (labels, theories, our story, diagnoses, personnel file) can also inform the information and assumptions we have about people, behaviors, and specific situations. Sometimes, when supervisors make assumptions, we also make conclusions and, therefore, may not feel the need or desire to listen. Sometimes, we may have already formulated our next response and/or developed a plan of action in our minds, before we have even heard entirely about the topic or issue the employee may be speaking about. Suspending our assumptions may be one of the most difficult challenges; however, it is absolutely necessary if we are going be fully present and listen to what someone is truly talking about.

Consider Valerie's situation above. As soon as she mentioned that she needed more of a challenge at work, her director, instead of listening, made an assumption about what she meant. We witnessed how that turned out.

Our Need or Desire to Problem Solve

Many well-intentioned supervisors want the best for their workers. They also want workers and the work that they carry out to be as productive and efficient as possible. In an environment that demands more with less, many supervisors and managers find themselves supporting their workers through problem solving. This is great, however, on many occasions; workers just need their managers to listen—to validate and affirm and to support them in figuring some things out on their own. Unfortunately, many supervisors and managers quickly launch into "problem-solving mode" when workers come to speak about an issue or situation. The problem with problem solving too quickly is that sometimes supervisors do not have enough information or the meaning of the experience or situation to problem solve effectively. If we do no have accurate information or meaning, what are we solving? We may be creating bigger problems.

Once again, we can consider both Valerie's and James's situations from earlier. Rather than listening a little more from their employee's perspectives for accurate information and meaning, the managers moved quite quickly to interpretation and problem solving. When problem solving is fraught with assumptions and interpretations, we can actually create more problems and increased stress and conflict between the people involved. Sometimes the stress and conflict is an immediate consequence (James), and other times it can take some time to develop and surface (Valerie). We will return to Valerie's scenario below and James's scenario in Chapter 7 to illustrate the positive and productive impact listening can have on a variety of work situations.

Our Own Responses

Our responses, if we are not cautious, can be real barriers to listening effectively. Also, if we are not careful, our responses can shut down the possibility that our employees may want to talk to us at all. In addition to this, sometimes our responses may even present formidable barriers to building trust and demonstrating respect, integrity, and empathy.

I have witnessed countless interactions, usually in the context of employees making suggestions, providing input, and/or giving feedback to their supervisors, wherein the response by the supervisor did not convey that they were open and interested or that they wanted to hear what it was the worker was saying. Unfortunately, four of the most common personal responses that supervisors/managers make when provided with developmental feedback or experience statements containing a higher than normal level of emotion or energy from their workers are *defensive, dismissive, consoling,* and *problem solving.*

Let's consider these four different responses in the context of two specific examples wherein different types of statements are provided to the supervisor. The first is a situation where there is high energy and emotion regarding a specific person in a situation, and the second represents a worker providing feedback to the supervisor as a suggestion for something better.

Example #1

A worker barges into the supervisor's office without knocking and states in an angry voice, "I hate that team leader! He is such a jerk!"

Defensive Response: "Listen here—don't talk about Walter like that! We both sat in on the interview and agreed to hire him!"

Dismissive Response: "Oh really. On our bad days, we can all be jerks sometimes too, you know."

Consoling Response: "Don't let it get to you. Give it some time, and I think things are going to get better."

Problem-Solving Response: "It's probably time to keep some distance from him, at least until you can figure out how you're going to make your different styles fit."

Example #2

An employee is feeling unsure about her work and has requested more support. The supervisor has asked if she could state what she might need. Her tentative statement was made reluctantly and with caution. "I think it would be helpful if you took a little more time to listen to my perspective and maybe . . . "

> *Defensive Response:* "What?! Listen better?! I am a great listener! I work hard at listening!"
>
> *Dismissive Response:* "Really, I do listen. Maybe if you could be a little more specific and clear about what you're saying, I could listen a little better."
>
> *Consoling Response:* "I'm sorry. I'm really doing my best here, just like you are, and I appreciate all that you are doing given the stress in the office."
>
> *Problem-Solving Response:* "You know what? You're absolutely right. This has been a goal on my performance appraisals for some time. I think I might sign up for a communication course. Yes, I really must work at this. "

In light of the two examples, it is not surprising to understand how such responses can be formidable barriers to listening effectively. When supervisors unintentionally respond in such manners, the implications run contrary to those of effective listening. Employees do not feel listened to. They do not feel like what they are saying is important. They do not feel heard, validated, or affirmed. In many cases, it is unlikely that they will share much more of their stories or their perspectives. This is an unfortunate consequence. What do their supervisors know about the situation or the employee's experience? Nothing. So how can they help support something better? They can't. In addition to the aforementioned implications, the greatest consequence of ineffective listening is that trust, respect, integrity, and empathy become jeopardized, and there is greater chance that the leader–member relationship will also be diminished.

Paraphrasing: Simple, Challenging, and Profound

Paraphrasing, also known as reflective or active listening, is probably one of the most basic communication techniques. However, trying to put this listening skill to use in a hectic work environment with serious time and resource constraints can be exceptionally challenging for any supervisor/manager. However, I have learned the exceptional value of paraphrasing, especially in the beginning of a conversation and/or at the start of a new working relationship. Paraphrasing is remarkably valuable during times of stress and/or conflict. That said, I find that if supervisors could paraphrase consistently and effectively, all workers would begin to experience that they are being listened to and heard.

The Goals of Paraphrasing

The goals of paraphrasing are quite straightforward. First, the main objective of paraphrasing is to provide the person that is speaking with the experience that they are being listened to and that the person listening has heard what the person speaking has said. Secondly, the next objective, which is often but not always a by-product of paraphrasing, is to encourage the person speaking to say more, to provide more information about their story. That's it.

Paraphrasing is not about asking "why?" Paraphrasing is not about offering your perspective or your story. Paraphrasing is not about asking all sorts of questions about what you are hearing or what you are interested in. Paraphrasing is not about rushing through to get to the information that you want to hear. Paraphrasing is about reflecting back to the person what it is you are hearing them say. Period. There will be plenty of time for exploration and discovery later in the conversation. Before someone will share more information that is meaningful, he must feel that he is being listened to and heard.

Structure and Tips for Paraphrasing Success

To ensure paraphrasing is more successful, there are several important preliminary considerations for supervisors.

- ✓ If possible, minimize distractions and interruptions.
- ✓ Make eye contact.
- ✓ Have relaxed body posture.
- ✓ Face the person.
- ✓ Use nonverbal indicators that you are listening—head nods and sounds like "mhmmm."
- ✓ Reflect what behavior you are seeing as a paraphrase if the person is not talking.

The above suggestions will assist supervisors in being increasingly present and attentive and often provide the experience that the supervisor is willing and ready to listen to what the employee has to say.

Paraphrasing, as stated before, is about reflecting back to the person talking what it is that she is saying or what you witness with her behavior. A paraphrase response can be conveyed as a statement or as a question. My personal preference is to paraphrase with curiosity so as to encourage more conversation, which is why I tend to use the paraphrase in an exploratory questioning and clarifying manner.

Let's return to Example #2 from above to illustrate what paraphrasing may look like as a statement or as a question in this particular situation.

Social Worker: *I think it would be helpful if you took a little more time to listen to my perspective.*

Supervisor: *You think it would be helpful if I took more time to listen to your perspective.* (Paraphrase)

OR

Supervisor: *Ok (pause), so you think it would be helpful if I took more time to listen to your perspective?* (Paraphrase)

Social Worker: *Yes, but that's not it really.*

Supervisor: *It's not?*

Social Worker: *You're actually a great listener. It's just that when we're in your office, there are tons of distractions and interruptions getting in the way of any meaningful dialogue.*

Supervisor: *Oh, so it's not that I'm not listening. It's just that there are many things interfering during our time together.*

A great by-product of paraphrasing, in addition to the results of workers feeling listened to and heard and sharing more, is that the supervisor, with this simple listening technique, begins to get a clearer understanding of what it is the worker meant by the first statement. This is the beginning of the pathway to the employee's story and provides the portal or doorway to learning more about what is important to the worker, what the worker needs, what she desires, and what she is good at.

Paraphrasing is a great technique for listening; however, it is limited in capacity for people to feel accepted and understood, an important experience for quality leader–member relationships and a quality leadership experience overall. Remember that when employees and managers describe the greatest leadership experience in their careers, that it is not uncommon for them to describe those supervisors or managers as being understanding, as really "getting it" or "getting me." Sometimes, they say things like, "The supervisor could really relate to what I was going through." Great leaders engage with their team members in ways that convey acceptance and understanding. This is also referred to as empathy and is among one of the key qualities of great leaders. Remember that empathy represents the ability of the supervisor to tune into the experiences and emotional needs of individual team members.

A technique known as empathic responding is a great tool supervisors/mangers can use when listening so that workers can feel like who they are and what they are saying is really being accepted and understood.

Empathic Responding to Approach Understanding

Empathic responding is a lot like paraphrasing but takes the supervisor's listening to a deeper level by incorporating the feeling and/or the emotions detected in what a worker is saying. Empathic responding offers leaders a way of communicating that recognizes and reflects the feelings and/or behaviors of a team member within a specific situation. Like paraphrasing, this simple technique can be difficult to practice. Several examples of empathic responding will be offered below. Each example will be preceded by a variety of simple empathic responding structures that, when followed, will assist supervisors and managers to shape an empathic response.

Empathic Responding Form

"It seems as though you feel (__FEELING__) about/because (__SITUATION__)."

OR

"When (__SITUATION__), it seems as though you feel (__FEELING__)."

Empathic Responding Example

Team Member: *I really like this new assessment format as it leaves more time to build relationships with our clients (smiling big and bouncing in her seat).*

Manager: *It seems as though you are happy and pleased with the new assessment because it supports relationship building with our clients.*

OR

Manager: *When you have more time to build relationships with clients, it seems as though you feel happy and quite pleased.*

Empathic responding, because it is geared toward reflecting the worker's experience as well as expressed emotions, can also include nonverbal signs or behavioral cues that, when reflected to the worker, may elicit more meaning as to what that particular experience might be.

Empathic Responding Form

"When I mention (__SITUATION__), it seemed to me that you (__OBSERVABLE BEHAVIOR__)."

Empathic Responding Example

Manager: *I am really looking forward to chatting about this in the unit meeting.*

Team Member: (He says nothing. However, he looks at his watch, lets out a sigh, and rolls his eyes.)

Manager: *I noticed that when I mentioned taking this up in the meeting, it seemed as though you let out a sigh, looked at your watch, and looked back a little with your eyes.*

Team Member: *Sorry, I didn't realize I did that. It's just that I really worry about the size of the meeting agenda. We put so many important things off until then. I'm worried we won't get to the priority areas.*

Let's return to Example #1 from the top. Because we have already reviewed how not to respond above, this demonstration will illustrate how paraphrasing and empathic responding can be used to effectively listen, create a better sense of understanding, and access greater meaning as to what the situation and the employee's experience within the situation is really about.

Example #1

A worker barges into the supervisor's office without knocking and states in an angry voice, "I hate that team leader! He is such a jerk!"

Supervisor: *Wow, you seem really angry.* (Empathic Response)

Worker: *No kidding! That team lead is such a jerk!*

Supervisor: *So he's not very nice?* (Paraphrase)

Worker: *It pisses me off that he let Joey, our client, out of the Secure Isolation Unit!*

Supervisor: *So you're angry because he let Joey out of the SIU?* (Empathic Response)

Worker: *Ya, he was supposed to be in there all day as a consequence for his behavior.*

Supervisor: *So he let him out too early?*

Worker: *No, that's not it! I can deal with that issue. It's everything else!*

Supervisor: *So you can deal with the early release. It sounds like there's more here* (Paraphrase) *and that there are other things that might also be making you angry.* (Empathic Response)

Worker: *Ya, ever since he came to the team, he has been undermining all of my decisions for disciplining the youth in our unit. I don't know if he's trying to make me look stupid, but that's how I feel.*

Supervisor: *Oh goodness. I can't imagine what that must be like, but it sounds to me that when you perceive him to undermine your directives, you get angry and frustrated because you feel that it is making you look stupid.*

Worker: *Ya. I don't like feeling stupid at work. It shakes my confidence and I start to question myself on everything, even the things I know I'm certain about and that I am good at.*

Paraphrasing and *empathic responding* are critical skills necessary for conveying an experience to the person sharing that they are being listened to and what they are saying is important. In addition, effective paraphrasing and empathic responding can result in the experience of the team member feeling validated, affirmed, heard, and understood. A wonderful by-product of these two great communication techniques is that they can result in the person sharing more meaning regarding what the situation is really about. Empathic responding can help access more of the deeper meaning within the story. It can be like peeling an onion. For instance, in the example above, there is so much more to the worker's experience that surfaces as the paraphrasing and empathic responding continue. *Effective paraphrasing* and *empathic responding* can also initiate and create an opening or pathway to more of the worker's story regarding important needs, values, goals, and strengths, aspects of the experience that are most important for the supervisor to get closer to understanding the worker's story.

Common Paraphrasing/Empathic
Responding Challenges and Suggestions

While the techniques of paraphrasing and empathic responding seem simple and straightforward, putting them into practice can be much more difficult than most might think.

The following are common challenges that have arisen in a variety of practice sessions with many social service supervisors, managers, and senior executives. Each challenge will be presented and followed by one or more considerations for minimizing and/or overcoming the identified challenge altogether.

> Challenge: It is not my way of communicating, and it feels ungenuine and gimmicky.

For many people, communicating in this way is not common for them. And like most new techniques or tools, trying them out in a not-so-usual way may feel a little awkward or uncomfortable. It will take some time to get used to this way of listening and communicating; however, be patient and give it some time. It is also important to find your own style and to keep in mind that you can paraphrase and/or empathically respond as a statement or as a question. If you want to feel and sound less gimmicky, try to be more genuine. This will take practice. Remember that practice, practice, practice makes better.

> Challenge: Won't most people feel that I am mocking them or being condescending as I continue to parrot what they are saying?

This is a common concern for most supervisors and mangers. It is important to keep in mind that employees have important experiences to share; they want to be listened to, heard, and understood. When you accommodate the need, value, and desire to be listened to, validated, affirmed, and understood, the person talking will be less concerned about how you are communicating. It is important to relax and trust the process. If you are feeling awkward and uncomfortable or if you feel as though you are not doing it right, you may want to inform your employees that you are trying something new. You may want to try a message like this, "I wanted you to know that I want to listen and communicate more effectively so that I can be a better leader for you and the team. I am trying out some new ways of listening actively and responding empathically. While I feel a little awkward doing it, I am working to get better."

This is an important message for several reasons. First, it provides people the opportunity to know that you are trying something new. This is helpful just in case they do sense some discomfort or awkwardness and allows them to attribute it to your brave efforts at trying something new. In addition to this, it may take off some of the pressure you might place on yourself for getting it perfect immediately. Finally, I believe that a supervisor or manager can rarely go wrong when she gives the message that she is trying out something challenging in order to provide better leadership to her members.

Challenge: I want to ask "why" immediately and get to the reason behind the first one or two statements.

Why questions are among the most common questions used when attempting to understand and/or "get to the bottom" of a situation. Unfortunately, the why question, no matter how gentle or respectful, can sound like the beginning of an interrogation. Also, the why question, when asked, may have a tendency to evoke a sense of blame, guilt, or shame and lead to a negative experience or a not-so-positive reaction. Sometimes why questions can be really difficult to answer. Can we really know why all the time? Do we really know the reasons behind all of our needs, values, goals, and/or strengths? Not really. Why questions, due to aforementioned experiences, may lead to those being asked why to answer, "I don't know." Why questions may unintentionally jeopardize a feeling of trust and safety and thereby negatively impact the leader–member relationship. Helpful tips on alternatives for why questions will be offered below in the discussion of *Helpful Discovery Responses and Questions*.

Challenge: I want to solve the problem immediately or as quickly as possible.

Most supervisors and managers operate in resource- and time-constrained environments where they are asked to do more with less. Given that they are helpers themselves and want the best for their workers, most supervisors have a tendency to want to solve problems quickly in order to help and move on to the next area of need. While this is noble in theory, there are several serious problems that may arise from attempting to problem solve too quickly. As we have seen from several examples so far, it is not uncommon that the first one or two statements made by a worker about a situation or his experience is often not what the issue or issues are really about.

Therefore, a premature attempt to solve a problem may lead to statement or particular issue as not being the right problem at all.

Sometimes workers want to be listened to or validated and understood around a specific situation or their experience within that situation. An attempt by a manager to problem solve too quickly may lead to the employee feeling rushed or unimportant. In addition to this, a worker who feels rushed to solve an issue that is not really a problem may feel invalidated, unaffirmed, or misunderstood. Finally, regardless of the reason behind a supervisor's own need and goal to move quickly to problem solving, despite good intentions, it may jeopardize the relationship between the supervisor and her member.

> Challenge: Paraphrasing and empathic responding are limited and do not allow me to go further or deeper into the worker's experience.

Inherent in the purpose of paraphrasing and empathic responding are these limitations. Paraphrasing and empathic responding are helpful for providing an experience of being listened to, heard, and understood. They are also very helpful for enhancing the relationship by conveying trust, respect, integrity, and empathy and for fostering an overall feeling of safety for workers. However, these effective listening techniques, while helpful for creating an environment and pathway to the employee's story, are limited for probing and moving deeper into an accurate discovery of specific needs, values, goals, and strengths. They are limited in their capacity for accurate meaning making.

These are the reasons why paraphrasing and empathic responding should be used in the beginning and throughout meaning-making discovery conversations and supplemented with the most effective questions and responses for accurate meaning making.

❖ DISCOVERY RESPONSES AND DISCOVERY QUESTIONS

Discovery of employee and team needs, values, goals, and strengths is at the core of a Responsive Leadership Approach. While paraphrasing and empathic responding create conditions and initiate a pathway to the employee story, *discovery* responses and questions are critical for understanding the depth of meaning contained within worker attitudes and behavior. Remember that *meaning making* takes information that we have about a person, whether it is positive or negative, and turns it into meaning by answering the meaning-making questions posed earlier: *What do we know about this from the person's perspective? What do we know about his or her experience within this? What are the needs, values, goals, and strengths that have been or are operating?*

Discovery responses and questions are used following paraphrasing and empathic responding. However, it is important that while paraphrasing and empathic responding should be used in the beginning of conversations, they are to be used consistently within and throughout communication and relationship building consistently. The following helpful responses and questions are used to delve deeper into the meaning of the employee behavior and/or situation to surface important needs, values, goals, and strengths within that particular employee's story, their lived experience. Remember that individual and shared needs, values, goals, and strengths are keys to understanding the meaning and value work and the work experience hold for the employee. In addition to this, individual needs, values, goals, and strengths are inextricably linked to individual employee engagement and performance motivators and, when accurately identified, offer the leader highly potent options for motivating and engaging their employees to perform optimally. I will present the list of *discovery* responses and questions below and then provide a brief explanation to illustrate the utilization of specific techniques, including when to use them, how to use them, and the positive implications of effective use. The *discovery* responses and questions are as follows . . .

- Tell me about that.

This is one of my favorite responses. I find it to be the best response to use after paraphrasing and empathic responding to meet the inevitable and limited stalling point in the conversation. It is gentle, respectful, and curious in that it conveys the message that the listener is interested and wants to hear more of the story. I also found this statement helpful when I was practicing the overall communication process. When I would get stuck or lost in what or how I was going to respond next, I would just say, "Can you tell me about that?" and the person I was listening to would continue talking and provide more information and meaning to his story.

- I would like to hear more about that (topic, statement, situation, feeling, experience).

Similar to the above statement, this particular response is a little more directive in that it assists to gently guide the person talking to a specific part of her own story. This is helpful because it assists in keeping the listener on track of the speaker's story, not onto a new topic that is of interest to the listener.

- Can you help me understand . . . ?
  - o What is that like for you?
  - o What was that like when it happened?

This is a gentle, empathic question that moves the person talking to express not only their perception of the situation but also the impact that particular experience had on him. This question is exceptionally helpful for revealing important aspects of the person's experience and often begins to surface needs, values, goals, and strengths.

- Are there other times that you feel like this?

This question helps take the person and his story to other times, situations, or experiences with other people that result in similar feelings and experiences. It provides an opportunity to surface consistent themes that are most significant to the person sharing her story. It is not surprising that similar experiences will also surface a consistency in the needs, values, goals, and strengths that are or were in operation within a variety of experiences.

- Can you tell me a little more about . . . ? (Go back to the specific topic, statement, situation, feeling, or experience within the same story.)

This question is similar to the first two but is placed later in the story sharing. This is a great question that can be used to encourage the person to return to an important part of their story. I like to go back and do what I refer to as "circle around" to establish that the consistent links I have made between needs, values, goals, and strengths are indeed the most important aspects of the person's experience—that they hold the greatest meaning and value within the employee's story.

- Can you tell me what you mean when you say_____?

So often when workers are speaking about their experiences, they use general terms, slang, or a variety of different nomenclature to describe their stories. While different words have different meanings for people, so too do the same words, especially when there are social, cultural, and/or geographical differences. Terms like *moody* and *challenging* or metaphors like "flat as a pancake" may mean something specific to one person but be interpreted very differently by another.

Clarifying what people mean prior to moving on too quickly in the conversation can keep one on track to a more accurate understanding of the worker's story. An example I use is the common response given by a supervisor or manager when a worker makes a subtle or direct accusation that the leader is being unfair. The most consistent response to this is often a defensive response—"I am not"—and followed by an explanation that justifies the leading defense. The interesting thing is that most supervisors who respond in this manner rarely if ever get to the meaning behind the statement. However, if and when supervisors can refrain from defensive or dismissive responses and respond with "Can you tell me what you mean when you say 'play favorites'?" often what happens is that a worker can recall a very specific date at a very specific time wherein a very specific incident or interaction occurred, taking the supervisor closer to discovering the meaning the statement holds for the individual worker.

- Avoid *why* questions.

This idea was presented earlier in the chapter as a challenge to paraphrasing and empathic responding. Given that *why* questions have the tendency to elevate emotions and/or evoke a negative response, I encourage supervisors and managers to eliminate this question from their vocabularies altogether. As a matter of fact, with many of the suggested communication techniques offered here, one can surface the meaning of a person's story without even asking "Why?" The following two suggestions are what I refer to as alternatives to why questions or why questions in disguise.

- "Really, (pause) . . . (followed by a paraphrase of the last statement made, posed as a question)?"
- What do you think that might be about?
- Ask the *million-dollar questions*.
    o What difference would that make? / What difference did that make?
    o How would that be helpful? / How was that helpful?

These questions are worth more to me as a leader than my combined 11 years of post-secondary education. They are simple yet transformative for two very important reasons. Firstly, the million-dollar questions can turn information into meaning almost immediately by illuminating a deeper understanding of what a person has stated. For instance, when a worker makes the statement, "I really like when you check up on me," I can assume I know what it means. However, I can paraphrase and/or use one of the million-dollar questions. By asking, "What difference does it make when I check up on you?" or, "Can you tell me how my checking up on you is helpful for you?" I may learn more specifically that checking up assists in the worker feeling supported, reassured, and that they like to know they are doing what is expected of them. This is important because without pursuing a greater understanding of what is meant, I may assume that "checking up on me" means whatever I think it means. And to be honest, it is almost always different from what is meant by others.

Secondly, and more importantly, the million-dollar questions can actually transform something that seemed impossible into the possible by illuminating a more accurate meaning within a statement or set of statements. Here is an example of what I mean:

Supervisor: *So can you tell me how you think I might be helpful?*

Worker: *I think you should just fire everyone in the program!*

Note: This is quite a request and is actually not at all possible. However, instead of getting angry, arguing, or lecturing the worker on policy around firing practices and so forth, it is important to make meaning of this particular statement by paraphrasing and following up with one of the million-dollar questions.

Supervisor: *Really, you think I should let everyone go?* (Paraphrase)

Worker: *Well, not everyone. Not Sarah, Raymond, or Jessica.*

Supervisor: *So what difference would it make if tomorrow, other than Sarah, Raymond, and Jessica, the whole team were fired?* (Million-Dollar Question)

Worker: *I think this would be a better place to work because there would be a lot less gossip and backstabbing.*

Supervisor: *So you feel that there is gossip and backstabbing in the office?* (Paraphrase)

Worker: *Absolutely!*

Supervisor: *Can you tell me a little bit more about that?*

In this case, the issue is not at all about firing the workers in the whole unit. There is a specific meaning embedded in the original statement made by the worker. Simply, paraphrasing and using a million-dollar question can assist in illuminating the meaning immediately. The worker is raising an issue about the perceived gossiping and backstabbing in the office. Interestingly, just as empathic responding can help "peel back" the story like an onion to the core of the meaning, the million-dollar questions can turn what initially seemed as impossible (fire everyone) into a specific issue that can be discussed and dealt with directly.

You can see why they are called *million-dollar questions*. They are invaluable for immediately illuminating the meaning and often the needs, goals, and values embedded within the employee's story. I encourage supervisors and managers to make a personal declaration; that is, when they hear someone state that they need or want something that seems inappropriate, unsafe, or altogether impossible, they should take a deep breath and ask themselves, "What do I know about this from this person's perspective?" and then pose one of the million-dollar questions. There is no need to get angry, frustrated, or confused or to argue, lecture, or attempt to problem solve when we really don't know the meaning of what a worker is saying or asking for.

- Allow for silences.

It is important that supervisors and managers allow for silences for many reasons. Silence helps us stay calm and relaxed and allows supervisors and managers time to consider and move through the various steps in the meaning-making process—to listen, work to understand, and focus on the needs, values, goals, and strengths that are operating for a particular person. In addition, silence allows workers the time to really consider their own experiences as they cultivate and articulate the meaning within their stories. For many employees, it may be the first time that someone has really asked for their perspectives as it pertains to the meaning of their experiences. Finally, allowing for silences offers the worker and the supervisor a space that allows more room for listening.

- Ask *direct discovery questions*.

While the aforementioned responses and questions for discovery are important for surfacing the meaning within a worker's story, direct discovery questions can be helpful if and when a leader is feeling stuck or lost in the conversation. This can happen if and when a worker provides a great many details about a variety of situations or when a worker provides a variety of explanations for the same experience and/or situation. When supervisors are feeling lost or stuck in a mass of ideas, details, and/or experiences, I encourage them to ask one or more of the following *direct discovery questions*:

- What do you feel you might need here? (Need Question)
- What is most important to you? (Value Question)
- What is it that you are hoping for? (Goal Question)

It is not uncommon for direct discovery questions to encourage the person sharing her story to move directly to important needs, values, and goals embedded within the story of her experience.

❖ MAKING MEANING OF THE CHALLENGE FOR VALERIE

Now that you are familiar with *meaning-making responses and questions*, let's return to Situation 1: A Challenge for Valerie, offered earlier in the chapter, so that we can move through the process in a manner that illustrates the overall *meaning-making process* and the subsequent benefits of utilizing the approach when communicating with employees.

Remember that in a conversation with her codirector, Valerie mentioned that although she still loves her job, she feels as though she would like to be challenged more in her work. Instead of making meaning of her statement, her well-intentioned manager made an assumption about her experience and went to his counterpart to interpret and manage what they assumed to be Valerie's experience. Let's take the scenario from beginning and observe what happens when Valerie's manager utilizes the meaning-making process offered within a Responsive Leadership Approach.

Codirector: *It's nice to see you Valerie. How are things going for you?*

Valerie: *Things are good generally. I still love my job. However, I have been feeling lately like I need more of a challenge.*

Codirector: *Really, you need more of a challenge?* (Paraphrase)

Valerie: *Ya, I think so. I've been doing this job for 10 years now.*

Codirector: *Yes, you have been at intake for a long time. Can you tell me what you mean when you say "more of a challenge"?* (Paraphrase and Responsive Question)

Valerie: *Well, I love my work with people. It's what I love the most. I love making a difference in my community. That's my family's priority. It's just that I'm good at what I do and I feel I can take on more.*

Codirector: *Take on more?* (Paraphrase)

Valerie: *Ya, I want to make more of a difference. I'm about six years from retirement, and I want to do more.*

Codirector: *Wow, only six years. And you want to do more before you retire?* (Paraphrase)

Valerie: *Ya, I do a lot of volunteer work in the community after hours, and I do a lot of good stuff in my job, but I would like to combine those a little more. You know, bring them together. I feel I can get more done at work, but I feel constrained just being in the office.*

Codirector: *Really, constrained being in the office?* (Avoiding "Why?" and Using Paraphrasing as a Question)

Valerie: *Well, I love working intake and helping individuals and couples out, but lately, there are a lot of slow days here in the office. And I think some people would be more open to mental health support if we reached out. You know, beyond this office and the big government building. Ha ha.*

Codirector: *Tell me more about reaching out, beyond this office and the big government building.* (Responsive Question and a Paraphrase)

Valerie: *Well, I think we would reach more people if we did more than wait for them to come to us. Also, I think it would increase my workload, which might give me the challenge I need.*

Codirector: *So getting out into the community more and increasing your workload might give you the challenge you need?* (Paraphrase)

Valerie: *Ya, both of those would really help me feel like I am making a bigger difference for the community. It would also be good for me because that's what I need and where I find the most value—when I am working more closely with the people of my community.*

Codirector: *So it sounds like when you are working closer with your people and feel like you are making a bigger difference, you experience the greatest meaning and value in your work.* (Paraphrasing and Empathic Responding)

Valerie: *Yes, absolutely. That's why I moved into intake years ago, because I could help close to 20 people in one day versus when I was providing counseling service and could only get to about five. I needed more of a challenge then, and I am feeling I need more a challenge now.*

Codirector: *Valerie, I am really impressed with your commitment to your community and to our program.* (Appreciative Statement— to be discussed in Chapter 5) *It sounds to me that increasing your caseload might be helpful at this time, and considering some outreach possibilities may also bring increased meaning and value to your work.* (Paraphrase and Empathic Responding)

Valerie: *Oh yes. I think that's exactly what I need right now. I realize I am on intake and we don't really have an outreach component. Is that possible?*

Codirector: *As a matter of fact, it is something we have been talking about at the director's team meetings. I think it is definitely worth exploring. How do you feel about coming along to the next meeting and sharing your ideas with the management team?*

Valerie: *Really?! I would love that!*

As you can see, Valerie's manager was able to use meaning-making responses and questions to arrive at a better understanding of what is important to Valerie—her needs, values, goals, and strengths. Even though the conversation between Valerie and her manager was fairly brief, it was not long before key aspects of Valerie's story were surfaced. We learned that Valerie has a strong need to make a difference and remain closely involved with the people in her community. Valerie has made her personal and professional goals line up with those needs and is looking to increase her workload in order to stay connected to the community and make a greater impact. Although strengths were not purposefully cultivated in this conversation, it is clear that Valerie is good at her job.

When the scenario was presented earlier in the chapter, Valerie's managers made a great deal of assumptions about what was going on for Valerie and made guesses as to what was important to her, what she might need, and what she might want for something better. They approached her comment "to be more challenged in the work" by interpreting and managing Valerie. Based on their interpretation, they deduced that giving Valerie a leadership position would provide the necessary challenge she was looking for.

In light of the information that was revealed in this conversation, it is not surprising that in the first scenario, Valerie left her position after being promoted to supervisor. She gravitated back to what was most important to her: to work frontline for a community program in her neighborhood.

❖ IMPORTANT COMMENTS ON MEANING-MAKING RESPONSES AND QUESTIONS

Over the last 10 years, I have found both the simplicity and the profundity in the meaning-making process absolutely astounding. The hardest part of the approach is to unlearn all of the things we have learned about interpreting and managing worker attitudes and behaviors. Just sticking to the responses and questions offered above will help supervisors and managers get access to the worker and the worker's story, thereby revealing important needs, values, goals, strengths, and other important performance motivators. When leaders can surface these important aspects of the worker experience, they will be in a better position to respond by providing the necessary support and guidance that has the greatest value and meaning for the worker. In addition to this, leaders who can engage and understand what is most important to employees are better able to keep their team members connected to the aspects of the work that keep them highly engaged and performing optimally, cultivating, connecting with, and enhancing the motivation that has always been there.

❖ SUMMARY OF IMPORTANT POINTS

- Quality leadership is dependent upon an accurate understanding of the unique needs, values, goals, and strengths of the individual worker.

- Leaders who can connect a worker's needs, values, goals, and strengths through work and organizational engagement are more likely to foster optimal worker performance and preferred outcomes.

- It is important that leaders recognize and minimize the various barriers that exist to an accurate understanding of a worker's story.

- Information is not *meaning*. Meaning can only be found within the unique experience of a worker's story.

- Problems and challenges that impact motivation, morale, and performance arise from the misunderstanding of the meaning a particular situation holds for the person and/or people involved.

- Quality leader–member relationships combined with effective and responsive communication are critical to access a pathway to the meaning within a worker's story.

- The operationalization of values is key to creating a quality leader–member experience for both the leader and the member.

- *Meaning-making questions* can help leaders avoid the pitfalls and perils of interpretation and management of member attitudes and behaviors.

- *Paraphrasing* and *empathic responding* are 100% within a leader's control and are key to initiating relationship building and gaining access to a member's story.

- *Discovery responses and questions* can help leaders move quickly and accurately to the core of an employee's needs, values, goals, and strengths.

❖ PERSONAL LEADER REFLECTION AND CONSIDERATIONS

- What values are most important to you as a leader?

- Consider asking individual members and/or the team overall to share their understanding of what important values might mean to them. What might they say these values look like in practice?

- How do you build *trust, respect, integrity* and *empathy* as you carry out your role as a leader?

- Consider a specific team member's positive behavior. What do you know about this from his perspective? What are the needs, values, goals, and strengths that are operating within the meaning of the team member's story?

- Consider how often you utilize listening techniques such as *paraphrasing* and *empathic responding* in your interactions with team members.

- Which *discovery responses and questions* are you already familiar and/or comfortable with? Are there particular discovery techniques that you would like to try out and/or improve upon in future conversations with members?

5

A Strengths Focus and Quality Leadership

Success is achieved by developing our strengths not by eliminating our weaknesses.

— Marilyn vos Savant

❖ A DIRE NEED TO EMPHASIZE STRENGTHS

Up to this point in the book, great emphasis has been placed on the importance of discovery and making meaning of worker needs, values, goals, and strengths as a means to foster quality leader–member relationships and to inspire and engage workers to feel better, develop better, and perform better as they carry out their important roles of helping. While needs, values, and goals all form important aspects of a Responsive Leadership Approach, it is for very important reasons that a strong emphasis be made regarding a strengths focus as a key ingredient in enhancing worker morale, engagement, commitment, and overall performance—a need for an emphasis so strong that a focus on strengths and quality leadership warrants its very own chapter!

There are several very notable reasons for making the strengths focus aspect of the Responsive Leadership Approach a stand-alone chapter in this book. First, a focus on values, needs, and goals is already quite common and forms an integral aspect of frontline worker training, performance development, and most approaches to supervision and employee management. A focus on strengths, however, while theoretically and philosophically in line with social service values and guiding principles is less common and, from the experience of many workers in the field, does not make up an integral aspect of employee supervision, performance development, and/or performance management. As a matter of fact, when it comes to most performance management approaches, in particular, a focus on employee strengths is often rare altogether and in some cases nonexistent.

A second reason for making an emphasis on strengths in supervision and management a necessary focus has to do with the reality within the current political, bureaucratic, organizational, training, work, and service-delivery realities of social services. Many of these social service dimensions are actually antithetical and/or provide countercurrents or impediments to the use and sustainability of a strengths focus within supervision and/or management. Finally, promoting and illustrating a strengths approach in supervision and management is critical because consistent operationalization of a strengths perspective in leadership is difficult to do and maintain, especially if it is not the most common modality utilized by most supervisors and managers. In addition to the myriad of social services context challenges that exist as impediments to a strengths focus, the reality is that many supervisors and managers have not been taught to operationalize a strengths-based approach in practice. Most of us can understand what a strengths-based approach is philosophically and in principle, but most supervisors and managers have not been taught how to apply, integrate, and/or sustain a strengths-based approach in practice with their team members.

It is for these reasons and many others that a strengths focus as it relates to quality leadership occupies a full chapter in this book. The remaining discussion will focus on the challenges that exist to utilizing and sustaining a strengths-based approach to social services supervision and management, including the negative implications a problem-saturated environment has on supervisors, workers, and clients. In addition to this, the discussion will outline what a strengths perspective in leadership can look like and will make strong linkages between a strengths focus and quality leadership. A variety of strengths-focused tools, strategies, and practice examples will be offered. Finally, the chapter discussion will conclude with a clear illustration of the powerfully positive implications of a strengths focus in the context of supervision and management in order to create a greater quality leadership experience for all team members.

❖ CHALLENGES TO A STRENGTHS
FOCUS IN SUPERVISION AND MANAGEMENT

The Importance and Relevance of a Strengths Focus

Very few people would disagree about the importance of utilizing a strengths perspective in the context of social services supervision and management. More than ever, a focus on strengths forms an integral cornerstone to most frontline-person and family-centered helping interventions and is consistent with social service philosophy and guiding principles. Many social service workers find a strengths perspective favorable and in line with their personal and professional values and goals for helping. Focusing on strengths with individuals, families, and communities is in line with the way most frontline social service workers prefer to work. In addition, many organizational and program missions and visions have incorporated and/or reflect the importance of a strengths focus within operational support and service delivery. It is in this light that a strengths-based organizational and management approach seems like it would make sense and be commonplace. Unfortunately, however, there exist a myriad of environmental influences and challenges that unintentionally operate as impediments to the utilization and implementation of a strengths-based approach in supervision and management.

Social Services: A Problem-Saturated Environment

In order to gain an understanding of the incongruence between the importance of a strengths focus in theory and what is actually happening in practice, we must consider the overall environment—the context in which supervision and management of workers occurs. Social services in general maintain a predominantly problem-oriented focus, and the realities that challenge a strengths perspective occur at every level of the system, impacting and thereby influencing the way worker supervision and performance development training occur and how these processes are carried out in the field.

Most social services organizations operate from mandates that maintain a focus on safety, risk assessment, risk management, and reduction of harm, albeit in the context of promoting overall well-being and health. Unfortunately, what is inherent in most problem-oriented paradigms and service delivery approaches is that the area of inquiry and/or focus of attention is centered on what is not working or what needs to be fixed. Such a focus inevitably leads to a starting point of inquiry and operation based on deficits, weaknesses, threats, dysfunction, and deficiencies. A problem orientation is prevalent and evident at all levels across various social service sectors and influences the context of most approaches to the structure and process of social services supervision practice.

Political agendas, bureaucratic priorities, and legislated mandates also influence and impact operations and service delivery models, subsequently shaping the focus and process of supervision sessions. For instance, most helping agencies utilize a biomedical approach as a foundation for assessment and intervention. In addition to this, many programs and service delivery models are highly influenced by the fiscal need and encouragement of and/or a politically mandated use of the *DSM* (*Diagnostic and Statistical Manual of Mental Disorders*) as a requirement for intake, assessment, and intervention. Because supervisors and managers are providing guidance and support for workers operating within the predominantly biomedical and *DSM*-driven paradigms, a great deal of case management and support discussions are focused on the attainment of well-being by fixing or changing dysfunction, deficits, abnormalities, erroneous thinking, and/or pathological behavior. Although strengths-based assessment and intervention has become a more important aspect of social services intervention and support, the reality remains that in practice, a focus on strengths does not take up a great deal of time when it comes to supervisor–member discussions around supportive case management reviews. Instead, the predominant supervision focus continues to be around crisis situations, stressful challenges, problems, and problem solving.

Problems With Training

Social service training endeavors to prepare supervisors and managers with the knowledge and skills to educate, coach, support, develop, and delegate tasks to their team members in a way that enhances the consistency and quality of supportive service being provided to clients. However, like the overall context of social services in general, most supervisory training programs take a problem orientation and problem-solving focus. Supervisors and managers are presented with many theoretical models and orientations for understanding a variety of people and systemic problems in order to understand and solve them. A focus on strengths is often omitted from the traditional problem-solving approach because the initial starting point for inquiry is on what is "wrong" and/or what needs to be fixed. Supervisors and managers are trained to ask "Why?" and to gather information so that they can assist in successfully solving a variety of problems. In essence, they are taught to assess and interpret situations so that they can manage to problem solve them successfully. There are curricula that attempt to incorporate a focus on strengths, but it is often minimal in comparison to the predominantly problem-oriented approaches offered. In addition, when curricula offer a segment on strengths-based supervision, I have found that the emphasis pertains more to the *looking* for strengths, falling short, however, on the skills and tools for a tangible and practical application of a strengths approach to supervision practice.

A key area that often forms a core element of supervisor and manager training is employee performance development. Most approaches to employee development operate from an overall behaviorist approach, meaning that supervisors are encouraged to learn a variety of human-behavior and system theories and models in order to interpret the attitudes and behaviors of employees so that they can develop more capable, confident, and competent employees. While employee development and management represent positive endeavors geared toward enhancing staff capacity to work toward better outcomes for clients and organizations overall, a behaviorist approach contains an inherent bias toward interpreting and managing employees, versus engaging and understanding their individual experiences. In addition to this, most developmental and behavioral approaches focus on competency development from the perspective of a deficit-based and/or performance-weakness model, once again minimizing the emphasis and/or omitting altogether a focus on employee strengths.

Problems With Professional Development

Finally, when it comes to supervisory training curricula for working with "challenging" employees, most approaches to performance management for supervisors take on an "undesirable performance" lens while emphasizing management of performance through the interpretation of a variety of human-behavior models and theoretical and developmental orientations, all geared toward managing or changing poor employee attitudes and behaviors in order to bring about more desirable outcomes. In my experience as an academic and a trainer in a variety of course modules, very few performance management approaches contain a focus on strengths.

Performance development and performance management are actually the same thing; however, the former term is often used in the context of proactive and positive employee development whereas the latter term is often used in a not-so-positive context, usually when an employee is struggling with competency development and/or is involved in some sort of discipline process. This dynamic is evident when a manager is talking about an employee plan. Often when we hear someone referring to a performance plan, it's in the context of regular performance appraisal and development. However, when we hear reference to a performance management plan, it is often in the context of a "challenging worker" and/or a worker who is demonstrating and/or engaging in "undesirable" behavior. Regardless of what term is used and/or the context, both performance development and performance management processes operate from a deficit base and/or performance weakness stance. The predominant focus is on development of the undesirable performance behavior. In my conversations with thousands of frontline workers, their experience in general has been that performance development focuses on areas of weakness or required development and is often lacking in a strengths focus. Similarly, a performance management plan rarely contains a focus on strengths as the behavior that is being targeted is often problematic and the documentation that has been gathered to build a plan is often focused on areas such as undesirable, inappropriate, or unprofessional attitudes and/or performance.

An important contextual reality that challenges the consistent utilization of a strengths focus within supervision and management is that the above-mentioned problem orientations are often in operation in a highly stressful, crisis-oriented, fiscally and resource-restrained environment where workers and supervisors are expected to do more with less. When supervisors have a strong desire to help workers solve a variety of people and systemic problems in the context of perceived time and energy limitations, they are naturally encouraged to get to the problems quicker for the sake of overall efficacy. Unintentionally and inevitably there is less space and time for a discussion of what is going well, a discussion and subsequent development regarding team-member strengths.

Problems With Managing Performance Problems

While many workers in various fields report that their experiences with performance evaluations and appraisals are less than satisfactory, worker reports of performance management and discipline range from negative to outright humiliating. At a time when workers are struggling to perform in a preferred and expected manner, when they are probably feeling less than confident and capable, a strengths perspective would be helpful to provide a more positive experience of themselves and/or their work. However, often when performance management is initiated, the process and the impacts move in the opposite direction of a strengths approach.

Most approaches to employee discipline are based on the principles of punishment, and the problem-oriented and deficit-focused processes within performance management do little to motivate workers to change their behavior. When reprimands, progressive discipline, and suspensions are utilized as logical consequences and when support and clear direction for change are lost within a disempowering and intimidating process, an employee's capacity to be engaged and positively motivated is seriously limited, if not curtailed altogether. It is my experience that a strengths focus is missing altogether when employees are being reprimanded or disciplined for undesirable and/ or poor performance. At a time when a strengths focus should be utilized, it seems that most managers' time and energy are placed into a "tunnel" focus, searching for problems and/or justifications for reprimanding, suspending, and even terminating a worker from their job.

Unfortunately, when workers have a negative experience within the process of performance management and/or discipline, they are less likely to be positively engaged in the process. Approaches to discipline that are deficit focused and punitive often encourage what seems to be compliant behavior, when efforts and energy—instead of being placed in the work—often are geared toward "laying low," dodging responsibility, or just doing what is necessary to get through the shift. This type of engagement with the work does little to bring about preferred performance and outcomes for the clients being served.

❖ A PROBLEM FOCUS AND IMPLICATIONS FOR WORKERS

Optimal employee engagement, motivation, and performance are dependent upon two major factors: (1) the quality of the leader–member relationship and (2) the support and development of the employee's capacity to carry out his role of helping to the best of his abilities. An emphasis on deficits and weaknesses within a problem orientation to supervision and/or management can present a formidable challenge to both of these processes, with a negative result for employee, team, and eventually client outcomes.

Chapter 1 emphasized the reality that many workers across the social service sectors are unsatisfied with their supervisors and/or their experience of supervision overall; they are disillusioned with the quality of leadership. It is my belief that the predominant emphasis on problems over strengths in the context of supervision and worker development, which continues to persist in social services, is in large part the contributing factor to such a stark and concerning reality.

To put it bluntly, a predominant focus on problems, deficits, and weaknesses just does not feel good. When employees consistently hear what they are not doing well or what needs to be changed in the context of supervision and performance development, it can create feelings of negativity and pessimism and a sense of blame. As a matter of fact, in highly stressful situations, a strict focus on problems can lead workers to feel judged or criticized by their manager and lead to feelings of shame, guilt, and even fear. It is these types of experiences that can be detrimental to the quality of the leader–member relationship, compromising trust, respect, integrity, and empathy. A problem orientation is less than inspiring or motivating for frontline workers.

One of the greatest dilemmas of a work environment predominantly focused on problems at the expense of strengths is that it can engender and perpetuate serious value incongruence. One of the greatest impediments to good practice occurs when workers are expected to operate outside of or out of step with their values. Many workers experience a confusing contradiction when they are encouraged by their organization and supervisor to work from a strengths-based perspective in practice yet experience the opposite in the context of their own support and development. For many workers, this experience can be disconcerting. For others, it may be disillusioning and/or demoralizing altogether. Regardless of individual worker experience, a common consequence of working within a set of incongruent and conflicting value sets is that it is less than motivating or engaging. For many workers, it can be demobilizing.

Problems Limit Worker Potential

The negative impacts resulting from a predominant and persistent focus on problems are immeasurable. As a matter of fact, it is my belief that a problem orientation actually curtails the identification and development of human potential. We know that quality leader–member relationships are essential for accurate discovery of the employee's story and the subsequent development of her capacities.

When workers experience a low level of trust and safety in the context of their professional relationship with their manager and they fear the possibilities of being judged or criticized, there may be a reluctance to be honest about the information they might need to know or the things they may be struggling with. When overall safety is compromised, honest communication between worker and supervisor begins to break down. When communication breaks down, a supervisor's ability to access the employee's story is seriously compromised. When discovery is compromised, development of the worker's capacities and the delivery of preferred outcomes are subsequently compromised.

When employees withdraw from open and honest dialogue with supervisors in an attempt to keep themselves safe, they hold back not only their limitations but also their potential and their strengths! Yes, this is a major consequence when there exists lack of safety and trust: people hold back. And when workers hold back, they also hold back what they are capable of, including their strengths, talents, and potentialities to perform optimally!

I believe that this dilemma represents one of the greatest pitfalls and perils of a predominant deficit and problem orientation. When trust and safety within a leader–member relationship are compromised and a problem-oriented approach to supervision and performance development are operating, it is not uncommon for workers to hold back; that is, their efforts and energy may be going into refraining from expressing or asking questions in order to avoid making a mistake or asking a question about what they feel they should already know. This becomes problematic because, as stated previously, by holding back, workers are unable to demonstrate what they are capable of, thereby limiting the manager's understanding of the employee's story, in particular his strengths and potential capabilities. This dynamic becomes even more problematic when employees that are struggling with performance are placed on a performance management plan and/or some sort of disciplinary process.

Unfortunately, what can unintentionally be created is a reciprocally determining self-fulfilling prophecy. What I mean by this is that because most performance management approaches are problem-focused, often punitive in nature and altogether lacking a focus on strengths, there is a tendency for workers to feel criticized, judged, incompetent, and even blamed for their poor or undesirable performance, representing a less-than-positive experience. It is at this juncture that the potential for difficulties between the supervisor and the worker can be exacerbated. The more a supervisor "puts on the pressure" through a traditionally punitive and problem-oriented approach to performance management, the more likely a worker will alter her behaviors in response to that pressure. And because the supervisor is missing the meaning of the employee's story, there is all sorts of room to misinterpret the meaning of the particular attitude and/or behaviors.

Two great examples of this operating dilemma can be found in the scenario of Barb and Brandon in Chapter 3 and in the scenario of

James, which was initiated in Chapter 4. In both cases, when the manager was asked to comment on the strengths of the worker or on what is going well, they came up short. As a matter of fact, both managers stated that there was "nothing good" at all going on with the worker in the situation. However, we know from Brandon's experience that his story contains a plethora of strengths and, as we will see from James's situation, offered in Chapter 7, things are not nearly as bad as they seem there either. As a matter of fact, they are not bad at all!

As stated before, the impacts and consequences that arise when a strengths approach is limited or missing altogether in the context of supervision and worker development are multifarious and immeasurable. A predominant focus on problems and limitations is linked to jeopardizing the quality of the leader–member relationship as well as curtailing the development of worker potential. We can also surmise that negative implications affect a worker's sense of well-being, job satisfaction, motivation, development, engagement, and ability to perform optimally. Such experiences have a tendency to impact the whole team and create a contagion that contributes to the perception of the overall work environment as negative, thereby adding stress and contributing to intent to leave and eventually burnout. And because we know that a worker's perception of the work and experience of self and the work are inextricably linked to practice decisions and client outcomes, we know that a management approach limited and/or void of a strengths perspective can actually be hazardous for both employees and their clients.

❖ USING A STRENGTHS APPROACH TO ENHANCE QUALITY LEADERSHIP

A strengths-based approach within leadership can have a profound and positive impact on how employees perceive the work, themselves in the work, and their experience of the overall work environment. Prior to reviewing the multifarious advantages of operationalizing a strengths focus in the practice of supervision and management, I will attempt to define and illustrate what I mean when I refer to a strengths-based approach in leadership.

What Is a Strengths-Based Approach?

In my travels, I have come to learn that many social service employees, including supervisors and managers, have a limited understanding of what a strengths approach might be. When I used to interview people for a variety of positions in social services, it was commonplace for me to ask interviewees, "What do you understand as a strengths perspective or strengths-based approach?" Responses revolved around a similar theme: being positive, focusing on the positive, or when the negative is outweighed by the positive. Some responses would go a little further to articulate and reflect that a strengths approach, in addition to focusing on the positive, is also about reframing negative situations in a positive light. For instance, an employee who might be identified as argumentative can be described as assertive and independent thinking. A strengths approach within supervision and performance development is much more than being positive.

The Responsive Leadership Approach, which I refer to as a relationally and strengths-focused approach to supervision, maintains five important steps. These five steps are so important that I refer to them as *musts*, and when operationalized, they represent the strengths-based component of Responsive Leadership. The five *musts* are

- prioritize a strengths focus,

- define strengths,

- search for strengths,

- build on strengths, and

- leverage strengths in the pursuit of individual and shared goals.

Prioritize a Strengths Focus

The positive and profound implications for employees and clients alike can only be fully realized when a strengths focus is prioritized as an integral component of quality and effective leadership. Prioritization of a strengths approach to supervision and management moves beyond technique and is built on several key foundational principles.

- All people are resilient, have strengths, and posses the capacity for change and growth.

- Reality can be constructed as negative or positive, simply by one's focus of inquiry and attention.

- Purposeful operationalization of strengths can enhance efficiencies for approximating and attaining important objectives and preferred outcomes.

When a strengths approach is made a priority within supervision, the positive benefits for employees and clients are immeasurable.

Define Strengths

Before we can search for strengths, we must be able to know what exactly it is that we are looking for. I assumed for a long time, even into my career as a strengths-focused practitioner and trainer, that people knew what strengths were. I think this was one of the challenges workers and supervisors struggled with in adopting and utilizing a strengths approach in practice.

So in order to embark upon the operationalization of a strengths approach, it is important to know what these things we call strengths are. I like to use a fairly broad definition of strengths. I define strengths as basically anything that can be identified, used, or leveraged to assist, support, and/or enhance the development of individual, team, community, organization, or system potential and overall capacity to achieve important goals. Strength is a noun and strengthen is a verb; it is important to remember that even our strengths can be strengthened.

Let me explain. All people have internal and external strengths. Internal strengths are all of the things that we contain within us and our beings, things like values, beliefs, attitudes, knowledge, skills, experiences, opinions, ideas, interests, culture, dreams, aspirations, languages, talents, abilities, uniqueness, potential, and so on. External strengths are those things that exist outside of us, such as people (family, friends, acquaintances, coworkers), places, successes, actions, interactions, school, sports, hobbies, church, groups, community, work, extracurricular activities, and so on. While this list of strengths may seem very general and quite broad, it is purposeful as it provides the largest pool of resource possibilities to draw on when developing our own or others' capacities.

There are a variety of ways to understand and approach the operationalization of a strengths focus in the context of supervision. However, regardless of variance and differences within strengths practice, it is critical that we understand what we mean by strengths and what it is they look like, an essential element necessary for carrying out the following "must."

Search for Strengths

There is a great deal of truth to the proverb, "Seek and ye shall find." The message is both simple and profound. If we search for strengths, so too will we find them, and as a matter of fact, they are everywhere. One of the main problems in our current social services system is that most supervisors and managers have been predominantly taught to search for, focus on, and fix problems, not to search for, build on, and leverage strengths. If we are going to find strengths, we must make it an essential part of our role as leaders—to look for strengths.

Just as was stated above, I encourage all supervisors and managers to consider making strengths inquiry a priority focus in supervision and performance development. In doing so, I like to use the analogy of looking for loose change to illustrate the benefits to making a paradigm shift from not looking to actively searching for strengths.

If you made it your mission starting today to look for loose change all of the time and everywhere you traveled, there is no doubt that you would find more than you ever have. The interesting thing about loose change is that it was and is always there. However, when you don't look for it, you will not see it. As a matter of fact, you may even walk by it all of the time and not notice it at all. Furthermore, by not seeing it, you may accidentally step all over it and even bury it further down, and if and when someone encourages you to go back and find the loose change, it may be harder than ever to find!

Strengths are like loose change. And like loose change, if we aren't looking for it, we won't find it. In high-pressure situations, where there is stress and conflict, like in the scenarios of Brandon and James, strengths can be more difficult to see and/or experience, so much that even when the managers are encouraged to seek the positives and strengths in the situation, they cannot. Again, it's not that the strengths aren't there; they have been eclipsed by the negative or buried altogether.

When we make it a priority and our mission to search for employee strengths, we see strengths everywhere; not only do workers have more strength than they realized themselves, we find that they have more strengths than we could have imagined. However, in a problem-oriented and deficit-focused system, it can be difficult if not impossible to see and experience our own and others' strengths. We must actively search for strengths if we are going to find them.

A Necessary Paradigm Shift

I have to admit that when I began my journey two decades ago to make a strengths focus a priority in my work with other people, it wasn't easy. I, like many of my social services counterparts, was trained to interpret situations and manage them with a variety of problem-solving tools and strategies that often started with focus and intervention geared toward what wasn't working and what needed to be fixed.

Early in my career, I was responsible for providing clinical and performance supervision to approximately 175 youth-care workers, through 22 program managers and supervisors. It was almost impossible to keep up with regular supervision sessions, never mind keeping up while trying out a new and awkward strengths approach to supervision. I remember feeling that it was going to be impossible to speak to strengths—that we didn't have enough time to get to that "fluffy" stuff. It was around this time that a good friend and colleague suggested in a joking manner, "Why don't you just start with what you can't fit in and see what happens?" This idea got me thinking about making strengths more of a priority. So in order to counter the crisis-oriented pull to talk about problems, I placed a sign above the chair where my team members would sit for supervision sessions. It read in bold capital letters, **"WHAT'S GOING WELL?"** No matter how busy, chaotic, or ambitious our case-conference agenda would get, I started with that question. Yes, I was going to fake it until I could make it! It is my position that faking it until you make it is not a bad thing if our goal is to make it. Yes, I needed a prompt. Yes, it didn't feel smooth or genuine for some time. But the benefits, which I will speak to throughout the discussion, began to outweigh my discomfort. And after awhile, I made it. I did not need the sign anymore as the question, "What's going well?" was imprinted on my brain, and the question began to permeate all aspects of the work, including team meetings and performance development sessions.

Start With Strengths

A search for strengths starts with a positive and appreciative inquiry into what is working or what is going well. While at first not an easy paradigm shift from focusing on problems, I was able to rewire my brain to remember the three words, *start with strengths*, when I am considering individual attitudes, behaviors, and or complex situations. I learned very fast that this simple shift in perspective felt better; buffered stress, especially in challenging situations; and illuminated some positive dynamics and important elements that were operating outside of my awareness. Another great discovery I made was that almost all situations are not as "bad" as they may at first seem; if we look for strengths, we can actually find them.

Another very important discovery I made early on in my use of strengths-based explorations was that not only was I unaware of many of my employees' strengths, many of them lacked awareness of their own assets also. In addition to this, I learned that most workers seemed to have an easier time listing their weaknesses and/or areas for development than identifying their own strengths. One of the most difficult questions for my team members to answer was, "What are your strengths?" Although this presented a barrier to strengths exploration, it encouraged me further to make a declaration to two strengths-oriented priorities within my supervision process and approach to employee performance development.

The first priority was to make my active search for members' strengths a purposeful and perpetual aspect of most engagements. It was important for me to increase my understanding and knowledge of team member strengths. In addition (and this brings me to my second priority), I made a commitment that once I made important strengths discoveries, I would do what I could to bring those strengths to the team member's attention also. I made what I refer to as the three As a regular aspect of my individual and team member interactions. I did what I could to *acknowledge, admire,* and/or *appreciate* strengths. Furthermore, I began to use a set of very helpful strengths-oriented questions to assist with the cultivation and identification of strengths.

Strengths-Oriented Statements and Questions for Surfacing Resource Possibilities

Searching for strengths is the most important aspect of a strengths orientation to supervision and performance development. I refer to the term *resource possibilities* as strengths are resources in and of themselves, and they also help illuminate additional strengths as resource possibilities that can also be built on and leveraged to support enhanced worker motivation and engagement and optimal performance. I will demonstrate how *meaning making questions,* offered in Chapter 4, can be useful in exploring the meaning of strengths in a manner that illuminates additional strengths and other potential resources.

I like to use a set of strengths-focused statements and questions as a regular component in my practice and interactions with all workers and team members. It is not uncommon for workers and colleagues to hear me make *acknowledgment* and *appreciative statements* in almost every interpersonal exchange. I also utilize *appreciative questions, exception questions,* and *better questions* as strategies for exploring strengths within a multitude of interactions and a variety of situations.

Acknowledgment and Appreciative Statements

It is important for the supervisor/manager to make these types of statements. Other team members can also be encouraged to make acknowledgment and appreciative statements as they help bring a worker's attention to positive and affirming strengths that have been noticed by others. These types of statements acknowledge, admire, and/or appreciate the important strengths of team members. Sometimes the strengths that are being identified are operating outside of the employee's awareness.

Acknowledgment and *appreciative statements* can look like this:

- I like the way you interact positively with clients.

- I appreciate that you talk less and listen more with your clients.

- You have a great sense of humor, which is helpful for keeping some of our meetings light.

- Thanks for being on time to our sessions. It helps me stay on track.

- I like that you value collaboration and empowerment. I can see it in your meetings with clients and team members.

- You are great at keeping your case files in order. That is indeed a skill I am trying to get better at.

Appreciative questions, like the preceding statements, are helpful for encouraging individual workers and teams to explore and consider the things that they appreciate and/or admire about the work, the team, and/or themselves. Appreciative statements and questions are great for cultivating and identifying individual and team strengths that can be built upon and leveraged in the pursuit of important individual, team, and/or organizational goals. As stated before, it is not uncommon for *appreciative questions* to illuminate strengths and additional resources that were just outside of our awareness.

Appreciative questions can look like this:

- What's going well?

- What do you appreciate about your work this week?

- Are there positive aspects to working here? What might those be?

- Can you tell me something you did that is in line with your values?

- What are you most proud of?

- If you could acknowledge one or two things about yourself, what would they be?

- If you could acknowledge one or two things about your team, what would they be?

Appreciative questions are great for illuminating a variety of strengths and resource possibilities. However, they are also key to providing insight into the employee's story, and they are great for surfacing important needs, values, and goals. This is exceptionally true when *acknowledgment* and *appreciative statements and questions* are combined with *discovery questions* offered in the previous chapter.

Supervisor:	*It's great to see you today, George* (Acknowledgment and Appreciative Statement). *That was a great meeting this morning* (Appreciative Statement). *You did a great job as the chairperson, moving the meeting along and staying on track* (Appreciative Statement). *What do you think you did well?* (Appreciative Question).
Worker:	*I guess I kept things on track. I think I did a good job sticking to the agenda but also giving people an opportunity to speak on issues and important items.*
Supervisor:	*Ya, I thought you did well at that also. Can you tell me more about giving people an opportunity to speak?* (Discovery Question as a Paraphrase)
Worker:	*It's important to stay on topic, but I think it is more important to give our team a voice on the recent changes to standards of practice.*
Supervisor:	*What difference does that make? How do you think that might be helpful?* (Million-Dollar Questions)
Worker:	*For starters, it's important that we assess whether the team has an understanding of the changes and that our program promotes collaboration and empowerment. I like to do what I can to make those values work. They're important to me.*

The above scenario demonstrates that when *appreciative statements and questions* are combined with *discovery questions*, important information regarding worker needs, values, goals, and strengths can also be surfaced.

Exceptions and Exception Questions

I was introduced to the idea of *exceptions* through solution-oriented interviewing earlier in my career. *Exception questions* are based on the idea that no matter how difficult and/or challenging a problem is, there are often exceptions to the problem. Accordingly, this idea of exceptions means that there are times and/or situations when the problem wasn't so much of a problem. It is up to us to look for the exceptions in difficult or challenging situations so that we may discover the strengths and resources available in the exceptional times. When we can discover what was happening in the exceptional times, we are able to uncover and illuminate resource possibilities that have been ignored, minimized, and/or overlooked.

Exception questions can look like this:

- When is the problem not so much a problem?

- Can you tell me about a time when you were able to get your work in on time? How did you do that?

- Can you tell me about a time when you felt anger toward a client and did something other than yelling at him?

- During your probationary period, you had excellent attendance at work. How were able to do that? What was happening for you that helped you get here regularly and on time?

- Can you tell me about a time that you felt team members were not on your back? What were you doing to make that happen?

When we are successful at uncovering real strengths and we gather the details around those times, we are better able to develop a plan geared toward overcoming the problem and developing possibilities for enhanced and sustained success.

Better Questions

I have always struggled with the terms *perfect* and *best* as these terms are difficult to define. In addition to this, I often wondered if perfect and best were even attainable, especially given that both terms connote a fairly ambitious end point. Two other issues I had with these lofty terms were that they were exceptionally subjective and that different people had very different ideas about what best and perfect were— what they looked like. The biggest problem I have with perfect and best is that when they are used as benchmarks to set goals, they can turn up a great deal of pressure to reach a target that may be unreachable. For many people, this has a less-than-positive or demotivating effect and can lead to a sense of helplessness and/or disillusionment.

I prefer using the word *better* and the term *getting to better*. It is my belief that everyone can define what better is for themselves, even just a little bit. I believe this because most people can understand for themselves which things they would like to get better at and/or with. Maybe it's better in a specific performance area. Maybe it's a better attitude. Maybe it's to have better relationships with colleagues or clients. Maybe it's to feel better at work. Most people can consider what better looks like for them. The great thing about the concept of better, much unlike best, is that it is often definable and attainable. Better can also be set and reached in small or larger increments of gain. Better is a temporary destination on the journey to individual and or team development. Once we arrive at better, we can then define and move to the next destination of better.

One of the greatest outcomes of focusing on better is that most people who are struggling with learning and/or developing capacity have actually experienced better at some point in time. An exploration of better can lead to the positive exceptions to challenges and difficulties as well as illuminate a variety of strengths and resources that were operating at that time. In addition to this, *better questions* are quite versatile in that they can be used not only to focus on the past but also to consider *better* in the future. *Better questions* can encourage individuals to consider and envision a preferred future where things are better. Such an exploration often reveals important and meaningful information about what better would look like and how it may be approximated and/or attained. I refer to the two types of *better questions* as *better past* and *better future*.

Here are some examples of *better-past questions*:

- Can you tell me about a time when things have been better for you?

- Based on your experience, when has a program or team been better?

- Can you tell me about a time in your career when you experienced better supervision and/or management?

- Can you tell me when you had a supervisor or team leader that made things better?

- Have there been times in your career when you were feeling and/or doing better?

When *better-past questions* are combined with *meaning-making questions*, they can reveal important employee needs, values, goals, and strengths. Here is an example:

Supervisor: *Can you tell me about a time when things were better for you at work?*

Worker: *It was when I was working with my old team in the southern office.*

Supervisor: *Really, your team at the other office? Can you tell me about what made it better?*

Worker: *That team really knew how to have fun* (value), *and I like that because it's important for me to have a positive working environment* (need/value/goal).

Supervisor: *So having fun and working in a positive work environment are important to you?*

Worker: *Yes, absolutely. Don't get me wrong, I also like to be focused and productive* (value/goal) *because we are an essential service and families depend on us* (value). *It's really important for me to have balance at work* (value). *However, I also strive to get everything done so I don't have to come in on the weekend* (goal).

Supervisor: *How is not coming in on the weekends better for you?*

Worker: *It's the only time I get to see my family* (value/goal). *My children are growing up fast, and it's important for me to see them as much as possible* (value/goal).

One can see that, even from this brief engagement, the use of *better questions* and *meaning-making questions* has surfaced important needs, values, and goals, including some potential areas of strength.

Here is an example of the use of *better-future questions*:

- What are the first things you would notice if things were a little better at work?

- Imagine I meet you in six months and everything is better. What is happening for you? Where are you? Who are you working with? How are you feeling?

- If things were just a little better for you, what would work look like?

- How will you know when things are better? What will be happening?

- When your team is doing better, what will that look like for you?

As with *better-past questions, better-future questions* can be combined with *meaning-making questions*, to reveal the details of what *better* can look like while surfacing important employee needs, values, goals, and strengths.

Example:

Supervisor: *So can you tell me what would be happening in one month that would indicate that things were better for you at work?*

Worker: *I would be the director of the agency.*

Supervisor: *Really. And what difference would that make for you? How would that be helpful?* (Million-Dollar Questions)

Worker: *I would have some control over the communications that come through to our unit.*

Supervisor: *So you would have control of the communications?*

Worker: *Well, maybe not control, but I would do a better job of minimizing all of the information, and I would definitely take out some of the higher level system points. As a matter of fact, I would probably cut the number of communications in half.*

Supervisor: *How would that be helpful? How would that make things better for you?* (Million-Dollar Question and Better Question)

Worker: *It's not just for me. It's for the whole team! People are overwhelmed as it is just with the work and the caseloads. We do not need all of the extra e-mails and information about big systemic issues that we really can't do anything about.*

Supervisor: *So what has that been like for you?* (Discovery Question)

Worker: *It adds more stress. It adds more confusion. It takes up time and energy. On top of that, because I'm the team leader, I have people lined up at my door asking me for clarifications on the communication or just venting about the possible changes to mandates and standards of practice. It's overwhelming.*

Supervisor: *Can you tell me what you mean when you say overwhelming?* (Discovery Question)

Worker: *I get frustrated and a little angry at the director. I feel helpless that my team gets more stressed and confused than they have to be. I spend so much time taking care of them that I have difficulty getting to my own work. I've got people on my caseloads that really need me. Because the team is so important to me, I feel like I can't let them down. If there were more of a balance in the communications, there would be more balance in the unit.*

Supervisor: *So you are hoping for more of a balance in the communications?* (Paraphrase)

Worker: *Well, at least a balance . . . ya, just having information in the communications that is necessary and directly relevant to the work. We need a filter or something.*

Supervisor: *So you think a filter of some sort might be helpful. Can you tell me about that?* (Discovery Question)

Worker: *When I worked with the Inkster Team, our team leader was responsible for reviewing executive communications so that only the relevant information went through to the team. The higher level stuff was still important and was communicated at the larger unit meetings.*

In this scenario, the supervisor is able to get a clearer picture of what better might look like for this particular employee. With the use of *better questions* and *meaning-making questions,* the supervisor is able to cultivate and surface the important needs, values, and goals of the worker that will be helpful in moving toward an understanding of options that may or may not be available.

When we keep in mind the broad definition of strengths that was provided earlier, we can see that there are strengths embedded in needs, values, and goals that can be identified in this particular conversation. The worker needs a balance to be able to support the team and get work done. This worker values getting the work done, teamwork, efficiency, relevant communications, and commitment. This worker hopes to lower the stress, confusion, and extra workload for the team and for himself. In addition to this, he has indeed experienced a time when things were better. Although the scenario above was ended, the conversation could have continued to demonstrate additional details pertaining to the *what, when*, and *how* aspects of the worker's story as they pertain to strengths. There are many strengths surfaced in the worker's story that, if and when the supervisor requires, can be built on and leveraged in the pursuit of important individual and shared objectives.

Build on Strengths

Once strengths are identified, they become more concrete and tangible, making it increasingly possible to build on them. Building on strengths in the simplest terms means to construct or to develop them further. Strengths can be developed further so that they can have increased substance and more fortitude and integrity. What I mean by this is that even our strengths can be strengthened. For instance, an employee who is great at connecting with and building relationships with clients can continue to improve upon and/or develop this area further. This is mostly true because there are so many different skills and behaviors that exist within connecting with and building relationships with clients. For instance, here are just some of the skills required: making appropriate eye contact, listening effectively, empathic responding, balancing listening with verbal responses, and commenting on something that is important and meaningful to the client. When we look at values, knowledge, skills, and talents within strengths, we can begin to see the possibilities for building on them and developing them further.

Building on strengths becomes increasingly important in situations where workers are only just beginning to acknowledge and learn about their own strengths. Given that "What are your strengths?" is one of the most difficult questions to answer for employees, it is not uncommon for many workers to be learning about their talent capacities when they are engaged in a strengths-based exploration in the context of supervision and/or performance development. In addition to fortifying existing strengths, building on strengths can be accomplished when strengths are built into a worker's performance plan and/or to balance out or support specific areas noted for worker development.

Building on worker strengths is possible only when those strengths are made concrete and tangible. This can be accomplished when they are documented in specific and behaviorally measurable ways. This is one of those moments that might seem like common sense; however, I am astounded by how many times managers do engage in strengths-based inquiries, yet nothing is written down. Sometimes the difference between strengths perceived and strengths achieved is the written word. Simply put, strengths have less value when they are not noted or made tangible and accessible.

This is the reason why strengths must be captured in a specific and descriptive manner, in as many places as possible, as often as possible. Managers can begin to identify, capture, and even begin building on strengths right from the first contact and/or in the interview process. I encourage the programs I work with to incorporate strengths-based questions within the employee interview/screening process. The following are some examples:

- What is it that you appreciate about our program?

- What would you say are your greatest strengths?

- What organizations have you worked for in the past that you would say did things better?

- Can you tell us what you appreciated most about the last team you worked on?

- Please tell us about a time when you encountered a value conflict in your work? What was that like for you? And what did you do to work with it or through it?

The answers to these questions can surface important needs, values, goals, and, specifically, strengths of the person prior to him becoming an employee. I encourage supervisors and managers to consider utilizing some of the questions offered in the Preferred Leadership Profile (PLP) in the interview process. In addition to this, when important strengths are written down, they can be passed on to the supervisor who will be assigned the worker when hired.

Documenting strengths is key to a strength-building capacity. Unfortunately, in the current social services systems, supervisors and managers are not encouraged to capture strengths as much as they are encouraged to document problems. "Document, Document, Document" is practically a guiding axiom that represents a mantra for supervisors in most environments I've worked in. Supervisors and managers are commonly encouraged to document when there may be a foreseeable problem with worker attitude or behavior and/or a situation. I often find that supervisors and managers are encouraged to document under not-so-positive circumstances and often in situations where a case is being built for one of several reasons: to hold someone accountable, to begin building a performance management plan, or to begin forming a case that will justify terminating a worker for poor performance. Interestingly, I have never heard about a situation where managers are encouraged to "Document, Document, Document" around strengths or success or when someone has held a positive attitude or behaved and/or performed optimally.

A major problem I have with the encouragement of documentation primarily around not-so-good situations is to consider what reality is created in a personnel file when the thousands of successes are omitted and only the problematic behaviors or situations are recorded.

Because it is critical for leaders to build the capacities of their members, capturing strengths so that they can be developed further is critical. Strengths can be cultivated and captured in *any* interaction. In addition to the job interview, key opportunities for capturing strengths are during one-to-one supervision meetings, team meetings, and in the process of performance development sessions. I encourage all supervisors to look for areas in the current process and structure of supervision to build in mechanisms wherein strengths can be captured in detail.

The Preferred Leadership Profile has a strengths section built right in and encourages workers to identify any strengths that they would like to build on and/or develop further. I have found that room can be made for strengths on most forms of documentation that pertain to workers. In addition to encouraging leaders to document strengths in any and all situations, I suggest that they develop a running and ongoing list of employee strengths. I refer to this as an employee's *strengths index*. A strengths index does not have to be complicated at all. You can find two examples of an employee strengths index in Appendices C and D. The first index exists in the simplest form and represents a running list. The second example is a little more organized as it deals with specific skill/role categories that pertain to the particular worker in a particular role. I encourage supervisors to "Document, Document, Document!" strengths as often as possible. As a matter of fact, this list should grow as the supervisor and employee continue to collaborate on the cultivation, identification, and operationalization of strengths in practice. When strengths are captured in all employee-relevant documentation, they can be consistently reviewed, developed further, and leveraged in the pursuit of important goals.

Leverage Strengths in the Pursuit of Important Objectives

Supervisors and workers are consistently collaborating on a variety of organizational, professional, program, and client goals. In order to carry out value-focused and purpose-critical tasks optimally, supervisors work to support the enhancement of worker capacity to attain the most preferred outcomes for clients. Worker practice decisions and the subsequent outcomes that result from those decisions are a direct result of the competence, confidence, and engagement levels of the employee. It is this inextricable link between worker practice and client outcomes that makes employee performance development critical!

Performance goals that are meaningful and valuable for employees operate as motivators in and of themselves. However, for a variety of reasons, sometimes performance goals that require skill development and behavioral change can be difficult for some employees to approximate and/or attain. A strengths approach to supervision and performance development offers both supervisors and employees a great mechanism for enhancing employee competence, confidence, and engagement.

Strengths have been identified as one of the four major pillars of the Responsive Leadership Approach because they operate as key performance motivators for most people and they offer a plethora of resource possibilities for engaging employees in optimal development and quality performance. Because leadership is about inspiring people to work toward shared objectives, a strengths focus when combined with meaningful performance development goals can offer supervisors and managers a potent source for employee motivation, reinforcement, and expedited goal approximation and attainment.

As stated earlier, for a strengths approach to be truly realized, strengths must be prioritized, defined, searched for, built on, and then leveraged in the pursuit of important goals. Strengths are leveraged when they are utilized purposefully to encourage workers to set, strive for, and/or stretch toward important performance objectives. Supervisors can support workers to set goals by using the strengths identification process as a means to assess and/or surface important areas for desired growth and achievement. For instance, when workers gain an accurate understanding of their strengths as opposed to their limitations, they are provided with a broader set of possibilities for goals and growth. Strengths illuminate potential and possibilities, thereby creating a greater pool of professional development options that are meaningful and valuable. For instance, some team members have never considered being a team leader or supervisor until their own manager brought attention to the real potential and specified possibilities for such a goal. This is accomplished when supervisors list the concrete, tangible, and operating worker values, knowledge, experiences, and skills that are relevant to that particular role. When a strengths approach is utilized, possibilities and potential for worker growth and development are broadened. When workers can identify their own potential, they will be more motivated to set goals that are now in sight and within reach.

Once strengths are identified and developed further, they can be leveraged not only to set important goals for worker development but also to assist workers in striving for and/or stretching themselves toward those goals. Confidence, competence, and level of engagement arise from feelings of success. Let's continue considering a worker who has decided to set the goal of working toward a team-leader position. When relevant strengths, such as effective time-management and delegation skills and quality relationship-building capacities, are identified and elaborated upon, the team-leader position that once may have never been considered by an employee can now seem like a real possibility. Real possibilities are great for motivating workers to strive for meaningful and/or valuable goals. Identified strengths are leveraged when they are built into a worker's professional performance plan in a manner that assists and supports goal approximation. For instance, worker strengths can be leveraged by placing the worker into situations such as mentor and/or unit meeting chair as a means to utilize identified skills in order to develop additional skills necessary for accommodating team-leader capacity. Additional skills such as problem solving and mediating team differences on decisions can be identified and worked on by the member on the journey to team-leader status.

Finally, leveraging strengths can also mean utilizing identified needs, values, and skills to stretch worker efforts toward important goals. Consider for a moment the proverbial "carrot" as a reinforcement and/or incentive to shape behavior/performance. However, instead of a "carrot" or some sort of token reward, identified strengths are utilized as motivators and reinforcements. When a worker has needs to belong to a team, have some control in decision-making, and see results aligned with her values of collaboration, empowerment, and accountability, the goal of team leader can actually accommodate and reinforce this worker's needs and values. If and when a worker struggles in the process of working toward the goal of team leader, her supervisor can remind her that the end goal is worth the extra effort and work as it is in line with her own needs, values, and capabilities. It is this type of strength leveraging that can provide both supervisor and worker with potent sources of motivation and reinforcement simultaneously. In addition to this, because real strengths are being leveraged, worker confidence, competence, and level of engagement can be enhanced with important messages from the supervisor, such as, "You can do this," and, "You have accomplished similar tasks before, and you will be able to do it again."

❖ THE PROFOUND IMPLICATIONS OF A STRENGTHS APPROACH

It is my belief that quality leadership and a strengths approach are inextricably linked; a manager cannot create a quality leadership experience for members without operationalizing a strengths approach in practice. Practicing in this manner can have profound implications for workers, their teams, and the clients they are serving. As a matter of fact, the effects of a strengths-based approach in leadership can minimize the perceptions and experiences of workers that commonly lead to intent to leave and burnout.

Previous chapters have made mention of the many impediments to preferred practice that also impact a worker's perception of quality leadership experiences. Without reviewing all of the challenges again, there are several that are worth mentioning within in the context of the positive consequences of a strengths-based approach in leadership.

It Feels Good

Invariably, the first thing most people say following an exercise that compares a problem-focused interview with a strengths interview is that the strengths interview feels positive, refreshing, and uplifting— just good overall. Imagine if this was the only benefit. Even if nothing else changed in the work environment, we as helpers just feel better. That alone is a pretty good outcome, given that usually when we feel better as helpers, we do better. And usually the people we are helping do better also. Feeling good is great, but a strengths approach goes well beyond the positive experience.

A positive experience among workers in supervision with performance development and within team meetings can lead to what's known as a *positivity contagion*. Positivity is contagious. In addition to this, given that many workers in the social services perceive their work environment as poor or negative, a strengths-based approach may have positive implications for changing workers' perceptions of the organizational climate overall. It has been my experience that a strengths approach to leadership will inevitably lead to improved job satisfaction and team morale.

Affirming and Validating

A problem-centric environment leaves little room for understanding, knowing, and/or hearing about what we do well or do right. It is extremely affirming and validating to hear that we are saying and doing a lot of things right. Most people, to some degree, like to hear about their strengths as much as possible, especially in the tough times, when things may not be going well or when we feel like we are moving away from better. Being affirmed and validated around what we are doing well can act as a buffer, making us able to hear about or face with strength and courage the things we need to improve or develop further. Simply put, it's easier to hear the not-so-good stuff and know that we aren't all bad, especially if we hear about the good stuff first and hear that that we are actually doing good-to-great things also.

When employees are validated and affirmed as having strengths and capacities to succeed, it can be exceptionally motivating and rewarding. This is a critical point for two important reasons, especially when it comes to engaging and motivating employees to perform optimally. First, one of the major factors that leads social service workers to intent to leave and even burnout is lack of recognition by their supervisors and/or organization. A strengths-based approach is exceptionally rewarding as the recognition and reinforcements are imbedded as an inherent part of the process. Second, one of the most effective ways to shape and improve upon human attitudes and behaviors is through positive reinforcement. There is very little contrary evidence on the fact that from a behavior-modification perspective, positive reinforcement is one of the most powerful mechanisms for shaping employee behaviors. When we consider the strengths-based questions and responses offered above, we see that a strengths approach is, in and of itself, perpetually positive and reinforcing.

Sense of Real Competence and Confidence

One of the great things about a strengths approach is that it is more than just being positive. It is specific and tangible. It points in the direction of successes and concrete results from efforts and accomplishments of both the past and the present. Real success from real strengths results in real competency. A strengths approach provides the valuable message that people are capable; they have done it, they can do it, and they will do it again! A strong sense of competence and confidence are invaluable assets for workers who are carrying out the important role of helping others. Increased competence and confidence is directly linked to increased job satisfaction, motivation, engagement, and performance.

Hope and Optimism

A problem-saturated mode of inquiry in a deficit-focused environment that is perceived by employees as negative can be overwhelming and less than inspiring to say the least. Sometimes workers can feel so overwhelmed with negativity that they can become less mobilized and even incapacitated. When this occurs, it can actually block hope and lead to an overwhelming sense of helplessness. Identifying, building on, and leveraging strengths, among other things, is an exercise in *hope* building. A strengths approach provides a great deal of hope and optimism by illuminating the fact that there is more to us or a situation than just deficits, weaknesses or problems. Even if hope is all we have, it can be everything. Hope can sometimes mean the difference between giving up and getting up—giving in or giving it one more try. Hope and optimism can provide formidable injections of motivation, contributing to increased individual job satisfaction and providing a boost to team morale.

Additional Resources

One of the greatest things about a diligent and focused strengths inquiry is that it can turn identified strengths into additional resource possibilities that were previously unnoticed and/or operating outside of awareness. Just as a focus on dysfunction can illuminate all sorts of problems, conversely, a focus on strengths begets more strengths and successes. It increases the pool of possibilities—potential and available raw materials necessary for making the journey to *better*. Additional strengths will broaden the pool of possibilities for goal variety and performance development pathways. In addition, when identified strengths are built on and leveraged, approximation to goals becomes more rapid and efficient, and the attainment of preferred performance outcomes is much more likely.

Value Alignment

One of the greatest dilemmas facing workers across social services, which is also a major contributor leading to intent to leave and eventual burnout, is when workers operate for prolonged periods of time in a manner that is out of step with their personal and/or professional value sets. When supervisors operationalize a strengths focus in supervision and performance development, workers will experience greater alignment between their personal and professional values and the ways in which they are encouraged and expected to operate in their work. Given that values and working in line with these values are key sources of motivation for most social service workers, a strengths-based approach in supervision performance development will inevitably lead to increased worker motivation and engagement and optimal performance.

Positive Working Environment

It may be challenging, if not impossible, to change the political, fiscal, bureaucratic, and legislative challenges that translate into real impediments to preferred practice and quality supervision. However, we should consider the important question raised by Patti (2009), "How do we create organizational conditions that will lead to positive worker perceptions, attitudes, and behavior in order to bring about the highest quality and the most effective service?" (p. 117). I believe we may have an important part of the solution in the operationalization of a strengths approach in leadership. Strengths-focused approaches that operate in the context of supervision and performance development may in fact be one of the most potent forces available to leaders to inspire maximum worker engagement and optimal performance.

❖ SUMMARY OF IMPORTANT POINTS

- Social service systems can present real barriers and countercurrents to a strengths approach within supervision.

- Many current approaches to supervision and performance development do not operationalize a strengths approach.

- Performance management and employee discipline are often antithetical to a strengths approach.

- A strengths-based approach within supervision will enhance the quality of the leader–member relationship and quality leadership overall.

- A strengths focus in leadership is critical for enhancing worker job satisfaction, motivation, engagement, and overall performance.

- A strengths based approach in leadership maintains five priorities, which are to prioritize, define, search, build, and leverage strengths.

- A strengths-based approach in leadership has many positive implications for workers, teams, and clients.

- A strengths approach is a potent source of motivation and reinforcement that can lead to positive employee perceptions, attitudes, and behaviors.

❖ PERSONAL LEADER REFLECTIONS AND CONSIDERATIONS

- How does your understanding of a strengths-based approach to supervision and performance development compare to what was presented in this chapter? Similarities? Differences?

- In your practice as a leader, where are you operationalizing a strengths-based approach?

- Are there areas where you could do something different to more closely approximate a strengths-based approach to leadership in your practice?

- Does your organization and/or program support the operationalization of a strengths-based approach in leadership?

- Are there areas with respect to employee interviewing, documentation, supervision sessions, and performance development that can be enhanced or developed further to promote and/or endorse a strengths-based approach?

❖ REFERENCES

Patti, J. R. (2009). *The handbook of human services management* (2nd ed.). Thousand Oaks, CA: Sage.

6

Doing Quality Leadership

Practical Strategies for Inspiring

You may be theoretically rich but practically poor.

— Pushpa Rana

This book has worked, from the beginning, to simplify the concept of *leadership*. Leadership was defined as a process by which an individual or individuals inspire the attitudes and behaviors of others to engage in value-based and purpose-critical efforts in order to accomplish a set of shared objectives. Leadership is about inspiration—the capacity to be the source or cause to motivate, stimulate, and/or bring forth the positive attitudes and behaviors of others.

We know that quality leadership is inextricably linked to enhanced worker motivation, engagement, job satisfaction, and organizational commitment. Quality leadership also has a positive impact on practice decisions and subsequently on the positive and preferred outcomes for clients. Simply put, when supervisors and managers lead, their workers are inspired and so too are the people they serve and support. So far, this book has provided a variety of insights and key points on how supervisors and managers can inspire workers to feel better, be better, and do better as they carry out their important role of helping others.

Leaders can inspire by utilizing a *responsive approach to leadership* in the context of supervision and management. This approach posits that supervisors can inspire in key ways, such as

- making quality leader–member relationships a priority,

- operationalizing important and guiding values,

- getting to know the needs, values, goals, and strengths of workers,

- getting to know what motivates workers to engage and perform optimally, and

- utilizing a strengths-based approach in the context of supervision and performance development.

As stated previously, it was not my intent to present a model of supervision and/or management in the social services but to simplify leadership in a way that offers leaders in the field knowledge and practical strategies for motivating and engaging their team members to perform optimally as they carry out their work as helpers. Being a responsive leader is about having the capacity to tune into and respond to the needs, values, goals, and strengths of the people one is responsible for leading. While a Responsive Leadership Approach is indeed inspiring, there are many practical ways that a supervisor/manager can inspire workers to feel better, be better, and do better.

All supervisors can learn to inspire! And if you are already a supervisor that inspires, I already know that you are open to learning how to inspire even more. How would I know that? Because that's also what great leaders do—they never cease learning how to be *better* for themselves and for their people!

This chapter will provide you and all supervisors in social services with insights into important areas for consideration and offer practical strategies for *inspiring* staff and teams to feel *better*, be *better*, and do *better* as they carry out their work with children, youth, families, and communities. In order to best organize the tools and strategies offered herein, I have categorized specific areas based on the Key Performance Motivators outlined in Chapter 3. I refer to the seven categories as *domains for inspiration*. While there were more than seven Key Performance Motivators identified earlier in the book, all of them can fit within the identified categories and are relevant to the seven *domains* below:

- Relationship

- Vision and Values

- Mission and Goals

- Appreciative

- Personal and/or Professional

- Feedback

- Strengths Focus

As stated in Chapter 3, individual workers are motivated by different things at different times. It is important for the supervisor to figure out collaboratively with each worker which Key Performance Motivators are relevant for inspiration. Once the supervisor has an understanding of which *domain* areas are the most relevant to a worker, the ideas and strategies offered in each domain provide helpful sources of inspiration.

Prior to getting started and considering which domains are relevant to workers, it may be helpful for supervisors to encourage each worker on the team to fill out a Key Performance Motivator Appraisal Form, offered in Chapter 3. This may help identify which domains may be most relevant to the member.

The insights and practical strategies offered below have been informed by years of practice experience, evidence-based research, and principles of best practice. You may recognize some of the ideas and approaches offered here, as some have been mentioned, and build on tools already presented in preceding chapters. If you are already prioritizing some of these critical areas and are utilizing the subsequent strategies for inspiring and motivating your members, keep it up; you are making a positive difference for them and their clients. There may be some things below that stimulate thinking or feeling; some may remind you of things you already know are important, and/or some items presented may inspire you to try something new.

❖ RELATIONSHIP DOMAIN

A relationship that is based on *acceptance, understanding, trust, respect,* and *integrity* is absolutely essential as a foundation for staff learning, development, and performance. In addition to this, very few people will admire, cooperate with, or "follow" a leader when they have little to no trust and respect for that person. These relational ingredients are important as they provide the basis for safe and nonjudgmental communication and support. Great supervisors get to know their members' needs, values, goals, and strengths through relationships. The better a supervisor knows their members, the better able she will be to respond to their needs and desires and more likely she will be able to match supervisory support and resources accordingly.

Furthermore, up to this point, the chapters have demonstrated what most of us already know from our practice wisdom: that the supervisor–worker relationship and supervisor support contribute to improved job satisfaction, increased motivation and engagement, enhanced practice, and preferred outcomes for staff and clients. Relationships are key!

Here are some things you may consider doing to positively influence this factor for inspiration:

- Make relationships a priority

- Encourage members to fill out a Preferred Leadership Profile

- Get to know your members (needs, values, goals, and strengths)

- Ask workers to express what a preferred relationship looks like in practice

- Operationalize values of trust, respect, integrity, and empathy as well as key organizational values (see Chapter 4 for steps to operationalize values)

- Make efforts to stop in and say hi or goodbye to staff

- Make time for coffee or tea with staff

- Get to know what is important to your staff

- Schedule and keep uninterrupted time with members

- Take and make opportunities to do activities (individually or as a team), like relationship and team building

- Try to be accessible and approachable

- Make regular check-ins on relationships and the quality of supervision

- Do your best to be nonjudgmental

- Ensure you take what they say seriously and follow-up

- Try hard not to be quick to defend or dismiss member feedback/ input

- Ask staff about family or interests outside of work

- Make quick check-ins with members (individually and in group meetings) prior to business a priority

- Check out assumptions about members ("When in doubt, check it out.")

- Maintain confidentiality to the extent possible

- Do not ask workers to do what you haven't already done yourself or that you are not prepared to do

- Follow through on commitments

- Do what you say you will do (DWYSYWD)

- Ask staff what the best supervisor–member relationship looks like

- Be willing to be flexible with process and time around identified employee needs

- Encourage consistent unit meetings

- Encourage, promote, and attend staff social engagements

❖ VISION AND VALUES DOMAIN

Although *vision* and *mission* are often grouped together, they are not the same thing. Vision is the value-driven dream of where a program and/or organization hopes to go. It is meant to be global and inspiring. Mission pertains more to "how are we going to get there." Mission will be discussed further in this chapter. Some people are much more connected to the vision. These are those I refer to as the "values people." I am one of them. Like most values people, I am vision and value driven. We are passionate!

When it comes to motivating members to perform, nothing is as powerful as the cultivation and/or mobilization of *passion*. Passion usually arises from personal purpose, but more importantly, it originates from what people feel is important—their values. Most people choose social services because it is a profession that espouses or endorses values (social justice, compassion, empowerment, self-determination) that are in line with their own personal values. Organization and program choices are also often based on a preference or match between personal and organizational values. When members operate within alignment of personal, professional, and organizational values, there is rarely a lack of passion when the work is being carried out. Furthermore, operationalization of values helps answer the questions, "Why do we do what we do?" and, "Why do we do it in this way?" An impassioned answer to the question "What's important?" provides great impetus to passion, motivation, focus, and meaning. It connects members to their purpose—their *passion*.

Values also represent one of the most important cornerstones of the employee's story regarding what is most important. When workers honor specific values and can maintain a connection to them in the context of their work, they are more likely to be highly motivated and engaged to perform optimally.

Here are some things you may consider doing to positively influence this factor for inspiration:

- Make a connection to values a priority
- Complete a Preferred Leadership Profile with staff
- Ensure that *vision* is communicated and accessible to all members
- Ensure that program and organizational values are visible and accessible to all members, especially where they congregate or meet regularly
- Review steps to operationalizing values offered in Chapter 4
- Encourage staff to become familiar with the organizational/ program vision
- Ask workers to identify which values are most important and why
- Get to know why a staff member has come to your program
- Ask member what part of their work they are most passionate about and why
- Review the organizational vision and guiding values regularly
- Review guiding values at supervision or unit meetings
- Connect worker roles and responsibilities to vision and values
- Encourage member to connect personal and program values
- Encourage and model operation of key values
- Review with member how they apply values in their work (daily, monthly, yearly)
- Make pocket-size guiding values check list

- Encourage staff to consistently consider, "Why do we do what we do?"

- Encourage staff to articulate "why we do what we do in the way that we do it"

- Take time to review and integrate at least one guiding value at each staff meeting

- Take time to review and integrate at least one guiding value at individual supervision sessions

- Develop a team/unit charter made up of important team and/ or program values to guide value-based decision-making and work together

❖ MISSION AND GOALS DOMAIN

Mission and purpose-critical goals are foundational to organizational, program, team, and individual purposes. *Motivation, focus,* and *enthusiasm* are actually by-products of goals. If you take away a goal that is important to someone, you will take away those three key by-products. Most people seek out or gravitate to a job because its organizational objectives and mission are in line with their own mission and/or goals. If staff can accomplish their own goals while carrying out the organization or program mission, they will be connected to their purpose. Mission and goals also answer the questions, "What's the point?" and, "Why are we doing what we are doing?" The answers to these questions are something we all want to know, especially when work becomes difficult or challenging. Continuously connecting organizational and program objectives to our members' goals and their purposes is a great way to promote motivation, enthusiasm, and cooperation at work.

Here are some things you may consider doing to positively influence this factor for inspiration:

- Make a connection to the organizational/program *mission* and purpose a priority

- Complete a Preferred Leadership Profile with staff

- Ensure that the program/organization mission has been communicated clearly

- Ensure that all staff have clear understanding of roles, responsibilities, and expectations

- Ask member about his purpose and goals
- Make direct connections between worker goals and purpose-critical program objectives
- Explore staff anticipations (what they want) for their clients
- Explore staff anticipations (what they want) for their team
- Review the program mission with members regularly
- Connect roles and responsibilities to mission
- Have staff review mission and vision at unit gatherings
- Match job tasks, if possible, with staff member goals
- Assist staff to answer "What's the point?" and "Why do we do what we do?" as they carry out work responsibilities
- Allow space for member goals to shift or change
- Explore personal and/or professional goals for worker development
- Ensure regular check-in and support on developmental goals
- Conduct a "What's in it for me?" (WIIFM) discussion
- Support opportunities to set and meet professional development objectives
- Work to make professional development affirming, validating, meaningful, and valuable

❖ APPRECIATIVE DOMAIN

A major cause of intent to leave and burnout, as reported by many workers, is directly related to the lack of appreciation and/or recognition experienced in the field for the challenging and important work employees carry out.

Validation and affirmation are essential elements for feeling understood and accepted, which is an important aspect of the leader–member relationship described throughout the book. There are many challenging social service sectors, and it is not uncommon for members to sometimes feel misunderstood, unsupported, or devalued. Often, workers who are engaged in challenging jobs or experiencing stressful or difficult times simply want people (especially their supervisors and managers) to understand how hard the work is or how hard it can be. Acknowledging these realities with a supportive response can be exceptionally validating and affirming.

When members do not feel validated or affirmed in their experiences, they can begin to become stuck and frustrated and, after a while, feel devalued and even demoralized. Members need to be *acknowledged*. They also need to be *admired* and *appreciated* for the important, complex, and difficult work that they do—and not just for accomplishments but for efforts as well. I have made reference to the three *A*s of *acknowledgment, admiration,* and *appreciation* earlier.

For some workers, the three *A*s are exceptionally important and can operate as a type of currency for the social, emotional, and spiritual bank account. The three *A*s can also function like gas in the tank. When it runs out, worker motivation, engagement, and even cooperation can run out also. I have a saying I use during my training: "I can't afford to give you a raise, but I can stick a *P* on it and give you praise. And when I give you praise, I hope it lasts at least a couple of days."

Here are some things you may consider doing to positively influence this factor for inspiration:

- Make the three *A*s a priority with and for your staff

- Explore what the three *A*s mean to staff and individual members

- Accommodate specific needs "to the extent possible" with efforts at three *A*s

- Make private and public member recognition a priority

- Ensure regular and positive contact with members

- Make and keep uninterrupted time with members

- Develop and support a process for appropriate and safe venting

- Listen, listen, listen

- Utilize paraphrasing and empathic responding regularly

- Utilize meaning-making questions to understand with and connect to workers' stories

- Take what members say in feedback seriously

- Make and follow through on commitments

- Ensure that there is a check-in and check-out at each meeting

- Always check in with members prior to business

- Remember that no news is *not* good news—it's no news

- Try not to defend or dismiss what members are saying

- Attempt (to the extent possible) to match need for support with the "right" support

- Be creative—create a process for staff recognition

- Encourage staff members to demonstrate the three *A*s with each other

- Say "Thank you!" more often

❖ PERSONAL AND/OR PROFESSIONAL GROWTH DOMAIN

Social service workers want to do better for themselves and for the people they serve. Therefore, professional development is essential in order to work toward expected outcomes. In addition, many workers are motivated and excited by opportunities for personal as well as professional development. Consistent chances for individual capacity building can provide a rich and meaningful source of motivation, enthusiasm, focus, and cooperation for carrying out great work. Furthermore, personal and professional goals are another way of ensuring concrete and tangible progress in what I refer to as "a world of intangibles." It isn't surprising that many people from the social service industry fish, hunt, garden, or build something with their hands outside of work. They are desperate to see an end product or experience some type of accomplishment.

Personal and professional development frameworks, processes, and supports provide staff with a plethora of opportunities to connect to what is important to them while they carry out their work.

Here are some things you may consider doing to positively influence this factor for inspiration:

- Make staff capacity building a priority

- Have staff complete a Preferred Leadership Profile

- Explore what personal development would look like for workers

- Explore what professional development would look like for workers

- Offer opportunities (formal, informal, training, mentoring, etc.) for personal and professional capacity building

- Engage with members in a training-needs assessment

- Make professional performance development (PPD) meaningful, realistic, achievable, concrete, time-driven, positive, and supportive

- Offer opportunities for members to share PPD with other members and the team

- Check-in on personal and professional goals regularly

- Offer incentives or rewards to staff for capacity development

- Implement peer-appraisal process regarding professional goal development

- Implement self-appraisal process regarding professional goal development

- Match workers with other team members with similar goals

- Offer worker opportunities to mentor or be mentored in identified areas for personal and/or professional development

- Match member roles and responsibilities with member goals for development

- Role model by implementing consistent supervisor appraisals

- Role model by working on supervisory developmental goals

- Set a regular meeting with each staff member with the sole purpose of engaging in the three *A*s only

❖ FEEDBACK DOMAIN

Feedback is essential for knowing whether or not one is doing what he or she is supposed to be doing. Most people want to know, "How am I doing?" It is also critical for both personal and professional capacity development, and it is the conduit that carries the appraising information on behavior/performance. Feedback must also include a developmental component of what and how behavior or performance can be enhanced or developed further. Knowing how we are doing and what we need to do to get *better* or be *better* to attain personal and professional objectives is helpful as a checkpoint and a "where to next?" mechanism. Accurate and clear feedback is essential for effective and efficient work.

In addition to this, positive feedback is motivating. When it is positive and constructive, feedback is even more valuable. Positive feedback paves the way for the not so positive, if and when it exists. Furthermore, very few things are more motivating for people who are striving to make a positive difference than the message, "You are making a positive difference. Here is how you can make more of a positive difference."

Here are some things you may consider doing to positively influence this factor for inspiration:

- Make consistent feedback a priority

- Encourage staff to complete a Preferred Leadership Profile

- Ask workers to identify what feedback means and looks like in practice for them

- Discuss preferences for structure and process for the most meaningful and valuable feedback

- Ensure efforts are made at accurate, clear, specific, and meaningful feedback

- Maintain a positive attitude

- Work at being approachable and accessible

- Listen more than talk

- Focus on worker strengths prior to negative or constructive feedback

- When feedback is critical, focus on the behavior not the person

- Ensure that trust is built and maintained in all relationships

- Implement communication pathways for feedback

- Encourage and support self and peer appraisals so that peers may provide feedback to and for one another

- Explore the preferred feedback currency (what and how) found in the Preferred Leadership Profile (PLP)

- Keep feedback more positive than negative

- Ensure that feedback contains evaluative (what it is that worker is doing or not doing) and developmental (what they can do to improve) components

- Promote the principle of "No Failure, Just Feedback"
- Promote learning with open and ongoing feedback with staff
- Allow opportunities for members to provide you with feedback
- Be open to feedback yourself
- Take feedback seriously
- Demonstrate integration of feedback as soon as possible
- Encourage and allow the team to offer feedback in unit meetings
- Have a suggestion or feedback box
- Call staff to your office for positive feedback only

❖ STRENGTHS DOMAIN

Everybody likes to hear about what they are doing well. As covered in Chapter 5, a strengths focus has many benefits for a member and a staff. Often this paradigm is in line with the way workers want and are encouraged to work (value alignment) and starts from the point of asking what's right versus what's wrong. A focus on strengths points to concrete successes and real potentialities for development, growth, and productivity. A strengths focus illuminates important resources for moving in a direction that approximates preferred staff performance. Finally, an approach that makes strengths a priority provides hope, optimism, and sense of real competency, ingredients that are essential for inspiration, positive and effective staff performance, and achievement of preferred worker and client outcomes.

Here are some things you may consider doing to positively influence this factor for inspiration:

- Make a strengths focus a priority
- Encourage staff to complete a Preferred Leadership Profile
- Review the steps in Chapter 5 for operationalizing a strengths-based approach in leadership
- Explore member strengths (personal and professional) regularly and whenever possible
- Regularly ask, "What's going well?" as a starting point in individual and team meetings
- Develop and utilize a strengths index for members

- Integrate strengths-focused questions in the interview process, supervision sessions, and performance development processes
- Identify areas that capture strengths with respect to staff competencies and performance areas
- Acknowledge and appreciate strengths often
- Start with strengths in staff supervision
- Begin with strengths focus in unit/team meetings
- Integrate a strengths section into professional development and annual performance review frameworks
- Match member strengths with roles and responsibilities
- Utilize member strengths to mentor or build team capacity
- Include a strengths section on all self, peer, and supervisor appraisals
- Encourage members to note strengths in themselves, other members, the team, and the program
- Regularly schedule one meeting to talk only about strengths
- Rotate a review of member strengths in unit or staff meetings
- Build on and leverage member strengths in pursuit of personal, professional, and organizational objectives

It is important to keep in mind that the above *domain for inspiration* and the practical strategies offered are provisional only. They have indeed demonstrated success for enhancing worker motivation, engagement, and performance with a variety of workers at different times across a variety of social service sectors. However, with that said, supervisors and managers are only limited by their imaginations when it comes to inspiring their team members.

❖ SUMMARY OF IMPORTANT POINTS

- Leadership is about inspiration—having the capacity to positively influence the attitudes and behaviors of workers to perform optimally.
- Quality leadership and inspiration are linked to enhanced worker motivation, engagement, job satisfaction, and organizational commitment.

- When workers are inspired, they feel better, are better, and do better in their roles of helping.

- Supervisors and managers can inspire through a *responsive approach to leadership*.

- Key Performance Motivators can be captured and categorized into seven domains for inspiring: relationship, vision and values, mission and goals, appreciation, personal or professional development, feedback, and strengths.

- Supervisors and managers can enhance their ability to inspire through a variety of insights and practical strategies offered within the seven domains for inspiring.

❖ PERSONAL LEADER REFLECTIONS AND CONSIDERATIONS

- Have you completed your own Key Performance Motivator Scale, as encouraged in the Chapter 3 reflection?

- Were you able to connect with any specific domains over others? What do you think that might be about?

- Were there insights and strategies offered within the domains that you were already aware of or doing?

- Were there insights and strategies offered within the domains that stimulated ideas or thinking around possibilities for inspiration?

- Consider encouraging staff team members to complete a Key Performance Motivator Scale.

- Engage in a discussion of findings with staff who have completed the Key Performance Motivator Scale.

- Once you have determined collaboratively with members which domains might be helpful for enhancing inspiration, consider using one or two ideas or strategies for the most relevant domain.

7

Understanding and Approaching Resistance and Opposition

People don't resist change. They resist being changed.

— Peter M. Senge

Helping vulnerable people and those less fortunate within the social services field is an exceptionally rewarding endeavor. However, from the beginning of this book and throughout, we have uncovered and discussed the myriad of challenges and impediments to both preferred practice and preferred outcomes for both staff and clients alike.

Under ideal circumstances, working in social services can be stressful, but it doesn't have to be as hard as it is. Most supervisors and employees alike understand that working to make meaningful and valuable changes to enhance the lives of children, families, and communities can be fraught with a great deal of stressors and challenges. Some of the most challenging situations workers face are working with people who appear and/or present as resistant and/or oppositional to support and/or change. This is most true in sectors where clients are encouraged or even mandated to make changes in their lives for the well-being of themselves and others around them. Most of us in social services understand that we may face, for a variety of reasons in a host of complex circumstances, different types and levels of resistance or opposition from the people we serve and support. However, an area where we least expect serious stress and conflict resulting from resistance and oppositional behavior is with our own individual employees and/or our staff teams.

Employee resistance and oppositional behavior can be challenging for supervisors and employees alike and can cause a great deal of stress and conflict. The cost of employee resistance and opposition is unquantifiable. There are very large costs in time and resources associated with undesirable and poor performance behaviors of employees. The various approaches taken by supervisors, managers, and human resource specialists to "interpret" and "manage" employee resistance and oppositional behavior are not only exceptionally expensive in terms of time, energy, and money, they can unintentionally make the opposition and resistance worse!

This chapter is aimed at illuminating an important and effective means for understanding and approaching employee resistance and oppositional behavior in a manner that decreases and even eliminates the identified concerns. Using a Responsive Leadership lens, this chapter will offer supervisors and managers a unique perspective on what employee resistance and opposition are and offer insights and practical strategies on how best to understand resistant and oppositional behavior and engage employees to move from resistance to something better, enhancing motivation, cooperation, and optimal performance.

❖ WHAT ARE RESISTANCE AND OPPOSITION?

Employee resistance and opposition are common terms used when referring to attitudes and/or behaviors that appear to be incongruent with employee expectations for preferred behavior and practice. The types of attitudes and behaviors that are categorized as resistant and oppositional are complex and variable depending on the interplay of different people, situations, and environments. However, regardless of the type and context of resistant and oppositional actions or inactions, these employee behaviors are often referred to as "undesirable or poor performance," "counterproductive," "unprofessional," and even "inappropriate."

Employees who have been defined and/or described as being resistant or oppositional are often employees who appear to be less than engaged, motivated, cooperative, and/or committed to the work. As a matter of fact, some resistant and oppositional behavior can appear to be going against organizational needs, values, and priorities. Many managers who have had the experience of supervising workers who are perceived and experienced as being oppositional and/or resistant can attest to how difficult and challenging it can be to connect with, engage, and motivate these workers to shift in the direction of more preferred, positive, and productive behaviors as they carry out their work.

❖ TYPES OF RESISTANCE AND OPPOSITION

As stated above, the types of attitudes and behaviors that are categorized as resistant and oppositional are complex and variable depending on the interplay of different people, situations, and environments. However, there seems to be a continuum of behaviors identified by supervisors as resistant that range from least to most challenging.

The following have been identified as types of resistance and oppositional behaviors, ranging from subtle and aggravating onward toward increasingly concerning and outright violent.

- Avoiding appointments, expectations, or responsibilities
- Not talking or engaging with one's work, team, or supervisor
- Lack of cooperation/participation in meetings
- Apathetic and passive behavior
- Walking out of meetings
- Not following through on goals/commitments
- Answering, "I don't know," "I don't care," or, "Whatever"
- Saying "no" to almost anything
- Doing the opposite of what one is asked or expected to
- Private and/or public defiance
- Intimidation of others
- Destructive behavior toward property
- Violence toward others

It is my hope that managers and supervisors never have to experience aggressive and violent behaviors from any of their team members. As a matter of fact, it is my goal to work toward a day when supervisors never experience the attitudes and behaviors that are currently referred to as resistant and oppositional. However, before we can leave a place of oppositional and resistant employee behaviors, we must first arrive at an understanding of the meaning of such behaviors. What do we know about employee oppositional and resistant behavior?

❖ A REAL DILEMMA: MISUNDERSTANDING OF EMPLOYEE RESISTANCE AND OPPOSITION

I am a firm believer that what we think affects how we feel and determines how we act. It is our perception and understanding of a situation that will determine how we feel about it and, subsequently, how we will approach it. Therefore, how supervisors perceive and understand employee resistance and oppositional behavior will determine how they approach and deal with it. Important questions for gaining an understanding of how supervisors manage an employee's resistant and oppositional behavior are as follows: How do supervisors perceive and experience oppositional behavior? What have they come to know and/or learn about it? How have managers and supervisors been taught and/or supported to deal with an employee's resistant and oppositional behavior?

Resistance and opposition are often synonymous with negative circumstances or situations. Rarely do we hear someone talking about resistant and oppositional behavior in a positive light and/or in the context of an appreciative inquiry. Employee resistance commonly carries with it a consistently negative connotation. As stated earlier, the most common terms utilized for poor performance and undesirable behavior are deficit focused and can carry negative overtones. In addition to this, when resistant and oppositional behavior becomes really problematic, it is not uncommon to hear terms like *difficult conversations* and *resistant to change* as well as rigid words like *can't, won't, never*, and *always* to describe challenging behavior and the lack of possibilities and/or potential for preferred change.

In challenging situations, it is not uncommon to hear statements like, "She is resistant to change," or, "He fears change." If we reconsider the notion that what we think affects how we feel and determines how we act, I wonder what chance a supervisor has to reengage an employee who is perceived and/or defined as "incapable" of positive and preferred changes toward enhanced motivation, cooperation, and engagement with the work.

It is my firm perspective that, unfortunately, formal supervisory training around working with challenging employees has actually exacerbated the stress and conflict supervisors experience in situations wherein they observe a perceived lack of motivation, engagement, and/or commitment. I have touched on this perspective in the beginning and throughout the book. Supervisors and managers have been taught to use theories of human behavior, systems, and organizational development to explain and predict employee motivation and behavior. In addition to learning how to interpret the experiences and behaviors of others without the employee's actual involvement, supervisors have been formally taught and coached on how to manage that behavior, usually through behavior modification principles and practices.

It is unfortunate that in many cases, supervisors and managers have interpreted and attempted to manage employee behavior without the employee's actual involvement, not knowing her perspective or her story. Consider the situations of Valerie and James offered in Chapter 4. In both situations, the managers worked to interpret and manage the situation without the involvement of the people they were concerned about. One can see that when we operate outside of the employee's story, which holds the meaning related to their needs, values, goals, and strengths, we may actually invite more stress, challenges, or conflict. Yes, we may actually invite more resistance.

❖ COMMON AND PROBLEMATIC BELIEFS ABOUT RESISTANCE AND OPPOSITION

For years, I have been asked to help many managers and human resources professionals deal with employees and teams that are, according to management, behaving in a variety of oppositional and/ or resistant ways. The various employees and teams appeared much less than engaged, cooperative, motivated, focused, and/or committed compared to their collegial counterparts.

Many of the situations were getting worse, much like Brandon's (Chapter 3) and James's (Chapter 4) situations. It was not uncommon for most of the people involved to be experiencing high levels of frustration, confusion, stress, and conflict. Through exposure to and experience with many of these situations over the years, I have learned that a great deal of the frustration, stress, and conflict were less a result of the people involved as from the manner in which the situations were understood and subsequently handled.

When we consider the idea that what we think affects how we feel and determines how we act, it is critical to examine the beliefs or assumptions regarding resistance and opposition that are operating and how those ideas determine the ways in which challenging employee attitudes and behaviors are dealt with. I have come to identify five general beliefs that are common assumptions about employee resistance and opposition that, when operating in the process of employee and/or behavior management, can be problematic and exacerbate the situation. These five assumptions are covered next.

Assumption 1: Resistance is an intrapsychic phenomenon and originates from within the individual.

This belief is most evident in the fact that the first area of inquiry and focus regarding problematic or undesirable behavior is solely on the individual employee. The most common questions are "What is going on with this person?" "What is he or she struggling with?" and "Why is he or she doing that?" The area of focus and inquiry often begins with and stays on the individual and the individual's attitude and/or behavior. As the focus and area of inquiry expand to include the past, present, and/or future, the focus often remains on the individual and the individual as the problem.

I am surprised how often that the area of inquiry doesn't implicate other people or systems in general. It is still rare for me to hear the area of inquiry start outside the individual and work inward. One hopes for questions like "What have we done to support something different?" "What messages are we giving through our actions as leaders?" and "To what extent does our work environment permit, promote, and/or perpetuate these types of attitudes and behaviors?" As stated before, when a belief that the problem originates and/or lies with the individual, there is little if any room to consider implicating other people or the environment as possibilities for influencing or contributing to poor performance or undesirable behavior. In addition to the focus of inquiry and assessment on where the problem might reside, approaches to intervention, usually some form of behavior modification design, are often directed on changing the individual to bring his behavior into line with expectations. As a matter of fact, long before I became aware of this operating belief, I used to teach a course in how to do just that!

It was called "Managing Difficult Employees." The belief I am referring to is actually embedded in the title; accordingly, the difficulties reside within the person—the person is the problem!

Assumption 2: Resistance is a defense mechanism and/or manipulation.

It is my experience that, commonly, employees who present as resistant and/or oppositional are implicitly or explicitly accused of hiding something by being dishonest and/or manipulative. The idea is that employees who present with challenging or difficult behaviors are being defensive or have something to hide. Unfortunately, this seems to be a default for well-intentioned people who are frustrated and confused about the apparent incongruence between what an employee knows about expectations for conduct and his behavior that falls short of or outside of those expectations. Early in my career, like many supervisors, I was in similar predicaments on many occasions—confused, frustrated, and angry in my attempt to manage "challenging" employee attitudes and behaviors. I believed I had all of the information I needed, and sometimes I did (though I was missing meaning). So what was the inevitable conclusion when the focus was on the "difficult employee" as the problem? She must be hiding something or lying! So when the path to an inevitable conclusion is governed by an unclaimed and operating belief, performance management, and/or progressive discipline, two common behavior modification approaches make the most sense as options for changing behavior.

Assumption 3: Resistance is wrong or bad.

This belief is evident in the intent and level of energy expended to bring poor performance and undesirable behavior toward expectations; this is also known as compliance. As stated previously, the language used to define and describe oppositional behavior is negative and carries an element of blame to the individual employee. It is not uncommon to hear people use the phrase "performance manage out" when referring to managing the challenging attitudes and behaviors of some employees. In addition to this, most approaches to managing challenging employee behaviors stop, modify, change, or extinguish them versus working to understand and engage them. Finally, there is more evidence of this particular belief in the language and labels used to question and/or describe the person or situation. The question

"What's wrong with him?" carries with it the assumption that it is not a good thing. Also, as was discussed in Chapter 3, many negative labels and even diagnoses are used to describe employees that present as resistant and/or oppositional. Consider how well-intentioned supervisors described Brandon and James. They or their behaviors were not held in positive regard. As a matter of fact, both employees were on the road to being performance managed out.

Assumption 4: Resistance requires interpretation by experts.

Prior to elaborating on this point, it is important to clarify what I mean by *experts*. An expert is anyone who has an opinion about the employee a supervisor may be struggling with. It could be a coworker, past supervisor, or even a person that has never met him! However, with that said, there are some experts that have more expertise and authority than others, like HR professionals, trainers, coaches, consultants, and authors.

I am continually astounded—not surprised however—that due to the above operating beliefs, very rarely do managers and supervisors approach the employee directly. Often, for a variety of reasons, they approach one of many experts to discuss the employee and the employee's behavior to try to get insight on how best to approach the situation. They often start with the question "What do you think about this?" What they do not know is that this is the wrong question to ask and they are asking the wrong expert. The right question is "What do we know about this from the person's perspective?" The right expert is the person with whom we are dealing: the employee.

Assumption 5: Resistance requires strategic intervention or behavior management.

When experts are approached and encouraged to consider the employee's experience, they do this from their own perspectives. Because they are not asked a meaning-making question, such as, "What do we know about this from his perspective?" the supervisor and all experts consulted are left to build their understanding on information that is outside of the employee's story. As stated in other places in this book, what commonly occurs following the interpretation of the worker's story, based on all of the barriers listed in Chapter 3 (Organizational Impediments, Theories/Models, Our Story, Assumptions, Labels, Diagnoses, Personnel File), is that a plan is generated and usually imposed upon the employee. Endemic within this type of reaction is the belief that opposition and resistance require interpretation and, subsequently, strategic and behavioral intervention.

❖ A DIFFERENT PERSPECTIVE: RESISTANCE AND OPPOSITION AS INFORMATION

The Responsive Leadership perspective offered for understanding resistance and oppositional employee behavior flows from a set of ideas and beliefs that are quite different from those offered above. The following set of principles for understanding resistance and opposition is exceptionally helpful for understanding, approaching, and effectively engaging and resolving such situations.

Principle 1: Resistance is information.

Rather than being perceived as negative or bad, resistance and opposition are viewed as positive, meaningful, and valuable resources. Resistance is information! It is information that something is not right and/or needs to be explored further. Resistant and oppositional behavior does not necessarily mean that the employee is uncommitted, unmotivated, and/or uncooperative or does not want to engage or perform optimally as she carries out her work. There may be very good reasons why the employee or the team are not engaging or performing in an expected and/or preferred manner.

The information that we are missing carries with it the meaning in the employee's experience and the situation overall. Keep in mind that meaning is found within the employee story—the needs, values, goals, and strengths that are operating. Resistance is not something that we should fear and/or move away from. It is not something that we should try to extinguish or behavior-manage out. When resistance and opposition are experienced or apparent, to some degree, supervisors and managers must consider this important information and work toward gaining a better understanding by starting with the question, "What do we know about this from the person's perspective?"

Principle 2: Resistance is contextual.

All behavior occurs in a context where there are certain people, specific environments, and unique circumstances. In addition to this, individual perceptions and experiences are operating and vary depending on the multiple and interacting variables within each situation. This belief goes against the idea that oppositional behavior is something that originates from within the individual.

I have always been interested in how certain employees are star performers in some environments and then struggle in other situations, or vice versa. What do we know about this from their perspectives? It is important to consider the interplay between the employee's experience, needs, values, and goals and the fit between the operations of other variables within that environment. Consider the situation of Brandon in Chapter 3. He and his supervisor were struggling. However, because the supervisor was missing important information and meaning about Brandon's experience, the stress and conflict continued. As a matter of fact, it worsened.

This particular belief encourages supervisors, instead of starting with the employee as the focus of inquiry and asking "What's wrong with him?" to look to the other variables within the overall context. In addition, the idea that resistance occurs in a context encourages supervisors and managers to examine the fit and/or lack of fit between those environmental variables and the needs, values, goals, and strengths of the employee.

Principle 3: Resistance is often tied to relationship.

Throughout the book and within the context of Responsive Leadership, the relationship as a key element in quality and effective leadership has been paramount. Out of the multifarious variables involved in the context of varying environments is the employee's perception with respect to the quality of the leader–member relationship. There is a direct and negative correlation between the level of trust including emotional and social safety in the leader–member relationship and the amount of apparent and experienced resistant and oppositional behavior.

It is not a surprise that when employees speak of their greatest leadership experience ever, we hear about a time when they felt safe, understood, and validated in the relationship with the leader to whom they are referring. In addition to this, they also draw important connections and parallels to feeling open and honest with asking questions and even with providing feedback and/or direction to their leader. The converse is also true from my experience interviewing thousands of employees; they report increased reluctance and "holding back" when the relationship is less trusting and/or safe.

This particular belief about employee resistance and opposition encourages supervisors and managers to focus the area of inquiry on the quality of the leader–member relationship in order to search for meaning within the situation. And given that quality of the leader–member relationship can only be appraised by the member, this belief encourages supervisors and managers to start with the question, "What do we know about how the member experiences the quality of our relationship from the employee's perspective?"

Principle 4: Resistance often results from the interplay and operation of different values, needs, goals, and/or strengths.

To a large degree, this belief is represented in the aforementioned ideas; however, it is critical to pull out and make explicit the reality that there are various sets of needs, values, goals, and strengths in operation at any given time. Organizations maintain fairly clear values and organizational objectives and priorities that arise from a variety of identified and interconnected client, employee, and organizational needs. Leaders, as human beings themselves, have their own personal and professional sets of needs, values, goals, and strengths operating. Therefore, when the three main systems (employee, leader, organization) work together toward a common set of shared objectives, their individual and important needs and values are interconnected and consistently operating. It is when the three sets of needs, values, goals, and strengths are in alignment and/or are at their best fit that there is the highest level of employee engagement, motivation, and, usually, optimal performance. However, when those same variable are out of alignment and/or incongruent, there exists the greatest possibility for various forms and degrees of opposition and/or resistance.

❖ PROACTIVE APPROACHES FOR MINIMIZING AND EVEN ELIMINATING OPPOSITION AND RESISTANCE

It is my firm belief that a great deal of opposition and resistance can be avoided. Everything offered in this book up to this point is a proactive idea or strategy for minimizing the potential for opposition and resistance in employee attitudes and/or behavior.

When supervisors and managers consider that most social services employees are motivated, focused, and enthusiastic to help and that many social services environments can present serious impediments to preferred ways of working, it can open up greater possibilities for patience, compassion, and tolerance for attitudes and behavior that may be a result of challenging and trying work conditions. When supervisors and managers understand that frontline employees require quality leadership through inspiration, they can begin to implicate themselves and the quality of supervision and performance development in the equation of worker motivation, engagement, and capacity to perform optimally.

When supervisors acknowledge the inextricable link that exists among quality leadership, staff outcomes, and, subsequently, client outcomes, efforts can be made to enhance client outcomes through the development of leadership capacity. Supervisors and managers should understand that one of the best ways to inspire workers to be motivated and engaged and to perform optimally is by making meaning of the individual needs, values, goals, and strengths of workers and the role these variables play in preferred worker attitudes and behaviors.

The guiding principles and the techniques and strategies offered through the Responsive Leadership approach all work as effective and proactive approaches to avoiding, decreasing, and even eliminating oppositional and resistant employee behavior. It has been my experience and the experience of supervisors using the Preferred Leadership Profile (PLP), the Key Performance Motivator Scale (KPMS), the Meaning-Making Communication Process, and/or strengths-based strategies that issues relating to employee resistance and oppositional attitudes and/or behaviors are minimized and often become nonexistent. In addition to this, when resistance and opposition become apparent or are experienced, they are much easier to understand, and options for dealing effectively are often surfaced through the utilization of aforementioned ideas, tools, and strategies.

It is impossible to avoid and/or eliminate all resistant and oppositional behavior. However, as stated previously, there are things that can be done so that supervisors do not unintentionally invite, contribute to, and/or become the source of employee oppositional and resistant behavior.

❖ IMPORTANT CONSIDERATIONS FOR SUPERVISORS TO AVOID RESISTANCE ALTOGETHER

Over the years in my role supporting managers to enhance employee motivation and performance, I have learned that there are important areas to consider if supervisors are going to avoid causing, contributing to, or incurring resistance and opposition. In addition to this, if and when supervisors experience resistance and opposition, the following key areas are critical to check out as they may provide insight into the employee's experience and the particulars of a situation, which may lead to options for engaging and efficiently mitigating the identified concerns. These important areas are as follows. . . .

Employee Job Roles and Responsibilities

One of the biggest contributors that lead to intent to leave and burnout is role confusion. It is important that supervisors ensure all team members have clear knowledge and a detailed understanding of their respective roles and responsibilities as they relate to their particular jobs. When roles and responsibilities are not clear, it is not uncommon for employee confidence and competence to be impacted to differing degrees. This may lead to apparent hesitancy or reluctance, which may be perceived and labeled by supervisors as oppositional behavior.

Knowledge and Skill

This is an area that is often assumed and overlooked. Just because an employee is hired does not mean that he has the requisite knowledge and/or skills to perform in a manner that is expected. In addition to this, knowledge does not necessarily mean that the employee has developed the required skills yet. Sometimes supervisors assume that because an employee has the training that they should also have the skill. Therefore, it is important for supervisors to assess whether their employees possess the knowledge as a starting point and then assess the skill levels to carry out required tasks. When these important areas are overlooked, it is not uncommon for employee efforts and accomplishments to be defined as poor or undesirable and possibly perceived as oppositional and/or resistant.

Resources and Support

Many social services environments are exceptionally challenging and characterized by high caseloads and work demands with less than adequate staffing and funding. A lack of resources and support in an environment that demands more with less from workers can undoubtedly compromise employee motivation, engagement, and overall performance. When these realities are minimized and/or overlooked altogether, it can negatively impact a worker's job satisfaction, morale, and ability to carry out the work in preferred and expected ways. In addition to this, when serious impediments to preferred practice are intentionally or unintentionally overlooked, it sometimes can lead to judgment, criticism, or blame being placed on the worker and/or their capacities, further exacerbating the situation.

Leader–Member Relationship

At this point, the importance of the quality of the leader–member relationship should not be a surprise to the reader. From my experience, it is one of the most overlooked areas when it comes to understanding employee resistance and opposition. The importance of this variable is undeniable! The combination of research and practice wisdom presented in Chapters 1 and 2 emphasized and illustrated the critical role quality relationships play in enhancing worker motivation, engagement, and overall performance. As a matter of fact, there is ample research that demonstrates the inextricable link that exists between this particular variable and job satisfaction, organizational commitment, and organizational citizenship behavior. Conversely, it is true that poor-quality leader–member relationships as perceived by employees have a direct and negative impact on employee motivation, engagement, and overall performance. Therefore, it is critical that prior to and during moments when supervisors are experiencing apparent resistance and opposition that one of the first places they start with in the search for meaning is the quality of their leader–member relationship as perceived by the member.

Department/Division Structure and Process

Many social service working environments and the employees working within them are often subject to frequent fast-paced changes in mandates, legislative requirements, bureaucratic structures and processes, standards of practice, service delivery and program models, and staffing arrangements. Notwithstanding the unpredictable nature of and stress such fluid modifications bring, they are accompanied with learning and shifting requirements that create another layer of complexity and stress to an already demanding environment. It is important for supervisors to keep in mind that changing structures and processes cause stress but also that they require necessary time, support, and additional resources for workers to adjust, to the extent possible, to various structural and process alterations. When these particular areas are not considered, employees' behaviors to keep up with, manage, and/or cope with such drastic changes can be perceived and subsequently responded to as oppositional and/or resistant behavior.

Social and Emotional Safety

Research and practice wisdom are directly pointing to *trust, respect, integrity*, and *empathy* as key qualities found in affirming, validating, safe, and supportive supervision and management. More than 4,000 employees that I have talked to state that social and emotional safety are critical for social service employees. When workers feel safe from a leader's judgment, harsh criticism, and blame, they can be comfortable enough to ask questions and give feedback. I will never forget when one of my first supervisors in child welfare said to me at a time when I was nervous about the complexity and level of responsibility of my new job, "Don't worry, Steve; you are not going to be able to do it all or know it all. I'm here to support and guide you." I will never forget that moment. I felt so relieved that I didn't have to have all of the answers. Immediately, my supervisor was making me feel safe.

When workers feel safe, they are able to ask questions and give feedback to leaders without fear of some sort of judgment and/or repercussion. In addition to this, when workers feel safe, they are more likely to take appropriate risks or chances to extend themselves and test out their capacities. As stated in Chapter 5, workers who feel emotionally and socially safe and supported are able to demonstrate their potential and strengths. When it is unsafe, workers hold back, and in some instances, this may be perceived by the supervisor and/or manager as employee resistance and oppositional behavior.

Perception of Our Own Behavior

We all have our personal blind spots, meaning that we sometimes may not be aware of how our behavior is being perceived or how the perception of our behaviors may be impacting others. In a fast-paced, busy environment, it may be difficult to assess the attributions others may be assigning to our actions and/or inactions. It is critical that supervisors be aware of how their behavior is being experienced. Are they perceived as friendly, supportive, and approachable or as something less than positive—overly busy, threatening, or apathetic? How do we know what we know if we don't know what we don't know?

If supervisors do not know how their employees perceive and experience them, they may not understand how or why some employees might engage differently than others. For instance, if a supervisor is not aware that some employees view him as unapproachable because of how often he talks about being busy and overwhelmed, he may perceive staff reluctance to seek him out for support or direction as some sort of resistance or oppositional behavior. It is critical that supervisors create conditions and avenues for safe and accurate feedback on their behavior, so that they may be able to work at bringing their intentions in line with the perceptions of their team members.

Employee Value

Most employees appreciate that they are valued and that what they contribute to the team and the work is valuable. It is not uncommon for workers who are feeling less than valued or valuable to begin to disengage with some aspect of the team or work. This can be in some way related to role confusion, as stated above. It could also be related to lack of feedback and/or recognition for the important effort and accomplishments being achieved in the work. When supervisors are not aware of the possibility of this dynamic, employee behavior may be perceived as resistant or oppositional behavior.

Acknowledgment, Admiration, Appreciation

One of the major factors that contributes to employee intent to leave and/or burnout is lack of validation or recognition. It is not uncommon to hear social service employees state that there is a general deficit in the field when it comes to being appreciated and or recognized for the challenging and rewarding work they carry out day to day, month to month, and year to year. I have mentioned the three As at different points in the book. For many workers, the three As are like gas in the emotional gas tank, and when that gas tank is filled with some sort of acknowledgment, admiration, and/or appreciation, it can be energizing and motivating. In addition to this, the three As operate as various forms of positive reinforcement, which is a major factor in influencing positive attitudes and behaviors. However, if supervisors are not aware of employee needs and values related to the three As, they may be missing opportunities to engage and motivate team members. Further, if and when the three As are missing, some employees may be appear less motivated and/or engaged.

Employee Experience of Supervision and Supervision Sessions

We know that to a large degree, social service employees are dissatisfied with the quality of supervision, in general. Supervision as a mechanism of leadership can serve as a source to enhance employee motivation and overall engagement, especially when the employee experience of supervision sessions is a meaningful and/or valuable source of support and guidance. When supervision and individual supervision sessions are validating and affirming, when they are constructive and focused on strengths, and when they accommodate, to some degree, employee needs, values, and goals, supervision operates as a potent source of motivation and engagement. However, if and when supervisors are not aware of the lack of these important elements in supervision and supervision sessions, lack of employee motivation and engagement may be perceived as resistance and opposition.

Employee Personal Life

Work constitutes only one part of the employee's life. Sometimes the personal life and the subsequent experiences of an employee can impact the work. Sometime life challenges and/or stressors outside of work can impact the level of motivation and/or engagement level of the employee within the work environment. If supervisors are not aware of the potential for this dynamic, they may unintentionally interpret a lack of motivation or engagement or a dip in performance to be resistant or oppositional behavior.

As stated earlier, the above areas are critical for supervisors to be aware of and check out prior to but especially when resistance and opposition are apparent and/or experienced by the supervisor. In general, it is important for supervisors and managers to understand that there are many variables and situations that may or may not be contributing to employee resistance or opposition. However, it is my hope that if and when supervisors are able to tune in to these important possibilities, they are able to gain insight into and meaning from the possible causes and/or contributing factors.

❖ SIMILAR BEHAVIORS, DIFFERENT MEANING

The various contributing factors that lead to employee resistance and opposition are not only complex; they are unlimited and unique to the multifarious variables that are operating and interacting. This is why it is absolutely critical to approach each situation as unique and/or original—to start with what we know about the situation from this person's perspective.

My experience has taught me that the recipe for understanding and approaching resistance and opposition can seem much easier than the actual work in practice. However, as previously stated, resistance and opposition are inevitable and offer important information that requires supervisors to slow down and work collaboratively with the employee to make meaning of the identified concerns in order to lower resistance so that worker motivation, engagement, and overall performance can be enhanced.

I have found that when resistance and opposition are experienced and persist despite efforts by the supervisor to make meaning of the situation, that there are four general reasons for employee resistance and opposition that supervisors should be aware of and explore further. I refer to these as *under construction, issues of trust, legitimately confused,* and *purposefully manipulative.*

Under Construction

I use this term to refer to those workers who are new to the job or are in a role that has undergone changes to process, structure, and/or service-delivery approach. These workers are usually working to learn new knowledge and develop new skills in order to enhance their own and their teams' capacities to deliver the best possible outcomes for clients. It can be expected that their performance is going to appear less than optimal as their knowledge and skills are under construction. In addition to this, when workers are trying to master new knowledge or skills, it is inevitable that overall performance will dip until they enhance their overall capacities to adjust to the new job, the changes, and the requisite knowledge and skills that come with their new roles. It is important for supervisors to be aware of this dynamic so that employees are not unfairly judged or blamed for being purposefully resistant and/or oppositional.

Issues of Trust

One of the most common reasons leading to employee resistance and opposition has to do with trust. Often when there is apparent employee resistance, reluctance, holding back, and so forth, there is a good chance that safety and/or trust has not been sufficiently developed and/or there has been a breach in the level of trust between the leader and member. Trust issues are among the most difficult to assess with certainty. So many different variables can impact the trust in the leader–member relationship. Trust levels may or may not be affected by the actions and/or inactions of the current leader. Employees also bring their own history and experiences with relationships and trust, and those experiences may or may not be impacting their relationship with their current supervisor. In addition to this, it is important for all supervisors to know "You are not the first supervisor on the tour," meaning that there have been supervisors before you who may have negatively impacted an employee's perceptions and experiences of trust. It is important for managers and supervisors to know that trust issues often play a major role in employee resistance and opposition and that because relationships involve more than one person, this perspective implicates both the supervisor and the employee in the resistance equation.

Legitimately Confused

It is an assumption to think that everyone knows for certain his or her own needs, values, goals, and strengths that are operating in all situations. One of the most interesting revelations I have made on the journey to develop my own leadership capacity and to support the development of others is that some of us lose connection to our own needs and values. There are many reasons for this, including the fact that many social service workers, as helpers, can often place the needs of others before their own. Also, as discussed throughout this book, many workers spend their careers working in environments that are sometimes incongruent with their own values and preferred ways of working. Moreover, many social service environments are fast paced, workload heavy, and crisis oriented, which leaves little room for reflection and introspection on our own needs, values, goals, and strengths.

When workers are unsure and/or unclear about their own needs, values, and goals that might be operating when they carry out the work with others, they are not able to assess their own resistant and oppositional responses and experiences. When supervisors are able to explore employee needs, values, goals, and strengths that may or may not be operating in a situation, employees can provide valuable insights into times when they are most engaged or other times when there may be apparent resistance and opposition.

Purposefully Manipulative

Every once in a while, we will meet certain employees that I refer to as purposefully manipulative. These are the employees that place some or all of their own needs, values, and goals ahead of the team, the organization, and even ahead of the clients whom they are responsible to serve and support. These are employees that should not be charged with the responsibility of caring for vulnerable individuals, families, or communities. The good news is that these folks, I believe from my experience, make up less than 2% or 3% of the population. It is important for supervisors to be able to figure out who these employees are so that they can be helped out of the field of social services. One of my favorite sayings is "Leaders must help out their members to the greatest extent possible. Sometimes, however, leaders must help a member right out—out of the field altogether."

> *How do you know what you know*
> *if you don't know what you don't know?*

As strange as this question might be, it is critical to consider, with respect to understanding and approaching employee behavior, what is actually perceived as resistance and opposition. When an employee is demonstrating resistant and/or oppositional behavior, how do we know if the behavior is about *trust issues* or *legitimate confusion*? How do we know if the employee behavior is about *trust issues* or is *purposefully manipulative*? Interestingly, the behaviors can look exactly the same!

I encourage supervisors to think about two analogical questions: What is the difference between treading water and drowning? What is the difference between running to a train to catch someone you love and running from someone with a gun? The experiences feel different, but in both situations, the behavior can look exactly the same. Similarly, what is the difference between purposefully insubordinate behavior (not returning calls or e-mails, avoiding tasks or meetings, etc.) or the behaviors of someone who is scared and confused (not returning calls or e-mails, avoiding tasks or meetings, etc.). I use these examples to get supervisors to think about how one behavior can have many interpretations; however, the experience—the person's story—holds the meaning of the behavior that we are most concerned about.

Consider for a moment the situation of Supervisor Barb and Employee Brandon in Chapter 3. Barb made some assumptions about and interpretations of Brandon's behavior as purposively manipulative.

However, she was wrong. Brandon's experience and his behaviors were related to *issues of trust*. He feared that his supervisor was out to get him. He was not feeling safe enough to talk with her. Unfortunately, Barb was missing the meaning of Brandon's behavior, and the approach of progressive discipline made things progressively worse, and subsequently, Brandon was performance managed out.

We will have an opportunity below to revisit the situation of James offered in Chapter 4 in order to illustrate a Responsive Leadership Approach for effectively engaging employees who present as resistant and/or oppositional. However, prior to offering supervisors a process guide for approaching employee resistance and opposition, it is important to lay the foundational principles that guide such an approach.

❖ GUIDING PRINCIPLES FOR DEALING EFFECTIVELY WITH RESISTANCE AND OPPOSITION

Dealing directly and effectively with employee attitudes and behaviors that appear resistant and oppositional is probably one of the most difficult tasks a supervisor can engage in. As stated earlier, there is a reason why these are the conversations that have been deemed difficult— because they can indeed be difficult. With that said, it is important to remember that what we think affects how we feel and determines how we act. Based on the idea that resistance is not a bad thing and that it represents an indication of important information, I have outlined four key principles that have been helpful for myself and many supervisors and managers for understanding resistance and opposition in a way that has enhanced capacity for dealing with it the most positively and productively. The four guiding principles are as follows. . . .

Principle 1: Resistance and opposition are opportunities for discovery.

Resistance and opposition are gifts—opportunities for all involved to learn and grow. They are opportunities for discovery. Resistance is not something that we should run from, manage, or extinguish. It is an opportunity for us to learn more about our employees and for supervisors and managers to learn about themselves also. When we think of resistance and opposition as opportunities for discovery—to enhance the meaning and value of a situation in ways that will increase our capacity to be better helpers—we are more likely to feel excited, curious, and open versus suspicious, worried, and apprehensive, giving us a better chance for a positive and productive outcome.

Principle 2: Resistance and opposition must be honored and respected.

One thing I have learned over the years is that any and all forms of resistance and opposition must be honored and respected. I use a common North American analogy to elaborate on this point. There is a saying, "Respect the fire, or you might get burned." Over the years, working with thousands of employees, I have learned that resistance is important information that something is going on within a situation or between people. In many cases, it is a result of important, unmet, or conflicting needs, values, goals, and strengths that are operating. I have learned the hard way, through very challenging situations, that if and when resistance and opposition are minimized and/or ignored altogether, they do not necessarily go away or get better. As a matter of fact, whatever it is that is operating will continue and/or surface in a different way at a different time. In situations like Brandon's and James's, if these situations were dealt with differently, if the apparent resistance and opposition wasn't minimized, judged, or blamed, the two situations would probably have had more positive and productive outcomes for all involved.

Principle 3: People who present as resistant and/or oppositional have a right to their experiences—it is legitimate.

Earlier in my career as a supervisor, I was quite frustrated and even judgmental when I experienced serious opposition and resistance from some of my team members. My frustration, I later learned, was more about my own helplessness to deal effectively with the persons or the situation. In part, it was also due to the fact that I held some of the less-than-helpful ideas about employee resistance, as stated earlier. I remember not really appreciating employees that seemed angry or stuck and unable to move on in some area of attitude and/or development. However, over the years, I learned that there was nothing wrong with these people; they had legitimate reasons for their own frustration, anger, sadness, and helplessness.

When we consider that employee resistance and opposition signal the operation and interaction of important needs, values, goals, and strengths, it is easier to be patient, compassionate, and, subsequently, more tolerant in situations wherein employees appear resistant and/or oppositional. They have a right to their experiences. It is legitimate. It is not wrong or bad. Nobody is to blame. It just means that we are missing meaning in the situations and experiences, and it signals a need to begin the exploration with "What do we know about this from the employee's perspective?"

It is important for me to note as a tip for all supervisors that, over the years, I learned something very critical about employees who seemed "stuck" around an issue where there was a great deal of anger and/or frustration. In such situations, it was often about something that had happened in the past, and a worker needed someone to listen to his story so he could feel heard, validated, and affirmed in his feelings and/or experience within his story. Remember, needs do not go away until they are somehow met or satisfied in some manner. Now, whenever I feel or perceive that an employee seems "stuck" around a particular issue, I am signaled to slow down and really listen for unmet needs or incongruent values, or I look for personal goals that may have been blocked. Often, as stated before, I will find out, to some degree, that there are parts of the employee's story that require listening to, validation, and affirmation prior to moving on to problem solving and/or planning.

Principle 4: Resistance and opposition must be approached with the goal of understanding, not changing.

While the three aforementioned beliefs for approaching employee resistance and oppositional behavior are important, it is my belief that this is the most critical. I have made it clear that sometimes and unintentionally a supervisor's understanding and approach can make a situation more challenging and the outcome considerably worse. When the goal of a manager is to modify, stop, or terminate certain employee attitudes and behaviors, someone is automatically at risk of "losing" or having to give something up. Inadvertently and unintentionally, both supervisor and employee are at risk due to a competition inherent in the approach. Whenever people feel threatened because they might have to give something up, there is an increased likelihood that resistance and opposition will be evoked further, even if it is solely to hold on to one's own dignity and/or integrity.

I encourage supervisors and managers to approach resistance and opposition with the primary purpose of gaining understanding.

One should ask, "What do we know about this from the person's perspective? What needs, values and/or goals may be in operation here?" When we work to turn information into meaning in this manner, understanding the person and the situation becomes much clearer and neither party inherently has to give anything up. As a matter of fact, as greater meaning surfaces, both parties stand to gain a great deal. Understanding provides clarity to the unmet or conflicting needs, values, and goals. In many cases, when greater understanding of resistance and opposition surfaces, options for engaging the person within the situation are most effectively and efficiently achieved.

These four beliefs have been foundational and exceptionally helpful, in my experience, to understanding and approaching apparent and experienced resistance and opposition in a manner that is most positive and productive.

These guiding principles have been foundational and have informed the following procedural steps for approaching resistance and opposition when it surfaces and/or persists.

❖ REVISITING SITUATION 2 FROM CHAPTER 4: GETTING JAMES BACK ON THE FLOOR

In order to illustrate the process guidelines for *care-fronting opposition and resistance,* I thought it would be helpful to revisit the situation with James from Chapter 4. This particular situation is not uncommon from many other similar situations that I have experienced. It is a situation that seemed to be going from bad to worse. We can recall that James's situation finished with a less-than-preferred ending for all parties involved.

Although there is lots of information (assumptions, labels, interpretations, etc.) regarding James, his history, and his current behavior, there is little meaning. What do we know about James's difficulties in his other positions that led him to be moved around over the years from his perspective? Nothing. What do we know about James's refusal to get on the floor from his perspective? Nothing. The fact that the meaning of James's experience was missing from the equation is most likely in large part what led to many of the challenges and difficulties becoming increasingly worse.

To be as realistic as possible with this particular scenario, it's important to note that if James was indeed one of my team members, I would have utilized some of the tools offered in previous chapters.

However, in order to demonstrate the impact the tools can have, I will offer and utilize only small parts of the actual tools in the following process. I would like to illustrate how having even just a little bit of accurate meaning as it pertains to the important needs values, goals, and strengths of James can offer his supervisor the insight and leverage he needs to engage James in a manner that optimizes his motivation and overall performance toward preferred outcomes for him, his teammates, and the clients he serves.

❖ CARE-FRONTING JAMES: APPROACHING RESISTANCE AND OPPOSITION, A PROCESS GUIDE FOR LEADERS

The following steps offer supervisors and managers a process guide for approaching what seem to be experienced resistance and oppositional employee attitudes and behaviors. I refer to this approach as *care-fronting*, as opposed to confronting. Care-fronting, a term that I have been using for more than 10 years, refers to the process of approaching a challenging situation and/or topic in the most honest, straightforward, respectful, and dignified manner—a way that, to the extent possible, cares for the relationship and the integrity of all parties involved. The steps in the care-fronting process are as follows:

1. Inform the member of the reason for the meeting and establish a time to meet that works for both people.

This is an important step as employees have a right to know why it is that a meeting is being called. I believe that employees should not hear for the first time at the meeting why it is that they are being asked to report to a manager's office. I often say to supervisors that, especially under stressful and challenging circumstances, employees have a right to prepare themselves for the meeting. If they are not given a heads-up prior to the meeting, then it is not a meeting—it's an ambush.

Supervisor: *Hello, James. I was wondering if you are available sometime next week to talk more about your work, some of your goals, and how you have been feeling about being encouraged to get back on the floor with our residents. I would like to hear more about your concerns so that I can have a better understanding of how best to support you. Let me know which date and time works for you. Thanks.*

2. Be sure to review important information pertaining to member needs, values, goals, and strengths as they pertain to the work overall.

This is absolutely essential. Leaders inspire by knowing and understanding what it is workers need, what is most important for them, and what they hope for themselves and their clients as they carry out the work. In addition to this, by knowing and understanding the meaning of an employee's experience, a leader is better able to consider, engage, and respond to these important elements of the worker's story.

Look to the meaning in the notes and documentation from previous conversations and interactions with the team member. I encourage all supervisors and managers to review the Preferred Leadership Profile, the Key Performance Motivators Scale, the Strengths Index, and any other important documentation that may contain meaningful aspects of the employee's story.

In this particular scenario, the supervisor has reviewed James's documentation and has noted some important items that may be considered and leveraged in the conversation with James.
James's PLP:

Preferred Outcomes Section, Question #3: What would you define as the best team and/or work environment you would like to work within? Be as detailed as possible.

James states that he prefers a team that is supportive, where there is trust, support, cooperation, and "no BS," specifically gossiping or backstabbing.

Preferred Outcomes Section, Question #4: What do you think you can/will do to contribute to a team and working environment that you described above? Be as detailed as possible.

James was quite general and straightforward on his response to this question. James states that he is a team player and is willing to do what it takes to create a better team environment.

James's KPMS:

James's KPMS also provided the supervisor with important areas to consider and prior to and during the conversation with James. James's KPMS revealed that there were four items rated much higher than any other areas or set of items. These were as follows: a sense of control; personal and/or professional growth; the three As (acknowledgment, admiration, appreciation); and a strengths focus.

James's Strengths Index:

James's Strengths Index clearly shows that, despite his challenges, he is great at both verbal and written communication. He also has great skill in understanding and thoroughly completing all work-related documentation. He is dependable and reliable in these areas.

3. Appreciate efforts to attend the meeting and do a personal and professional check-in.

When the meeting commences, it is critical to appreciate the effort to attend the meeting. A personal and professional check-in is critical to connect and simultaneously strengthen the relationship with the member. In addition to this, a check-in provides the employee an opportunity to state how he is doing and share whatever is most meaningful and/or significant to him at the moment.

Supervisor: *Hello, James. Thank you so much for coming to meet with me. I really appreciate that you made the time for us today. I think it is important that we connect.* (Three As—Appreciative Statements)

James: *Ya. No problem. It's not like I really have a choice or anything. You're the boss, right?*

Supervisor: *Yes, I am the supervisor; you're right.* (Paraphrase) *However, I understand that work and life can get busy, and I wanted to recognize that I appreciate the effort. Also, it's great to have time with you as we haven't been able to connect as much as I would like to.* (Three As) How are you doing?

James: *I'm all right. Same old, same old, you know?*

Supervisor: *Same old, same old?* (Paraphrase)

James: *Ya, things are always the same here. Come in, do my job, try not to get in any trouble, and leave.*

Supervisor: *So things are the same.* (Paraphrase) *Can you tell me about trouble?* (Discovery Question)

James: *Well, I'm not sure I'm not in trouble. I'm in a manager's office again to talk about problems. So . . . it's a familiar drill, although I thought I was doing pretty good here.*

Supervisor: *So it sounds like you're not sure if this is more of the same. You've been here before to talk about problems, and you're not sure if you're in trouble.* (Paraphrase/Empathic Response)

James: *Well, is there trouble? Like can we get to what you wanted to talk about?*

4. Be positive and focus on strengths (what's been going well) and the three As (acknowledge, admire, appreciate).

Supervisor: *Absolutely, we can get to what we are going to chat about indeed. (Paraphrase) I also wanted to assure you that you are not in trouble. We are not here to talk about problems or trouble. One of my goals for this meeting is to let you know that I appreciate having you on the team. I don't get the opportunity to tell you that I really admire your contributions. I would agree with your statement that things have been pretty good overall. (Paraphrase/Appreciative Statements) Your communications are impeccable. You get things in on time, and the documentation is thorough. Really, your communication logs are so detailed that your colleagues have little question about what has been or needs to be done.* (Three As and Strengths Focus)

James: *I'm sorry sir, but I have to ask. Am I getting fired?*

Supervisor: *No. You are not getting fired. (Paraphrase) Can you tell me more about that concern?* (Discovery Question)

James: *Well, I have to be honest; the only time I hear about when I'm doing something right is just before I hear something really bad. And since we're talking about my not getting back on the floor and you're starting with all the good stuff, it makes me a little suspicious.*

Supervisor: *First off, I'm sorry that you have only heard the good things when they are followed by something bad. (Paraphrase) I would like you to hear about what you're doing well more often. And because this is different, it seems to lead you to feel a little suspicious.* (Empathic Response)

James: *Ya, that and you're actually listening to what I have to say. That's a little different too. It's not a bad thing. Just different. Really different.*

Supervisor: *OK, so it's not a bad thing.* (Paraphrase) *Good. I'm glad that you feel I'm listening.* (Paraphrase) *I really do appreciate your honesty and your feedback.* (Appreciative Statement) *I want to listen.*

5. Restate the purpose and expected outcomes for the meeting. Clarify your intentions and hopes for the meeting (understanding of situation, incident, or behavior). Be clear about what you hope for, and clarify what the meeting is not about. (Example: "I was hoping that we could gain an understanding of what has happened and work together towards something helpful or better. This is not a disciplinary meeting.")

While it is important to clarify the meeting's purpose, intention, and anticipated outcomes, clarifying what the meeting is *not* about is also essential. The purpose of this is to create conditions that lower anxiety and promote a more comfortable interaction. As supervisors, we want the attention and energy of the employee to be invested in the work and not on negative concerns and worries regarding *what ifs* and thought scenarios based on fears of what might really be happening. This fosters a more comfortable atmosphere wherein both supervisor and employee can be fully present and focused on the aspects of the meeting that are most important.

Supervisor: *OK, so you said you wanted to get to what we're here to talk about.* (Paraphrase) *As we discussed when we set the meeting, I want to talk with you more about your perspective on getting back to the floor—the question of whether you want to or not. I really want to gain a better understanding of how you see things, what you need, what's important to you, and what you hope for.*

James: *So you're not going to force me back to the floor?*

Supervisor: *No. That is not my intention. I really wanted to gain a better understanding of how you see things and, really, how we can make work better for you, for the team, and, most importantly, for the youth that we serve. I really want to hear from you. I do want to understand your decision to stay on accommodation and the impact that may be having on you, the* *team, and the service overall. You are not in trouble. This meeting is not about discipline. You are not getting written up. And I am not discussing this meeting with HR or anyone else for that matter.*

6. Ask the employee what it is that he or she hopes to get out of the meeting.

Supervisor: *So James, with that said, what is it that you are hoping to get from the meeting and our time together?*

James: *To tell you the truth, other than wanting to get this meeting over with, I haven't really thought about it. I'd like to hear more about the part of making work better for me. Ha ha. It's been rough for a while. Better for me usually means better for everyone else. I can be a handful. Ha ha.*

Supervisor: *So, if we talk about making things better for you and everybody else, that would be helpful?* (Paraphrase)

James: *Yes.*

7. Describe things in concrete terms. Explain as behaviorally measurable as possible what you have observed—no interpretations or assumptions, just the facts.

Supervisor: *OK. Good. I really want to get a better understanding from your perspective about your consistent refusals to get back on the floor when past supervisors have requested this of you. I know that since our time working together, there have been requests made by other team members to work at lighter duty, and it seems as though you have refused to cooperate with those requests. That's how I understand things. Is that clear?*

James: *Yes, it's clear.*

8. Ask the employee for his/her understanding/explanation/ experience.
   a. *Can you tell me how you understand what was/is happening?*
   b. *Can you please share how you see things?*
   c. *Can you help me understand what was/is happening?*
   d. *Can you tell me what that might be about?*
   e. *Can you tell me what your experience is?*

Supervisor: *That's been the main concern. I want to hear how you see things, from your perspective, of course. Can you tell me a little more about things being rough and you being a handful?* (Paraphrase/Discovery Question)

9. Support the discovery of the member experience and listen to the meaning within his story—the needs, values, goals, and strengths.

James: *Well, I haven't been happy for a long time. People have been forcing me to do what I don't think I'm ready to do. And what if I don't ever want to go back on the floor?*

Supervisor: *I would like to hear more about whether you want to go back on the floor ever.* (Paraphrase) *Can you tell me a little more about people forcing you to do things you're not ready for?* (Discovery Question)

James: *All I hear, not so much from you but from everyone before you, is that I must get back on the floor. You know what? No one has even asked me, "James, would you like to go back on the floor?" I actually really miss working with the kids. I just didn't expect to get hurt so early in my career. No one really gets it.*

Supervisor: *No one gets it?* (Paraphrase)

James: *How hard it was to go on accommodation after getting beat up by a kid. It was embarrassing. I never really wanted to go on accommodation, but my supervisor at the time, Ray, said it was a good idea. And for some reason, I was left there despite wanting to get back to work. When Ray left the company, I had been on accommodation for two years.*

Supervisor: *So it sounds like it was a tough time, being hit by that youth.* (Paraphrase) *I also hear you say that you never really wanted to go off the floor. Forgive me, James, but I'm a little confused. I hear you saying that you didn't want to go on accommodation, yet for the last several years, you have been refusing to get back onto the unit with the kids.* (Paraphrasing an Incongruence) *Can you tell me a little more about that from your perspective?* (Discovery Question)

James: *Are you sure you didn't read it all in my file? After Ray left, Jack became my supervisor. Let's say I don't think he liked me very much. The year that we were more than full capacity and short staffed on my line, Jack forced me to get back on the floor. It was a nightmare. I tried it because I really wanted to get back in it. The trouble was, I had no support. It was almost like I was set up to fail. Worst time in my career. It was the beginning of my regular visits with HR, and I was placed on my first of many performance-management plans. I took stress leave and, with the support of my doctor, went back onto accommodation and light duty.*

Supervisor: *Wow, James. I'm so sorry to hear that it was so tough and the worst time in your career.* (Empathic Response)

James: *To tell you the truth, it hasn't gotten much better. It seems as though, ever since then, I've had a target on my back. I always feel like someone is ready to write me up for something. I get passed around. It feels like I am being forced back to the floor to screw up for the final time. I'm not gonna be set up to fail.*

Supervisor: *So you feel like you're being targeted and set up to fail?* (Paraphrase)

James: *This might be the first meeting where I don't feel like someone is out to get me.*

Supervisor: *I'm not out to get you.* (Paraphrase) *I'm sorry that you feel that we have been.* (Empathic Response) *James, can I ask you a question that you mentioned no one has ever asked you?* (Paraphrase)

James: *Sure.*

Supervisor: *Do you want to get back on the floor?* (Goal Question)

James: *Some days, I don't even know anymore. I just feel like I am trying to get by without getting fired. It seems to be the main focus, the only goal lately. I used to really like my work. I had plans. It wasn't supposed to be like this, that's for sure.*

Supervisor: *It sounds like you are unsure and that lately the only goal seems to avoid getting fired.* (Paraphrase)

10. Encourage a focus on needs, values, goals, and strengths.

Supervisor: *Can you tell me more about what you mean when you say you had plans and it wasn't supposed to be like this?* (Paraphrase/Goal Question)

James: *Well, I'm not sure I know anyone who wants his image to be lazy, uncommitted, and insubordinate. I'm not sure anyone likes to be the main source of stress for his or her team and management. It's not what I envisioned when I signed up for this. It's been very stressful.*

Supervisor: *I'm sorry to hear that it has been so stressful for you.* (Empathic Response) *Can you tell me what you did envision for yourself in the job when you signed on?* (Paraphrase/Discovery Question)

James: *Well, I always knew that one day I wanted to be a manager. My father was a superintendent at the local mine. My brothers are all in management. I've always liked working with people, although that may seem hard to believe with my history. But when no one is there to take care of you, you have to take care of yourself.*

Supervisor: *So it sounds like you have a family of leaders.* (Paraphrase) *Can you tell me more about what you were hoping for when you took the job at the facility?* (Discovery Question)

James: *Ya. I knew that I liked working with kids. I used to volunteer at the YMCA, so I thought youth justice was a good fit for me. I admit, I didn't think the kids were going to be as tough as they are, or the managers for that matter. Ha ha. Just kidding. The kids I can handle. It was Jack.* (pause and big sigh)

Supervisor: *Yes, it sounds like you and Jack had a less-than-positive experience.* (Paraphrase of Nonverbal Communication) *Now that I hear you talk about what you hoped for in the beginning, it makes me think of some of the information I read on your PLP, the leader profile. I noticed that you really value a trusting, supportive team that works well together. I also recall that you actually had—and maybe still have—aspirations to be a team leader one day. Are these things still important for you?* (Goal Questions)

James: *I know it may not seem like it from my attitude and behavior over the last while, but yes. However, I think I've almost given up on the team leader thing, especially here. I will always value good teamwork. I know that my refusal to go back to the floor causes stress for some of the others who need a turn.*

Supervisor: *That sounds tough. You really want to support the team and you know that staying on accommodation causes stress for the other guys.* (Paraphrase/Comment on Incongruence)

James: *Ya. Doesn't make sense, does it? I know if I go off accommodation this time and it doesn't work out, I'm gone. There will be no chance to go back. I don't want to screw up again.*

Supervisor: *I hear that you're worried about it not working out.* (Paraphrase) *Can you tell me a about what it would look like if it worked out—if things were better this time?* (Better-Future Question)

James: *I wouldn't be left to hang. Not set up. I'd be supported.*

Supervisor: *Can you tell me what you mean when you say you'd be supported?* (Discovery Question)

James: *I would have some clear direction and support around difficult decision-making. I would have someone to talk to when I had a tough situation. Support, you know? Some guidance. Positive feedback on what I'm doing well and where I can improve. You know different from just hearing that I'm screwing up. As a matter of fact, I don't think I've ever really been supported at all in the time that I've been here.*

Supervisor: *So things would be better if you felt you had that type of support?* (Paraphrase) *What difference would that make for you?* (Million-Dollar Question) *How would it be helpful if you had the support you felt you needed and hoped for?* (Million-Dollar Question/Needs- and Goals-Focused Question)

James: *You and everyone else would probably see a different James. I would do my best. I might even be a team leader. I can't remember that last time I actually tried. If I tried, maybe I could be a manager one day—a better manager than Jack ever was!*

Supervisor: *So are you saying that if you had the kind of support you feel you needed, that you might work toward that dream of becoming a manager one day?* (Paraphrase)

James: *Well . . . (pause) . . . this is a little strange.*

Supervisor: *Strange?* (Paraphrase)

James: *I came here today thinking that I was getting closer to being fired, and now we're here talking about my goals—the one I had years ago—of working towards a management position. It's strange.*

Supervisor: *James, let me ask you a question. If you had the support you needed and you were sure that you were not being set up to fail, would you consider working toward that first step as a possible mentor or team leader?* (Paraphrase/Goal-Focused Question)

James: *Well, to work in that direction, I guess I have to first consider getting back on the floor. Right?*

Supervisor: *Well, an important part of a supervisor's job is to role-model relationship building with the youth and to be on the floor from time to time.*

James: *Well . . . (pause) . . . I guess I better get back on the floor then!*

11. Share what you heard and your understanding and experience of the situation. Attempt to clarify and summarize needs, values, and goals.

Supervisor: *James, please let me know if what I'm hearing is in line with what you're saying and what your experience is.*

James: *OK.*

Supervisor: *It seems to me that there is still value in the work. You value your team and you value the youth that you work with. It also seems to me that when you are supported, you value having important goals to work toward, and you value doing and being your best. Unfortunately, you have had some not-so-good experiences that have led to stress and conflict at work. In addition to this, you seem to have lost a connection to some of your important goals—to work with youth and your team in the way that you would prefer and to work toward taking* *on a management position one day. It also sounds to me that you might be reconsidering that journey toward leadership and that getting back on the floor may be an important step toward realigning with some of the values and goals that are important to you.*

James: *Yes. I think so. Yes. Yes.*

Supervisor: *I also heard that your need to have assurance that you are not being set up and that you won't be hung out to dry is critical. I also heard from you that if you are going to consider moving back onto the floor that you will do so only if the right supports are in place. Is that correct?*

James: *Absolutely, sir.*

12. Work to align or fit the member's needs, values, goals, and strengths with what you need and want from the member in his/her work.

Supervisor: *James, I want to tell you that I appreciate your honesty here, and I am impressed with your commitment to the team and to the work. We are actually not that far off, you and I. I really want you to do your best also. The kids, the team, and this program are very important.*

James: *Yes, sir.*

Supervisor: *Your values of working with youth, teamwork, and the good work overall are very much in line with what this program stands for. I admire anyone that is willing to work toward a leadership role, especially someone who has had a less-than-positive experience with management. I do want to talk a little further about what better support might look like for you this time around. However, before we get into what it might look like, I would like to talk about what it has looked like in the past, when you felt as though you had the support you needed in moments, even if it was just a little.* (Exception Question) *In addition to this, prior to identifying the supports needed, I think it would be important to chat about where you feel things are going well and where you are succeeding and possibly look at the things we can build on as you move forward.* (Strengths Approach)

Jams: *Sure.*

13. Focus on workers' exceptions and strengths—when are they succeeding, what are they succeeding at, and how have they been and how are they now able to succeed.

Supervisor: *Can you tell me about a time when you felt you were getting the support you needed on the floor?* (Exception Question)

James: *Well, there was very little, if any. Ever. I mean Ray was a nice guy, but he wasn't very supportive.*

Supervisor: *So you really feel as though the support was lacking.* (Paraphrase) *Can you tell me about a time when you were feeling successful, even just a little bit, prior to accommodation and/or even when you gave it a try a while back?* (Exception Question)

James: *I know for sure it was when I was on shifts with the people I knew I could trust. Definitely not when Jack was on my shift.*

Supervisor: *OK. People you trust.* (Paraphrase) *What difference did that make for you? How was having people on shift that you trusted helpful?* (Million-Dollar Questions)

James: *I felt secure because they were dependable and they knew what they were doing. And if I had a question, they could help me out. Also, with people that you trust, you can talk openly about how you really feel about a decision or policies or even how you feel about some of the difficult clients.*

Supervisor: *OK. Anything else?*

James: *Well, I know I was feeling successful when we divvied up the tasks on the floor each week and we knew who was documenting, who was in on crises, and who was in charge of shift change and stuff like that. I like it when things are orderly and not all over the place. A set schedule really helped as well. As a matter of fact, when we used to come in 15 minutes before shift, it helped us with connecting, especially the days when there wasn't a lot of action on the unit.*

Supervisor: *So it sounds like you're at your best when you are working with people who are dependable and reliable—people who you can count on and trust. It was helpful for you to have a set schedule and divide the tasks up into parts so that they were clear and easier to manage. Coming in early for shift change to connect was helpful also.* (Paraphrase and Strengths Focus)

James: *Yes. Those things helped me, and I think the team also, do better.*

Supervisor: *Thank you for sharing that. This is very helpful.* (Appreciative Statements) *Was there anything else you could think of that contributed to you feeling better and doing better in your work?* (Exception Question) *Can you think of anything that was better, even just a little, when you attempted to get back on the floor before?* (Better Question)

James: *Actually, I do remember. I remember that when I started, because we had low numbers on the unit, I was able to work a couple hours a day on the floor for the first while. Then, shortly after that, the unit across town closed, and we were swamped with their kids. Jack forced me back on to the floor full time . . . without any support.*

Supervisor: *Can you tell me what difference the two hours a day made for you?* (Million-Dollar Question) *I ask because I'm not sure we can do that with the numbers of youth we currently have.*

James: *It was good to ease in after being away. I needed some time to get oriented to all of the parts of working on the floor again. It was good to digest it in parts. Also, I could focus on the things that I was good at. My unit partners supported me to work on the things I remembered, for starters. That was helpful.*

Supervisors: *So easing into the role again and getting oriented to the job was helpful to make it more manageable.* (Paraphrase) *And it seems like focusing on the things that you were comfortable with and knew well also helped.* (Paraphrase)

James: *Yes. Actually, when we talk about it like this, I really feel I could do this.*

Supervisor: *So you think you're willing to give it a try? Ease in to getting back on the floor?*

James: *Ya. I think so. I would like to try it again. Yes.*

14. Begin developing a plan out of discovered resources.

Supervisor: *OK. We've covered a lot in this meeting. I really appreciate your effort in working toward something better for you and for all of us.* (Appreciative Statement) *Let's consider what a plan might begin to look like. And then we can talk about the supports you might need in general and what you might need from me.*

James: *OK.*

Supervisor: *OK. Based on what I've heard, I am going to throw out some ideas, some things to consider, and you can let me know what you think. I want to hear more about your goal of becoming a team leader and moving toward management. I think that today, however, we should focus on the plan to get you back on the floor first. Once you are feeling better about that, we can have a look at the bigger picture. What do you think about that?*

James: *That makes perfect sense. I wouldn't even expect you or the other managers to think that I'm close to ready for that move. I would like to first prove it to myself that I can do this and then to you.*

Supervisor: *Given that you feel it would be helpful to ease into the position again, how do you feel about starting one or two days per week in the beginning? It's up to you. In addition to this, since you feel getting oriented to the role again is helpful, might I suggest the job-orientation seminar that we run each month? I believe it is scheduled for new hires Thursday next week.*

James: *I like the idea of one day at first, if that's OK. I want to be sure this time. I think the orientation would help. It's a little embarrassing given that I have been here for so long, but this isn't about ego. It's time to get back on track. I'm willing to do what it takes.*

Supervisor: *I heard that you prefer to work with people you perceive as reliable and dependable. Of your current team members, who would you feel the best about working with on shift? Because if we can partner you for the first while with people you feel most comfortable with, we will try to make that happen.*

James: *To tell you the truth, I feel pretty good about everyone right now. I do know that Sarah, Bradley, John, Eric, and I click pretty well. They would be my preferences, but I feel pretty good about all of the team.*

Supervisor: *Great. I think it's good that you feel pretty good about all members.* (Paraphrase) *I will talk with those you mentioned and see if we can work out a schedule that works for all of you. Also, I know that Eric, John, and Bradley all like to come in shortly before shift change. That's also important to you. Speaking of scheduling, the quarterly schedule is due to be made. Would you like to work on that with Eric and John?*

James: *Yes, that would be good.*

Supervisor: *Also, because you have impeccable communication and documentation skills, we can have you focus on things like intake meetings and intake reviews and documentation.* (Building on Strengths) *That would also give you a little exposure to the new clients. You can ease into client contact if that helps also. I'm not sure if that would help*

James: *Yes, sir. I would really like to get some positive interactions with kids under my belt. The tough stuff will come. It always does.*

Supervisor: *I would really like the team to be involved in some of this planning, seeing as it is going to affect them. What do you think of that?*

James: *It makes sense. I'm a team player, sir. I know that most people are looking forward to me moving off accommodation and getting back to the floor, so I think it will be good for all of us. I've got nothing to hide. I'm ready to do this.*

15. Clarify, if needed, roles, responsibilities, expectations, and preferred performance.

While this is an important aspect to the process of approaching opposition and resistance, it is important to note that, given that James is clear on his expectations and roles, this is a less important step in this particular scenario. However, in this situation, the supervisor will review roles, responsibilities, expectations, and preferred performance as a course of review for clarity and shared understanding.

Given that James appears cooperative, focused, engaged, and motivated, there is less of a need to review these elements in detail. It is important to note that because a lack of role clarity, including responsibilities and expectations, can lead to perceived reluctance and opposition, it is critical that when new goals, objectives, and arrangements are set, these areas are also reestablished. This will minimize confusion and enhance clarity and certainty for all parties moving forward.

16. Brainstorm ideas for support. (This may or may not involve consequences.)

It is the type and level of opposition and resistance and the implications of the particular behavior or set of behaviors being discussed that will determine whether a consequence will be established in the event expectations are not met. In this particular scenario, because the implications of James not following through and the impacts on others will be minimal, there will be no need for consequences to be discussed if James doesn't stick to or work toward the agreed-upon plan. However, in other situations where certain resistances and opposition have serious implications and consequences for team members, clients, and/or the organization overall, it would be important for consequences to be identified and discussed at this juncture in the process.

Given the particulars of James's scenario, a discussion of support is all that is necessary at this point. However, that said, given his history with lack of support and his identified need for support, this particular part of the process holds great importance.

Supervisor: *James, can you tell me what support for this plan might look like?*

James: *Well, the plan overall is pretty supportive. I like that we are going to start slow and focus on the things I know I can do. We can look at increasing the days each week, if that's OK?*

Supervisor: *So it sounds as though you feel the supports are built in?* (Paraphrase) *And if we consider each week whether to increase the number of days, that would be helpful?* (Paraphrase) *How do you think I can be the most helpful in supporting your success as we develop this plan further and follow through?* (Need-Focused Question)

James: *Regular check-ins will help. I think that feedback on what I'm doing well and where I can improve will be helpful. I think if we can set small check-ins and one monthly meeting for the first bit that would help.*

Supervisor: *OK, James. This is a great start. I believe we can set up weekly check-ins by phone, or I can pop by if that's OK. And then we* *can schedule in some monthly meetings to support your development to get back and excel on the floor. How does that sound?*

James: *Good. It sounds really good.*

Supervisor: *James, I want you to know that I appreciate your honesty and your efforts today to work toward something better for yourself.* (Appreciative Statements) *I can really see and feel that you care about your work, your team, and the youth we serve and that you are willing to make changes that will benefit all of us. That is a true asset.* (Strength Focus) *What do you say we take a little time to think about what we chatted about today? I will put what we talked about into e-mail and send it to you. Do you think you have time toward the end of the week, say around 2 p.m. on Friday? We could get together and put a little more detail and create a timeline for this plan once we've had some time to think about it further.*

James: That sounds good.

17. Provide opportunities to try out the plan.

James and his supervisor will work together to detail a clear and concrete development plan with objectives, identified supports, and timelines. James will have many opportunities to work on the plan with support from his supervisor.

18. Follow through and evaluate.

Follow-through and consistent evaluation are important aspects of all professional development and support plans. However, in situations where there is serious and/or long-standing opposition and resistance, they become even more essential. In James's particular situation, wherein he has felt "set up" and "hung out to dry" by management in the past and where he has clearly stated a fear of being "set up to fail," follow-through and careful evaluation are critical for James and his success.

❖ SUMMARY OF IMPORTANT POINTS

- Resistance and opposition are often referred to as poor performance and/or undesirable behavior.

- The costs and consequences of employee resistance and opposition are great and impact employees, clients, and the organization overall.

- How supervisors think about employee opposition and resistance will affect how they feel about it and thereby determine how they respond to it.

- Employee opposition and resistance are not bad things; they provide information that we are missing meaning in a situation.

- Many of the principles and strategies offered throughout the book operate as proactive approaches for decreasing and eliminating opposition and resistance.

- Supervisors and managers must be aware of the multifarious dynamics and circumstances that can lead to employee opposition and resistance.

- The four guiding principles offered can assist supervisors in approaching resistance and opposition in the most positive and productive manner.

❖ PERSONAL LEADER REFLECTIONS AND CONSIDERATIONS

- Consider a time in your career when, as an employee, your values, needs, and/or goals were not being met or accommodated. What was that like for you? How were you behaving at that time as a result? Could your attitudes and behaviors have been interpreted as resistant and/or oppositional?

- Consider your own beliefs and assumptions about employee resistance and opposition. Are they in or out of step with the idea that resistance and opposition are information about important situational and/or experiential meaning?

- Think about an employee that you have struggled with in the past or are currently struggling with. What do you know about his or her behavior from his or her perspective? What are the needs, values, goals, and/or strengths operating for this person?

- Reflect back on a time when you or someone else you know approached an employee who was perceived or identified as being oppositional. Compare the process and interaction that was used with the process of *care-fronting* offered above. Was it similar? Were there differences? Could something have been done differently in order to achieve a better process and/or outcome? What might that be?

8

Epilogue

I am only one, but still I am one. I cannot do everything, but still I can do something. And because I cannot do everything, I will not refuse to do the something that I can do.

— Edward Everett Hale

L eaders are not immune from the stressors and multifarious challenges characteristic of most social service work environments. It can sometimes feel overwhelming and can lead many of us to question on some days if the stress is really worth it. There may be times when we may also doubt whether we are actually making a positive difference for the people whom we are responsible for supporting. I believe that it is for these reasons that the opening quote continues to be my favorite.

Never underestimate your abilities and/or the possibilities for making a positive difference in the lives of those you lead and in the lives of the people they too are responsible for. Even something we may perceive to be minor can in fact have positive and profound effects that are far-reaching. I will never forget a moment, years ago, during a common and difficult discussion I was having with a mixed group of 25 frontline supervisors and managers from youth justice, child welfare, and mental health. The somber topic revolved around how difficult and challenging our respective work environments were for working in ways that we preferred. An important question was being considered in the context of this conversation: How can we make a positive difference in a tough system that takes us away from the front line and the people that we are here to help? Out of the many like-conversations I have had with social service managers, there was a profound revelation made within this particular dialogue that I think about almost every day in my work with leaders. The 25 managers engaged in this particular discussion were responsible for the well-being of 8,000 children and youth! Eight thousand kids were on the receiving end of the practice decisions the workers these managers were responsible for made, an average of eight people with an average of 20 cases that averaged 2 to 3 children per file—8,000 children and youth!

Leadership within the helping field comes with great responsibility. Because leadership and worker outcomes are inextricably linked and worker outcomes directly impact the people we are responsible for, it is critical that our leadership actions and interactions be of the greatest quality possible. It was my intention, through this work, to enhance the meaning, value, and quality of your leadership efforts so that you may improve the capacity of your members in a manner that translates into higher quality service for the people they are responsible to and care for.

❖ WHERE TO GO FROM HERE? FINAL LEADERSHIP REFLECTIONS AND CONSIDERATIONS

It was my hope to stimulate thinking and feeling in a way that affirmed, validated, and maybe even inspired your experience as a leader. I understand that inspiration can fade, which is why the following reflections and considerations are offered—so that you may take steps to develop your capacities further and so that you may inspire yourself and those you are responsible for today and every day after.

Know Yourself

One of the most important things you can do for your people is to continue to know yourself better. As discussed previously, a challenging work environment can disconnect all of us, to differing degrees, from our own needs, values, goals, and strengths. To be more responsive as a leader, it will be important for you and your members to be purposeful in your reflections. Consider making it a priority to connect with what is most important to you—what you value, what it is you hope to accomplish, and what it is you feel you need to be more effective as you carry out your role as a leader.

Start With Strengths

Prior to looking at the areas that you would like to develop further, start with your strengths. If you are wondering why, you may want to review the positive and profound implications of a strengths focus offered in Chapter 5. Once you start looking, you will find many things that you are doing well. Consider building on those areas that you are already doing well as a leader and then move toward additional priorities that are important to you and your team members.

Develop a Plan

I always say that best is an effort and better is a destination. You can do your best, give your best, and try your best, but you can never be your best. You can always be better. Consider what better leadership capacity means to you. Consider what it looks like. My hope with this work was to affirm and validate what you are already doing well and to provide insights, strategies, and tools to develop your capacity further. You may have already started making use of some of the methods presented.

It is critical that you develop and record a plan; write it out or document it in some way. This can be the difference between whether the plan is merely perceived or actually achieved. Be sure to start with your strengths and start with small, realistic, and achievable steps. Remember that better can develop in increments, and small steps can add up to massive results. Consistent efforts at better can sometimes take us well beyond what we once thought best was. Share your plan with people who care about you and support your development. They will serve as valuable resources on your journey toward better leadership.

Construct Pathways for Feedback

Leaders cannot accurately assess their own effectiveness as leaders. Remember that the quality of leadership is determined by the perceptions and experiences of others—most importantly, the members.

Feedback from others is essential and operates as the key ingredient to initiate and enhance leadership capacity. It is important to do what you can to make as many avenues possible for people to provide you with feedback. More importantly, those avenues must be easy to access, comfortable, and safe.

Take ALL Feedback Seriously

All feedback is important. Remember that all behavior contains needs, values, and goals that are operating. When someone attempts to provide feedback, there is something going on, something being communicated that we must pay attention to, whether it be positive or not so positive.

It is the latter type of feedback and the ability to take it seriously that may be one of the most difficult aspects of leadership. When this happens, it is important to be aware of the possible reaction to defend or dismiss the feedback. Stay calm and tune into you. You may want to ask yourself this *meaning-making question*: What do I know about how I'm feeling in response to what I'm hearing? There is a good chance that you will learn something about yourself. Anger and frustration are often a result of our own needs being unmet, our values being challenged, and/or our goals being blocked. When leaders take all feedback seriously and work to actively integrate the meaning embedded within it, they will advance their own leadership ability, thereby enhancing the quality of the experience for their members.

Practice, Practice, Practice

Getting to better takes practice. Consider the amount of time and energy most professional athletes put in to their own skill development. They practice at practice so that they can be better in the game. Professional athletes rarely practice something new in a game situation as the chance of poor performance may interfere with their end goal. Consider your goals as a leader. Do you practice in the game or out of the game?

It is critical that leaders take the time to practice and sharpen their leadership skills. Remember that when leaders do well, so do their people and the people they serve. Consider setting some time aside to practice. You may want to connect with the people you trust who support your development so that you may practice, practice, practice.

Have Fun

It may be strange for some to see "have fun" as the final consideration in a book on leadership; however, it may actually be the most important one. It is not uncommon, when people are reflecting on the greatest leadership experience in their careers for them to mention fun as an aspect of that experience. Fun is important in most situations and becomes even more important to keep things positive, to buffer the stress of the challenges inherent in tough times and trying work environments. Fun makes good days great and the worst days better.

Consider connecting with the things that you appreciate about the work. Consider the things that contribute to work being positive, exciting, and fun. Consider asking your team members individually and/or as a group to share the things that contribute to their experience of work as positive, exciting, and fun as they carry out their very important work.

Appendix A

❖ **KEY PERFORMANCE MOTIVATORS SCALE (KPMS)**

The following list of items identifies important employee motivators for enhancing engagement, job satisfaction, performance, and organizational commitment.

For each item below, please rate on a scale of 1 to 10 the level of value and meaning each has for you. A 1 represents the item that holds little if any value and/or meaning for you, whereas 10 represents the item that holds the greatest value and/or meaning for you.

Quality Relationships

1--5--10

Comments:

_____

_____

_____

_____

Personal and/or Professional Values

1--5--10

Comments:

_____

_____

_____

_____

Vision and/or Values

1--5--10

Comments:

_____

_____

_____

Mission and Goals

1--5--10

Comments:

_____

_____

_____

Tasks of Interest

1--5--10

Comments:

_____

_____

_____

Personal and/or Professional Growth

1--5--10

Comments:

_____

_____

_____

Make a Difference/Results

1--5--10

Comments:

_____

_____

_____

Three *As* – Acknowledgment, Admiration, Appreciation

1--5--10

Comments:

_____

_____

_____

Constructive Feedback

1--5--10

Comments:

_____

_____

_____

Sense of Control

1--5--10

Comments:

_____

_____

_____

Strengths Focus

1--5--10

Comments:

_____

_____

_____

Leader–Member Discussion Points

What were your top four Performance Motivators?

Which of the Performance Motivators do you connect with the least?

Do you think there might be ways to enhance your connection to Key Performance Motivators in the work and/or the work environment? What might that look like?

Is there anything else we have not yet discussed that you feel is a source of motivation for you? If so, what might that be?

Appendix B

❖ PREFERRED LEADERSHIP PROFILE

NAME _____

Position/Title _____

Date _____

❖ VALUES

1. In familiarizing yourself with the mission and vision of the organization or program, what stood out as significant or meaningful for you?

   _____
   _____
   _____
   _____
   _____

2. Does the organization or program's vision and mission resonate or connect with any of your personal values? What values might those be?

   _____
   _____
   _____
   _____
   _____

3. Do any of the organizational or program's goals or objectives reflect or resonate with any of your personal goals? What are they?

_____

_____

_____

_____

_____

4. What is it that brought you to your current position?

_____

_____

_____

_____

_____

5. What are the things that keep you there?

_____

_____

_____

_____

_____

6. What's in it for me (WIIFM)? This is not a selfish question. We are all in certain roles or jobs at different times for different reasons. Sometimes it can be about
   a. making a positive difference,
   b. working to advance in one's career,
   c. earning a living,
   d. gaining experience,
   e. enjoying a challenge, and/or
   f. fostering personal growth.

   In your current position or job, what would you say is or are your WIIFMs? What's in it for you?

_____

_____

_____

_____

❖ PREFERRED OUTCOMES

1. What do you see as your role (not your title) with your clients?

2. What is it that you hope to accomplish—day to day, week to week, month to month, year to year—with your clients? What do you want for them?

3. What would you define as the *best* team and/or work environment you would like to work within? Be as detailed as possible.

4. What do you think you can or will do to contribute to a team and working environment that you described above? Be as detailed as possible.

❖ STRENGTHS

Professional Relevance

1. What would you say are some of your professional strengths? What are you good at? What have coworkers (past or present)

appreciated, acknowledged, and/or admired about the things you do or how you interact with others at work? List as many as possible.

_____

_____

_____

_____

_____

_____

_____

_____

2. If not yet listed, what are some of your experiences, skills, talents, knowledge, or attitudes that you think would enhance the work we do to improve the overall capacity of the team and the organization? List as many as possible.

_____

_____

_____

_____

_____

_____

_____

_____

Personal Relevance

1. What would you say are some of your personal strengths? What do you feel like you are good at?

_____

_____

_____

_____

_____

_____

_____

2. What are your interests, hobbies, and talents as well as your connections to family, friends, community, and culture that you admire and appreciate about your life?

_____

_____

_____

_____

_____

_____

_____

_____

❖ PERFORMANCE SUPPORT PREFERENCES

1. What goals or aspirations do you have for yourself as they relate to professional performance and growth? These should be what you feel are important, not what others have defined as important. Please list at least two.

_____

_____

_____

_____

_____

_____

_____

_____

2. Are there aspects that you would like to improve upon or enhance in the area of your identified strengths?

_____

_____

_____

_____

_____

_____

_____

_____

❖ PREFERRED LEARNING PREFERENCES

1. In your own words, how would you say that you learn best?

_____

_____

_____

_____

_____

_____

_____

2. Below are several examples of learning styles. Which would you say you prefer? On a scale from 1 to 4, with 1 being your greatest preference and 4 being your least preferred, how would you rate each learning style?

   A. _____. **Thinker** — I like to logically think things through. I like to learn about the theories and models for new ideas and ways of working. I like to sit back and analyze or synthesize information to make sense of it. I would prefer to read about a model or a new approach rather than jump in and try it out. I like to have the time to question and probe assumptions.

   B. _____. **Reflector** — I like to stand back and observe from different angles and perspectives before making a conclusion. I prefer to have accurate information and data gathered from different people and different sources. I like to watch activities, listen to discussions, or observe a group in order to put things together and learn about what needs to be done next.

   C. _____. **Sensors** — I like to involve myself and jump into new experiences and learn from that experience. I try to be open-minded and not skeptical of new ideas or ways of working. I thrive on the challenge of new and unique experiences—the newer and more exciting the better. I love brainstorming activities and role-playing exercises. I need to be involved.

   D. _____. **Actor** — I want to try ideas, theories, and techniques out in practice to see if they work. I like to experiment with applications. I can't wait to get back from training to try things out. I like when things are straightforward, practical, and down-to-earth. If there is a better way (because their usually is) to do something, let's find it and try to do it.

❖ QUALITY SUPERVISION AND SUPPORT INGREDIENTS

1. Consider a time when a management, supervision, or a coaching or mentoring experience was exceptionally meaningful, effective, or the most valuable? What made it so great? Please **list the qualities or the ingredients** that contributed to that experience of supervision being so wonderful.

_____
_____
_____
_____
_____
_____
_____
_____
_____

2. Consider your best manager, supervisor, coach, or mentor ever. What were the qualities or ways of acting or interacting that made him or her the best. **List as many qualities** as you can think of.

_____
_____
_____
_____
_____
_____
_____
_____
_____

❖ UNHELPFUL SUPERVISION AND SUPPORT INGREDIENTS

1. Consider a time when supervision and/or support was not meaningful, effective, or valuable. What made this experience so poor?

_____
_____
_____

_____

_____

_____

_____

_____

_____

_____

_____

2. Consider a manager, supervisor, coach, or mentor (without identification) that you were less than satisfied with. In what manner did he or she act or interact that made the experience less than satisfying? **List as many unhelpful actions or interactions** that made the experience what it was.

_____

_____

_____

_____

_____

_____

_____

_____

_____

_____

❖ MANAGEMENT/SUPERVISORY SUPPORT: STRUCTURE AND PROCESS PREFERENCES

1. When you consider your role, relevant job requirements, and responsibilities, what do you feel are your needs for supervision and support sessions? Do you feel you require more? Less? Please explain.

_____

_____

_____

_____

2. How often would you prefer supervision and support sessions? Please explain.

_____

_____

_____

_____

_____

3. Is there a time of day that you feel better suits you for supervision and support sessions? Please explain.

_____

_____

_____

_____

_____

4. Do you have a preference for the location of supervision and support sessions? (Examples: my office, your office, boardroom, hallway, on site, off site, other)

_____

_____

_____

_____

_____

5. Can you identify what your preferences might be for the process of supervision and support sessions? Please identify by checking the identified preference box on the list below. Feel free to add more, if you like.

- Individual sessions

- Group sessions

- Formal

- Informal

- Conversational (back and forth)

- One-way (supervisor to supervisee) with advice on work, progress, and goals

- Lead with strengths
- Lead with concerns
- Lead with areas for development
- Collegial dialogue
- Questions and answers
- Case discussions
- Formal learning or teaching
- Acknowledgment of what's going well
- Focus on performance areas (PDP)
- Opportunity to ask questions
- Consultation on performance and advisement
- Directed (just tell me what needs to be done)
- Practice or role-plays

Other:_____

_____

_____

_____

_____

_____

❖ CURRENCY FOR COMMUNICATION, FEEDBACK, AND SUPPORT

While there are many criteria and qualities that result in effective communication and feedback, such as clear, respectful, straightforward, concrete, clear expectations, and so forth, not all people require or prefer the same approach. Our "currencies" for communication and support may vary. Therefore, please note some of your preferences for how you would like feedback. What are the *dos* and *don'ts* that should be observed when there is a need to provide you with constructive feedback? In other words, for feedback to be effective and received, what do others need to pay attention to?

The following is an example for John Doe.

John Doe's dos and don'ts for effective and meaningful feedback

DO	*DON'T*
Be positive	*Yell at me*
Let me know you want to talk	*Ambush me*
Give me time to respond	*Expect an answer immediately*
Be respectful	*Talk over me*
Give me a chance to tell my side	*Make assumptions*
Be patient	*Interrupt*
Make the time	*Try to squeeze in something that needs time*
Do it in private	*Do it in public*
Respect confidentiality	*Tell others*
Give it to me straight	*BS me*

Please take a moment to list as many *dos* and *don'ts* that should be observed when providing constructive or developmental feedback.

DO   **DON'T**

DISCUSSION AREA

Is there anything I can do to make supervision and support more meaningful, valuable, or productive for you?

Are there things I need to consider or avoid in order to make supervision and support more meaningful, valuable, or productive for you?

Appendix C

❖ STRENGTHS INDEX

Date: _____

Employee Name: _____

Program: _____

Position: _____

Appendix D

Date: _____

Employee Name: _____

Program: _____

Position: _____

Communication

Relationships With Clients

Team Member

Documentation

Case Management

Index

Lightning Source UK Ltd.
Milton Keynes UK
UKHW020617200522
403285UK00009B/836